Letters from Simon

Letters from Simon

I. H. Paul

International Universities Press, Inc.
Madison   Connecticut

INTERNATIONAL UNIVERSITIES PRESS and IUP (& design) ® are
registered trademarks of International Universities Press, Inc.

Library of Congress Cataloging-in-Publication Data

Paul, I. H. (Irving H.), 1928–
    Letters from Simon / I. H. Paul. — [Rev. ed.]
        p.   cm.
    Includes bibliographical references and index.
    ISBN 0-8236-8130-0
    1. Psychotherapy. I. Title.
RC480.P39   1996
616.89'14—dc21   96-444465
                                                                         CIP

Manufactured in the United States of America

CONTENTS

FOREWORD

Twenty-two years ago, I wrote a treatise on psychotherapy in the form of letters addressed to a nephew.* The present book is based on a revision of it, and contains much that is new. Still, enough of the original has been retained, as have the fundamental points, that *Letters to Simon—Revised Edition* would have been a fitting title if I had decided to publish my new and revised letters. Instead I have written Simon's letters back to me.

My chief reason for this is that the revisions and additions were made in the course of teaching students. Their questions and criticisms were instrumental in a reexamination of my position on some key issues, as well as taking up new ones. Rather than counting on my letters to convey those questions and criticisms, I decided to try presenting them directly. I discovered that Simon's letters could readily incorporate the salient material from mine, while at the same time examining and discussing them in a fresh and interesting way. I am confident that the lessons of "Letters to Simon" are adequately aired when they are paraphrased and summarized in his letters back. Moreover, as you will learn, he shares my letters and discusses them with a fellow student. So it isn't only "him" taking the lessons, it's "them." She and he do not see eye-to-eye on all issues, and I believe their differences of opinion, not to mention their clinical judgment, are instructive.

Reading about therapy in advance of doing it has proven of such limited value that anyone who writes a didactic treatise might want to defend it, if not also apologize. I justify my effort with the claim

---

*Paul, I. H. *Letters to Simon*. New York: International Universities Press, 1973.

vii

that there is a certain value and necessary function to acquiring a reading knowledge of psychotherapy's concepts and techniques, and by emphasizing that my intention is only to supplement, not replace, what has proven to be the method of choice: supervision. But I am convinced, as well, that reading about therapy maintains its value not only before and during the beginning stages of actually doing it but also after the student has become a practitioner, for we are learning all the time. Therefore, though my intended audience is a student in the usual sense of the term, I've had a larger audience in mind, the student in the strict sense of the term, and much of what I have written can, I believe, be of interest and value to my colleagues.

A treatise on psychotherapy—even one that promulgates, as mine does, a particular method of therapy and a specific set of techniques—may merit no apology. But when it is written in the form of letters, then it needs mentioning that the subject lends itself to a discursive and informal treatment. In any case, I found that my intention, which was to articulate techniques concretely and explicitly, and spell out their basis in rationales that are clinical and comprehensive, could be served quite well by the flexible letter format—and especially when the letter writer feels at liberty to use a variety of literary devices.

In the interests of keeping the focus on the treatise and reducing distraction, personal remarks that would fit for such letters are kept to a minimum, and, starting with letter 5, even the beginning and ending salutations are dispensed with. I have provided titles for the letters, both as a guide to the topics covered and for the purposes of a table of contents. Since the letters are so discursive and the same issues are examined—and then reexamined from different perspectives—at various places, I have furnished an index that maps and traces every topic, and was designed for the reader who wishes to examine issues coherently.

I make some use of footnotes, mainly to provide the source of a citation or a mentioned publication. Otherwise, references to the published literature are sparse, for I judged that acknowledging my debt to those who have taught me, crediting those who have influenced me, and applauding those who share my views would be both unwieldy and unnecessary.

I do, however, wish to acknowledge, credit, and applaud my students, for it has been my practice to require them to provide critiques of my work, and I have always made it clear that I felt free to appropriate theirs—which is extensively reflected in this book. Four of them have also read parts of the manuscript and given me concrete, detailed, and valuable help. They are Eliot Jurist, James Ogilvie, Daniel Rothstein, and Lauren Silverman.

A fifth, Sharone Bergner, gave me a critique that ranged from copy editing to revising sections to rewriting entire letters, and it extended to reformulating basic issues. For authors to exonerate those who have helped them ("the views, nevertheless, are mine, not theirs") is customary, but Ms. Bergner cannot so easily be exonerated. It isn't hyperbole to say that she must bear a substantial responsibility in respect both to the language and the ideas of this book. This is not to say that she concurs with everything; I did resist some of her suggestions, and brushed aside some trenchant criticisms (including some that were directed at the letter format itself). I have no doubt that some day soon she will write on psychotherapy and have the chance to spell out our differences. In the meantime, however, she has to be fully identified with this book.

ONE

FOUR QUESTIONS

Dear Uncle,

I'm surrounded out here, on one side by behaviorists and on the other by interpersonalists. The handful of us who cling to the middle are considered eclectic, and branded reactionary. Our "talking cure" is an anachronism, a relic from the medieval age of psychoanalysis. Where we once owned the science and the culture, the modifiers have the science and the interpersonalists lay claim to the culture. From where I'm standing, ours is the rearguard action of a futile fight against the wave of the future.

As you know, however, I have a soft spot for the traditional, "dynamic," psychotherapy (and I've noticed that those of my teachers who happen to be in therapy just happen to be in some form of it, which must mean something), so I'm going to try it out and see for myself. No, I haven't found an analyst yet, but I have found a suitable clinic patient. I will start seeing him next semester, and I have started reviewing my course notes and textbooks.

I've also had this thought: since I happen to have a favorite uncle who is a practitioner of the traditional therapy, I might take some advantage of it. And since I happen to know that my favorite uncle enjoys teaching, if not proselytizing, I figured it would not be too presumptuous of me to ask him some questions. They are specific and concrete questions, and there are four of them.

1. What instructions do you give your patients to orient them to therapy? Do you ask them to free associate and tell you everything that comes to mind? This is a problem, I understand, because if they do it at all, patients free associate only sporadically and selectively. Do you tell them to do it anyway?

1

2. What if my patient, in the first or second session, say, says, "What do you want me to tell you?" or "What should I talk about?" How do I respond? Do I ask him for some case history ("Please tell me something about yourself, what's your problem, for instance?"), despite the fact that he was already subjected to the clinic's exhaustive intake procedure? I'll feel funny (and phony) pretending that I knew nothing about him. Not only will I have read the application that he filled out but I'll have read a comprehensive diagnostic report that was based on a series of clinical interviews. Moreover, he might resent having to repeat everything he told the interviewer, and wonder why I'd want him to. Then should I say something like, "I want to hear it in your own words"? What reasons do I give if he asks me why? (He isn't likely to be satisfied with the answer, "One of my teachers says we should.")

3. What about frequency of sessions? Daily is unfeasible, of course, and hasn't been regarded as necessary for decades. I'd like to know what you regard as optimal for our brand of therapy. Once a week is the norm in our clinic and it seems to me too big a departure from tradition. The clinic will allow two sessions per week, and with my supervisor's backing I can probably push for three. What would you advise?

4. What personal information, if any, are you willing to divulge? Say a patient asks you, in the first or second session, whether you are married and have children, how do you respond? Or say my patient asks me how old I am, how should I respond? I find it hard to imagine myself saying, "I'm not going to tell you anything personal about myself," it feels so cold and off-putting. Do I have no other choice? And should I first ask him why he asked, even though that feels both off-putting and evasive?

My prospective patient is a forty-five-year-old homosexual, so I won't be surprised if he asks me those questions. He is enrolled in a program for advanced computer technology, and he might also ask me how much I know about computers. Do I tell him that I own a Macintosh, love to format, and am expert at playing Tetris?

As you see, my questions are concrete. Our teachers and text-books lean heavily on theory and generalities, and are stingy when it comes to details. It's the details I need because, as you know, I'm a stickler for them. I know that you are, too, so I'm sure you won't be unempathic. In any case, I hope you don't feel imposed upon.

Simon

TWO

THE BASIC INSTRUCTION
AND DIRECT QUESTIONS

Dear Uncle,

Thanks for the answers and also for the interpretation. The answers are exactly what I need, and the interpretation is, as they say here, on target. I gladly acknowledge the Passover allusion; it was unconscious, of course, but I'm sure it was probably there. Chanting the Four Questions at the seder, and getting all that kvelling for it, wasn't exactly bad for my pleasure principle. I'd like to believe that you were beaming at my current questions and that's why you took pains to answer them so explicitly.

But your four answers have begotten four new questions, so you'll have to forgive me for extending my request and asking for a second letter. Please notice that I am not asking you any why questions, which can go on indefinitely; these are what-if questions, which are at least self-limiting.

Our orienting instruction—we call it the "basic instruction"—is: "You can talk about the things you want to talk about, it's up to you. I will listen and try to understand. When I have something useful to say, I will say it." I can picture saying it to my patient with a clear conscience; it is succinct and sounds sensible.

It avoids the problem of pretending that I know nothing about him (in your private practice you face this problem, too, because your patients are often referred by someone who has given you information, either in writing or over the phone), and it isn't the free association instruction ("say everything that comes to mind"), which can be awkward. Instead of asking him to tell me what's on his mind, I say, "What you want to talk about." Neither do I say "you should" but merely "you can," and to make it clear I add, "It's up to you." This, as you mention, provides an instruction that is

4

minimally directive, and that's what I want because the therapy is going to be maximally nondirective (I won't ask you why, because I promised to ask you no why questions).

The second part of the basic instruction notifies my patient of what I'm going to be doing, and it's certainly a considerate thing to do. But in addition to "I will listen and try to understand," there's also "when I have something useful to say, I will say it." The problem here is that it says, in effect, "You say anything you want to, I will say useful things," and this sounds to me like a touch of asperity (there's a tacit "but" between the two phrases). So I think I'd rather word it this way: "I will speak whenever I have something useful to say, something that I think might be helpful"—which brings me to the first of my new questions.

What if he asks for a definition of "useful," do I respond, "Useful for you"? He might regard this as quite gratuitous. Should I instead take the opportunity to say something about self-inquiry? This strikes me as a good idea, but if it's a good idea, shouldn't I do it in the basic instruction instead of counting on him to raise the issue? After all, don't I want him to self-inquire, explore his behavior and his personality (not to overlook his neurosis), and maybe get to understand himself a bit better? Why would I want such a key issue to remain ambiguous?

What if he says, "But shouldn't I talk about my problems?" Won't it perplex him if I again say, "It's up to you"? Or would you suggest I say, instead, "I gather you believe that talking about your problems is the right thing to do here"? This feels wrong to me, if not challenging too, because if he responds, "Yes, isn't it the right thing for me to do?" am I going to say, "No, not necessarily, because I think the right thing to do is talk about what you want to talk about"? This strikes me as having started the therapy on an awkward, if not also an argumentative, footing.

I have heard that patients often begin their sessions by saying, "I don't know what to talk about today," or some variation on this theme. Now, simply telling them to talk about whatever they want to talk about isn't likely to be "useful" because then they might simply rephrase it and say something like, "But I have no idea what

I want to talk about." In any event, I expect my patient to look to me for some guidance in this matter and I'm eager to know what kinds of guidance I can give—what would be *useful*.

I'm emboldened to ask such questions because your letter goes into such explicit detail. You even go so far as to suggest that I might want to commit the basic instruction to memory and speak it exactly as you have written it. This surprises me. I have been given to understand that we therapists have to find our own style, and fashion our own personal way of talking to patients. You apparently don't think so. You seem to be suggesting that, even aside from the basic instruction, I actually repeat your words; and you imply that you always say these things to your patients in exactly the same way. I find this very intriguing.

It leads me to your prescription for answering personal questions. You have a set speech for it. When your patients ask you whether you are married, say, and have children, and it's the first time they've asked such a question, you routinely say this: "From time to time you will want to ask me a personal question. Usually I won't answer it, at least not right away; even if I intend to answer, I'll often wait." Then you pause to give them a chance to ask why.

However, if and when they do ask you why, or ask you any kind of question, personal or otherwise, you never respond with a "Why do you ask?" You do this presumably because for one thing it's a counterquestion, and for another it's a directive. You try hard to ask your patients no questions, and for two further reasons. One is that questioning has implications for your "role definition," defining you as the one who probes and pries. The second is, you want to keep the therapy session from turning into a clinical interview.

But patients will wonder why we don't answer their questions right away. If they ask for our reasons, we are of course entitled to put our policy into immediate practice and make no immediate response. This, however, would be unfair and could make a mockery of the matter. So we have to go ahead and say something more about it. We have a number of options.

As I understand it, you don't object to the rationale that many therapists use for delaying their answers to personal questions, even though it can entail an implicit, if not explicit, directive "please examine the motives behind your question." They say something to the effect that, "If I answered right away, then your reason for asking the question might, oh, recede into the background, let's say; the answer could cover it, in a way; and then you might not think about the reason and instead you might become preoccupied, let's say, with the answer."

My difficulty putting this rationale into words aside, it strikes me as appropriate for a direct question but not for a personal one. How likely is it, after all, that my answering the question will foreclose an examination of the reasons behind it? If my patient asks me whether I'm married, and I say I am not, isn't it reasonable to expect that he will now reveal his reason for wanting to know? And if I had greeted the question with silence, isn't it likely that he will become preoccupied with my silence and read one or two meanings into it?

Moreover, the rationale is a bit abstruse, and I can imagine him not getting the point. At the same time, though, I can imagine him getting it—and arguing it with, "Don't worry, doc, the reason won't disappear. Besides, what's so important about the reason? I want to know whether you have a wife and kids because it matters to me. Does your answer depend on why it matters to me? Will you answer a question only if I have the right reason for asking it?"

You apparently agree that the rationale is problematic. In practice you use a different one. The continuation that you recommend is this one: "I will wait because I'll want to think about the question and be sure that the answer I give you would be useful." This, I concede, is less abstruse and more straightforward, though it again begs the question of what "useful" means. And if the patient says, "So do you want me to tell you why the answer will be useful? Is that what I should do whenever I ask you a question?" would "it's up to you" be appropriate for a response? In a loose sense, it would, but in this particular context it strikes me as evasive and deflecting.

By the way, you didn't mention whether or not you intended to answer the question (or does this fall in the category of your delaying policy?). I'm assuming that you want to remain as impersonal as possible, so I'd guess that you would rather not tell them that I have an aunt and two cousins. But in your letter you imply that "it depends," and I can't help wondering on what.

You did write that it's one thing not to tell whether we're married and have children; it's another not to tell our age and whether we're a student. This hinges on the issue of credentials, and patients have a right to know our professional credentials. Thus, "Are you a student?" doesn't count as a personal question; it's a business question and should be answered.

Fair enough. But does my age count as a credential? It depends, you say. For some patients it might. If I have reason to suppose that my age might, for my patient, count as a credential, then I should go ahead and tell him. I don't have to be so certain that it is a credential, for whenever we err, we should prefer to err on the side of prudence, and a businesslike response is usually prudent. If it turns out that he had construed it as a personal question, I can tell him that the reason I answered it was that I hadn't been sure whether it was business or personal. This might come up when he asks whether I'm married, and I choose to define that question as a personal one.

Which raises a few more what-if questions. What if I happen to wear a wedding band, do I remove it before the sessions? And how do I manage to disguise my age, do I grow a beard and tint it gray? And if it were humanly possible to keep my gender from showing, would I want to keep it from showing? But I am now being frivolous—and I'd better sign off before I get silly.

As ever

THREE

"USEFUL," BUSINESS, AND PERSONAL QUESTIONS

Dear Uncle,

Direct questions are directives that are hard to resist. This is especially true for our patients, which is why you are loath to ask them. You are also reluctant to advise me on how to deal with my prospective patient's anticipated questions because you don't want to complicate and maybe subvert my supervision (that's the reason you ignored my question about frequency of sessions, isn't it?). But I'll choose a supervisor who is congenial to your (our) point of view, and sound him (her) out on the matter before we begin. In any case, you overcame your reluctance, gave me some more explicit instruction, and for this I am grateful.

My asking for a definition of the term *useful* didn't surprise you; it pertains, after all, to the key question of when and why I am going to be "saying something." You can't recall ever being asked the question by any of your patients. Your guess is that they construe "useful" as "helpful to you" and it thereby makes perfect sense. Still, the answer "useful for our work here" is better than "useful for you."

The distinction is a fine but important one because it is our patients' work that counts for the therapeutic process, and it's the therapeutic process that is going to be useful for them. If I understand your point, we regard the therapy itself as the agency that is instrumental in alleviating their suffering, and we construe our role as being responsible for the integrity of the therapy. This makes sense to me but it might not to them (so I hope my patient doesn't ask me the question).

Next you admonish me that at no time and in no way do I ever want to engage my patient in any kind of an argument. When I

9

discuss business with him, I have to take pains to avoid even the appearance of arguing, as well as of challenging his judgment. Would I ever want to argue about the schedule, you ask rhetorically. Would I want to challenge his ability to pay my fee? In point of fact, I don't want to be someone who ever challenges or judges him, and this applies when he says that he doesn't know what to talk about, and it applies whether or not I have treated the issue as business. The reason we mustn't expand the basic instruction—by telling our patients to talk about themselves, for instance—is fundamental to our form of therapy. To sum up your argument: our patients must be free to talk about whatever they choose to talk about, and we must therefore remain "neutral with respect to content."

Well, this sounds terrific on paper, and is an ideal state of affairs, but it strikes me as an idealized goal and therefore an unrealistic one. Short of that, I find it daunting. Will I be able to sustain such a stringent neutrality? What if my patient talks only about computers? Will I be able to keep from suggesting that he might benefit from therapy if he occasionally talked a bit about himself?

It's small comfort to know that this is also true for classical psychoanalysis, in that the "fundamental rule" asks for all thoughts and feelings ("anything and everything that comes to mind"), and says nothing about them being about the patient's self. Free association, to be really free, can have no strings attached. Similarly, volition, by definition, can never be dictated. Therefore, instructing our patients to talk about themselves, or suggesting just that they try and do it, is dissonant with the underlying spirit of our therapy. Not that we don't welcome their talking about themselves. Of course we do. We even expect them to. What we don't do is *want* them to. In this respect, as in so many others as well, we remain "desireless."

So when my patient asks do I want him to talk about himself, I can only respond, "I want you to talk about whatever you want to." This is the right response for my second what-if question. My, "I gather you believe that talking about your problems is the right thing to do here," felt wrong because it was wrong—it's an interpretation.

Any interpretation, no matter how superficial, is untimely here. Even saying, "I gather you believe that I want you to talk about yourself," is pointless because the issue is a business matter and business matters should be discussed and not analyzed. (Would we ever think of saying, "I gather you believe that I want you to pay the fee"?) As you write: "When they ask us a question, patients want an answer and not an interpretation."

We have to reserve our interpretations for the purposes of uncovering and discovering, for the work of analysis and understanding, inquiry and exploration—in short, "the vital work of psychotherapy." And even then, we have to make sure that each interpretation is thoughtfully formulated and carefully timed in such a way as to be minimally directive and intrusive.

I find this exciting, even exhilarating, but again daunting. Dealing with business matters forthrightly seems easy enough, and I can see the value in doing it. But defining certain matters as business can be difficult, you warn, and treating them accordingly is crucial for our form of therapy; its quality and effectiveness can depend on it. Yet our definition has to be elastic and may become fluid (which is very evident, for it surprised me that you would define the statement, "I don't know what to talk about," as business, I'd have thought it belonged to "the vital work of psychotherapy").

I can see that business—inasmuch as it refers to the format and structure of therapy—has to pertain to more than the mundane issues of schedule and fee. It also has to stipulate the range of ways in which our patients behave during the sessions, as well as the ways in which we ourselves behave. The chief stipulations for them are: (1) they must keep their appointments and pay the fee; (2) they must talk; (3) they must talk as freely and openly as they can. In order to talk freely and openly they may need to know what our qualifications are, so here we get into the matter of credentials. Patients require a range of qualifications, including many that are specific (you write "peculiar") to them. Often it isn't merely a matter of asking whether we are qualified as a therapist, or whether this therapy is right for them, but also "Are you the right therapist for me? Can I talk to you about certain subjects, openly and freely, and will you both understand what I'm talking about and be sympathetic to it?"

When my prospective patient sees that I am younger than he, he may feel that it disqualifies me. His asking me how old I am therefore translates into a question of credentials. Therefore, instead of saying, "You're wondering if I'm too young to be your therapist, I take it," which is already an interpretation, I'm better off telling my age and then asking whether it's a problem for him. And instead of doing it this way: "I am twenty-six, is that a problem?" which can come across as testy and challenging, or "I am twenty-six, why do you ask?" which can be equally challenging, I can simply tell him my age and see how he responds. If he changes the subject, I can interrupt and say, "Before you go on, I want to ask you whether my being twenty-six is a problem for you." The important point is that I haven't asked for his reasons, at least not so directly that he can't respond, "No, it isn't," and then continue with the new topic.

Of course, if he says it is a problem, then it must be discussed in the same way we'd discuss a problem with scheduling or fees: the discussion should be businesslike and not therapeuticlike. I have to be forthright about my beliefs and opinions, avoid questioning his beliefs and opinions, and be careful not to use any interpretations to influence the outcome. This is because interpretations must be reserved for the vital work of therapy; they should never be coopted into the service of resolving practical problems.

Your lesson is well taken. I shall be ready to say something like, "It is my opinion that my age doesn't disqualify me; I don't believe it will prevent me from understanding the things you'll talk about" (and I can substitute "the clinic's opinion" for the opening phrase, for the clinic has, after all, assigned me to him). The same can be said when the issue of my heterosexuality comes up, and it also applies to my knowledge of computers.

Similarly, "I don't know what to talk about," can be treated as business, especially if he says it early on or in response to the basic instruction. At such times it might be in the same category as "I can't afford your fee." But would I not ask him to please explain how come he can't afford the fee? This seems like a natural thing to do, and I'm sure I would probably do it. You, however, are sure that you would not. For one thing, you aren't sure you really need the information, and, for another, the question can imply that you are a person who is going to be judging his reasons and evaluating his reasoning—so he had better be circumspect and not feel so free to talk about everything he wants to talk about.

On the other hand, however, your reasons, Uncle, have apparently been judged by me, and my questions and arguments have given you pause. I'm referring to your policy for answering personal questions. It's been years since you've given it any thought, and you agree that it has the problems I mentioned.

The first part, "I will often wait and not respond right away," is all right, though in practice you usually do respond right away, either by answering the question or by saying that you prefer not to tell whether you're married and have children. If you are asked why, you will say, "Because in my experience, you are likely to benefit more from therapy if you don't know personal things about me." By putting it on a pragmatic basis ("my experience") you minimize the possibility of argument. In my case, the final phrase ("and be sure the answer I could give you will be useful") can be omitted, and since I can hardly appeal to "my experience," I might substitute "because this form of therapy works better when you don't know personal things about me." This keeps matters at the level of objective fact and personal opinion, which is where all business matters should be kept, and it minimizes the potential for dispute and the passing of judgment, which is what all therapy matters should minimize.

Finally, thanks for taking my frivolousness seriously (I appreciate that you treat all of your patients' remarks as meaningful). You're not sure it doesn't make some sense to remove a wedding band and you see no good reason not to do it. But we can hardly hide our age and mask our gender, not to mention our physical appearance and manner of speaking. This merely means that we cannot be entirely impersonal, or for that matter, completely neutral; it doesn't mean we shouldn't maximize it within the limits of what is practical and feasible. I understand your point, and I am interested to know what you think the practical limits are and how far we can feasibly push them.

But I have already taken too much advantage of you, and it's time I stopped interviewing you. When I begin seeing my patient, I will write you and tell you how things are going.

Thanks again and best regards,
Simon

FOUR

TECHNIQUE, THEORY, AND PRACTICE

Dear Uncle!

It's a great idea, your offer to continue our correspondence and give me therapy lessons. I'm not sure about your interpretation that it was my idea in the first place (maybe only because it embarrasses me). Still, it's exactly what I want, it's precisely what I need, and I gladly accept all of the ground rules you've laid down.

First off, you will set the agenda. It will be like piano lessons where the teacher has a pedagogical plan, puts it into practice with verbal instructions and demonstrations at the keyboard, and assigns pieces for homework. We can do the same. In fact, we've been doing it already and it seems to work fine. Inasmuch as our craft consists substantially of spoken words, it can feasibly be learned via written words—up to a point only, of course, because supervision is crucial and only practice makes perfect.

Then you will write to me and I will continue to respond. You will want to know how I'm assimilating your instruction, so I'll continue summarizing what you write; it's the way you'll know whether your points are coming across as you intended them. Teaching by textbook has limitations that verbal instruction needn't have, and we might compensate for them if I dutifully feed back everything you feed me (turning me into a regurgitating parrot pupil). You also want me to continue raising my questions and making my critical comments, so I will. Occasionally you will give me homework in the form of exercises and problems; in that way we can also work on "case material."

I'd like to believe it's not just to make me feel less demanding that you mention that you stand to benefit, too. Not only does examining our work guard us against complacency but it can uncover

15

ideas we didn't realize we had and beliefs we didn't know were so articulated, as well as exposing biases that have been unacknowledged and therefore not questioned (see how the regurgitation works!). So you will occasionally digress from teaching me how to do therapy and discuss larger issues, and it will be somewhat for your sake as well.

But you are not going to lose sight of the fact that what I need is a treatise and not a polemic. I know that expecting you not to write about psychotherapy in general, and also about theoretical matters, is expecting too much. Nevertheless, you promise to give me a concrete description and articulation of the form of therapy that you regard as optimal and ideal ("the one that I practice with those of my patients for whom I deem it to be appropriate, and which is for the others the form that I deviate from").

I also know that I can't expect a complete treatise and things will be left out. There will be no overlap with my courses on psychopathology, we won't study the etiology of symptoms and the diagnosis of disorders, and neither will we cover every aspect of therapy. We will be focusing on the basic and "average expectable" issues, and in a concrete way. This suits me fine, Uncle. It's all I need and all I want. The nuts and bolts. The way to build the thing and make it run, and keep it running till it has run its course.

My friend Susan (you met her last year when I brought her home during the spring break and you and she played Beethoven's sonatas for piano and cello one afternoon) wants to participate in our project. In fact, she is eager and enthusiastic, and practically insists on participating. Susan is a kindred spirit; she is strongly committed to psychoanalysis, and plans to enroll in our postdoctoral program for analytic training. So this is what she proposes: she and I will read your letters together; we will study and discuss them together; and she will help me write mine.

Your first two letters have laid some groundwork for us (Susan is counting on being included), your third letter lays down some ground rules. The chief one prescribes the right attitude we should have toward practice, the best attitude we should take toward theory, and the correct way to regard the relationship between practice and theory. I would sum it up in this homily: *"Be always respectful and rarely skeptical toward practice; be critical and also wary of theory; never let your theory dictate your practice!"* Skepticism has to be distinguished from criticalness, and when you admonish us to be respectful of practice you mean *practice* in three senses of the term: (1) the clinical experience of those who practice and the practitioners who preceded them (as in the anecdotal method); (2) the work it takes to become a skilled practitioner (as in practicing piano); and (3) the ways in which the craft is practiced, namely its technique. Sense 1 entails a recognition that the anecdotal method, which has fallen on hard times, isn't coeval with an appeal to authority. Sense 2 entails a recognition that ours is a craft that takes work and study. Sense 3 entails a recognition that technique, which has also fallen on hard times in many quarters, is not only helpful and valuable, it is absolutely indispensable to psychotherapy.

The points you make in respect to senses 1 and 2 are well taken, but I give them short shrift for three reasons: (1) to bolster your arguments you lean on analogies, especially on making music (and for my sake you throw in some tennis); (2) I am leery of analogies, especially when they are used for purposes of persuasion rather than illustration; (3) Susan and I are already persuaded.

Suffice it to say that when our piano teacher shows us how to play a piece, we don't ask for proof and neither do we say, "How do you know?" When our tennis teacher shows us how to serve, we don't demand any evidence nor do we say, "So what's your theory?" We might ask for reasons, to help us understand better; we might disagree with the instruction, for we don't abrogate our critical judgment; but we don't approach the lesson as if it were anything like a scientific proposition. Neither will being taught how to play pieces and hit backhands suffice to make us piano and tennis players; we have to practice. Points granted and not pursued.

On sense 3 you deliver a polemic, aimed at me. If you had known that Susan was joining us, you could have spared yourself and relied on her to persuade me. As a musician, she too knows the special value (and joys) of technique. There may be more than one good way to play a chromatic scale, but there are also bad ways. She likes to point out that there's never any question of no technique, there's only good and bad technique—technical mastery and a lack thereof. She enthusiastically seconds the passage where you write that a deliberate abjuring of technical measures is itself a technique.

I personally second the passage where you point out that just as it can't make us expert musicians it won't make us expert therapists but we can get pretty good by merely mastering technique. This is true for tennis, too, and it's reassuring. But when you ask how useful is it for a piano teacher to instruct me to play a passage "tenderly" without helping me find the best fingering, and you argue that no music can be played musically and no tennis ball well struck without technique, then you lose me. Not that I disagree, but I cavil. Words can clarify, analogies and metaphors can obscure. (Susan believes they can serve as quasi-theoretical models, but I have my doubts; we resort to them when the going gets rough has been my observation.)

I don't think it helps to regard therapy as a performance or a game; it's not a voyage or a repair job, or anything other than itself. Therapists aren't surgeons whose technique has to take precedence, and neither are we like pianists who cannot begin to play any music without a certain level of skill and facility. Ours is a healing art, and its craft component is distinctive to it. (Susan says I shouldn't lecture you like this.) I do, however, like the way you write about the professional aspect of being a therapist:

> "Can you play the piano?"—"I don't know, I've never tried," is a relevant joke; it can be transposed into, "Can you surgically remove an appendix?"—"I don't know, I've never tried," without losing its incongruity and humor. Consider, however, "Can you do psychotherapy?" The joke is no longer so funny because there's a popular point of view that all one has to do is try; anyone with certain talents and interests can go right ahead and be a therapist. After all, don't we regularly help one another with our emotional

and psychological problems? Don't we hear each other out with patience and compassion, giving comfort and advice? What else is psychotherapy but the good ministrations of people to people, helping them endure and overcome? What special skills are required that many of us don't already have?

Then you go on to say that your conception of therapy leads you to claim that the difference between a therapist and a friend who gives good counsel can be no less significant than the difference between a surgeon and a friend who removes a splinter, that the discipline of conducting therapy is no different in principle from the discipline of playing the piano, and it isn't merely operational, it's substantive. Your thesis is this: just as the surgeon and the pianist are defined by the fact of possessing technical skills, by being craftsmen, so the psychotherapist can (and should) be defined. I'll buy that.

I have a worry, though. I expect to be sufficiently self-conscious when I do therapy; I won't need any additional distractions. Having to say certain things in a certain way, and having to avoid saying certain things in any way, is intimidating. I find it hard to imagine that it will free me up and allow me to listen to my patient better. This is what you claim it will do—I sure hope you're right.

Susan worries that it might not be good for us to be given explicit techniques, for while there are good and bad ones, there may be no single set that will fit all patients and all circumstances. This applies to piano playing: there is one set of techniques for playing Mozart and a quite different set for Debussy. Much also depends on the instrument, whether it's a modern grand or an old clavier.

Analogies aside, her point is we must tailor (a metaphor!) our technique to our patients, and she favors your injunction that we shouldn't tailor it to us. Little should depend on the kind of person we happen to be; it should depend on the kind of person they are, and what their problems, needs, and circumstances are.

Technique has fallen on hard times. Not only have traditional techniques been ridiculed and caricatured in contemporary culture but many of our teachers regard the term as a pejorative ("mechanical," "rigid," and "lifeless" are three of their favorite synonyms), and not only does it reflect a misplaced emphasis but technique can be the nemesis of good therapy. You disagree strongly—and having studied your first two letters, this comes as no surprise. Still, the intensity of your conviction is remarkable. Doing therapy is not just an art, it's substantially a craft; not only is an emphasis on technique rarely misplaced but it's always on target; good technique is indispensable for good therapy. Our lessons will therefore be largely taken up with matters that are technical.

So we have to be clear about what technique means. The ways in which we put our intentions into action (or act upon our intentions) and put our therapeutic goals into practice, is your definition. You defend it by pointing out that therapists often obscure their techniques with such locutions as "deal with," "approach," and "address." What it actually means to deal with a patient's resistance, for instance, isn't spelled out; what exactly we say when we address it isn't specified. And when do we say it? And how do we respond to the range of likely reactions to our intervention? These are technical questions. As you write:

> The ways in which we define our role and structure the session, the ways in which we communicate our understanding and formulate our interpretations, these are matters of technique. By technique I mean such things as ways of asking and answering questions. When patients ask how old we are, we are faced with a technical problem—not with a technical problem alone, to be sure, for the question needs to be understood, but with a technical problem also. When they persistently come late—or repeatedly deny that our interpretations have any validity, when they report a dream, when they fall into silence, when they insist that they need us to be their friend and counselor—then our responses are determined in significant part by technical considerations. Many of the principles I will give you in these letters can be regarded as aspects of technique. When I write about interpretations, for instance, I will propose that they be succinct. That's good technique. Similarly, it may be good technique to avoid interpretations that are too deep or too

shallow, give priority to the here-and-now over the there-and-then, keep the transference in the background, deal with resistances in the business mode. And if we expect our patients to become more reflective and self-searching, there are ways to achieve it and ways to avoid subverting it. Succinctly put: the explicit ways in which we put our intentions concretely into action are matters of technique.

Next we take on theory. Before summarizing your remarks, let me mention that many of them are sketchy and some are tantalizing, raising questions that you promise to answer later on. (You mention parenthetically that you will need time to collect your thoughts, and when they are collected you will write us a theory letter.) In fact, most of the issues that you have raised in this letter are going to be taken up in the course of our lessons, and many of them more than once. You intend them now as "maps of the terrain and signposts." The specifics, and their attendant rationales, will have to wait (which is naturally frustrating but unavoidable).

You do confide that your attitude toward theory has changed over the years. You used to take it seriously and you suspect it had to do with the intellectual energy we young people have. (Who's being disingenuous now?) But you've long been uneasy with the facile way we therapists make our theory, as if it required no special expertise. Most of us are amateurs when it comes to theorizing and rarely do we consult the philosophers to make sure we're getting it right.

Well, as it happens, Susan and I are surprised that you have this attitude but we're not startled by it. We have a philosophy professor who has made us theory shy. She is leery of psychologists who engage without scruple in making theory as if it required no study of the history of ideas and training in logic. She likes to ask those of us in clinical psychology how we'd like it if, on the basis of her having been a patient, she wrote a treatise on therapy. And her course isn't going to equip us; at best it might help us discriminate good theories from the bad ones and know when a concept is a piece of art and not a doodle. She says the physical scientists have it easy: compared with the stuff we chew on, they are munching baby food. Theorizing on mental events, and on states of consciousness and acts of human volition, is not only high in calories and fat but it's tough chewing.

They have a way of becoming ideologies, that's why you've become leery of theories, especially as they are used to dictate practice. Anyway, your views on psychotherapy have been influenced more by practice, yours as well as that of your teachers, mentors, peers, and forebears, and this is as it should be. (Susan is reminded of Freud's analogy between theories and wives. We men husband our wives; publicly we protect their honor and good name even though privately we have doubts, being too familiar with their defects. I, in turn, am reminded of the analogy of the lab coat, whose original function is to protect us from the dirty data; we grow attached to it and continue to wear it after it has grown frayed and filthy, no longer serving its function; it has become less a handy piece of clothing than a uniform advertising our identity. Both of the analogies fit your position but I think mine is more fitting.)

To get back to our lesson: a therapy designed according to a theory of psychopathology is a therapy that stands and falls with it—and many a therapy has foundered on its theory. The theory flourishes while the therapy stagnates in neglect. In our zeal for theorizing, and also for diagnosing our patients and their problems, we lose sight of the practical implications of our ideas. Theories simplify, as they should, but they tend to oversimplify. Practice is never simple; it ought to have a firmer basis than theory provides.

Take for example the theory that posits that everyone who is neurotic is neurotic by virtue of a fundamental delusion, a pervading piece of self-deception.[1] We neurotics have formed our characters in the service of this delusion; every symptom, anxiety, and inhibition, every personal trait, evolves from and devolves into self-deception, and will dissolve when that self-deception is ameliorated. This is a strong theory, it demands a strong therapy, which turns out to be our familiar talking cure. Does this follow? If we

---

[1] My reference is to Hellmuth Kaiser's *Effective Psychotherapy* (ed. L. B. Fierman. New York: Free Press, 1965) and David Shapiro's *Psychotherapy of Neurotic Character* (New York: Basic Books, 1989). They are superb treatises and—my critical remarks notwithstanding—well worth studying.

started from such a theory would we want to arrive at a therapy session in which therapist and patient sit sequestered in a room and talk to each other? Why don't they play games, eat meals, go places? The theory mandates the use of confrontations ("Look here, you are deluding yourself!") and here is where it leads us astray. Confrontations have consequences that have more to do with the dynamics of therapy—not to overlook the more mundane dynamics of everyday behavior—than with the dynamics of neurosis. Even when made with warmth and sensitivity, they put patients on the defensive and marshal their worst defenses. Instead of self-awareness and sober reflection, they promote self-consciousness and embarrassment.

The point is, our opinion as regards the technique of confrontation should be predicated not on our theory of psychopathology but on our theory of psychotherapy. We should start not with pathology in general but with therapy in particular ("We don't want our therapy to be dependent on a theory, we want it to have a firmer basis than that").

But, to use a confrontation of my own, isn't this quite impossible? Psychotherapy can't be completely divorced from psychopathology; there must be a psychological theory supporting it. This is what Susan thinks. She's very interested in theory. (I, on the other hand, having no talent for it and having a cognitive style that is concrete, am content to be agnostic.) Susan believes we need theory to provide us with secure guidelines and help us set our goals. She takes the position that psychological facts are permeated by schemas that are theoretical in nature, that the distinction between our facts and our theories is artificial, at best, and misleading at worst, and she likes the aphorism, *"Facts are little theories and true theories are big facts."* [2] She also has a high regard for Freudian metapsychology, and is disturbed by the way our teachers dismiss it out of hand. She is eager to know your views on it, though she suspects that you're going to be disparaging. I, in turn, would like to know whether our form of therapy

---

[2] This is the philosopher Nelson Goodman's, and can be found in his *Ways of Worldmaking* (Indianapolis, IN: Hackett, 1978), p. 96.

implies an acceptance of a particular set of theoretical concepts and the rejection of others.

These questions aren't going to surprise you, because when you were a student, you and your fellow students demanded theory of your teachers in order to evaluate their claims. When they advocated a therapy procedure, you wanted to know why, and your wish would be satisfied only if they spelled out the theory behind it. The theory, after all, could be judged and more readily accepted or rejected than a bald prescription could. Well, times haven't changed much: most of us still want our teachers' rationales to be based on theory and not on the abominable appeal to authority.

But psychotherapy was never the product of theory, it was born and bred of practice. Bertha Pappenheim[3] wasn't relying on theory when she invented the talking cure. Freud's use of the couch was based less on the theoretical reasons he gave than on the traditional practice of hypnosis (subjects are hypnotized in the supine position); he stopped hypnotizing (and started psychoanalyzing) because he wasn't a good hypnotist and didn't like the way it made him feel. Even free association emerged from pragmatic considerations. Most of the subsequent innovations in therapy were inductive rather than deductive. Theory has followed practice, not the other way round.

Moreover, rationales needn't be based on theory alone. When a prescription is proffered and the question is why, the answer can be "Because that's the way people are—haven't you noticed?" For instance: you tell us to avoid confrontations, and when we ask why; you say it's because they corner patients and put them on the defensive—there's no theory here. Then we ask you why confrontations do that, and you say it's because people are disposed to feel cornered and react defensively when they are faced with unpleasant truths about themselves—this is a fact. The explanation for this fact is that people wish to avoid facing unpleasant truths about themselves. And why is that? "Because that's the

---

[3]Known as Anna O and reported in Breuer, J., & Freud, S. *Studies on Hysteria* (*Standard Edition,* 12:145–156. London: Hogarth Press, 1958).

way people are—and that's a fact!" Must we now explain *this* fact?

Well, maybe we do, but not in order to do therapy right. Put another way: no matter what the theory is, what explanation we can find for this fact, the implications for therapy are the same. There comes a point when our theory will make no difference. Where that point is, is moot, but what isn't moot is that a point exists—and it matters to us. We can't keep asking why ad infinitum; we have to find a point at which we stop (and we can get help from our philosophers in finding it, for there's a point of view among them that contends that the chief function of a theory is to help us stop asking why).

Therefore: on the issue of theory and practice we have to avoid the position that the latter must follow the former. Ours will be a practical bent of mind; our philosophy will be empirical and pragmatic. We won't disdain theory; some of it will sometimes be relevant and even helpful; rarely will any of it be decisive and indispensable. ("A therapy predicated on a theory is only as good as the theory," you write, "and we want our therapy to be better than that.")

But "our therapy" doesn't have a name. I won't ask why, Uncle, but I will ask you how come. Don't you find writing "my form of therapy" and "this particular method of psychotherapy" pretty awkward? Isn't it going to become increasingly awkward as we go along? I think it would be useful to give it a name, but Susan isn't sure. She distrusts the names that psychologists give to the events they study, and is disdainful of acronyms. I believe that, at the very least, they simplify prose. I appreciate that you'd be loath to name our therapy; names can be misleading, or pretentious, or both. They are often based on an exaggeration of small differences and they foster clannishness.

So I offered Susan a compromise and she accepted it. I propose solving the problem with a simple typographical expediency. Whenever you write "this particular method of psychotherapy," or any variation thereof, I will substitute "Psychotherapy" with an uppercase P, while *Psychotherapy* will denote "our form of psychotherapy."

26 I. H. Paul

To sum up: instead of asking what the theory is behind this or that practice, we'll ask what the rationale is. Insofar as the rationale uses clinical concepts, there is no quarrel. But when the concepts we use are predicated on psychological theory, then they needn't, and they shouldn't, play a significant role in Psychotherapy. (See how the name works?) This is an intriguing point of view, and provocative, and both Susan and I, but especially Susan, will be eagerly awaiting your lesson on it.

In the meantime our attitude toward theory will be as advised: civil and respectful but nothing more. We will ration our why questions and settle for rationales that are empirical, unabashedly taking recourse in the answer, "Because that is the way things are—haven't you noticed?"

Simon and Susan

FIVE

PSYCHOANALYSIS, THE THERAPEUTIC PROCESS, AND EGO AUTONOMY

Susan is happy that you've welcomed her aboard, I am happy that you approve of *Psychotherapy,* and both of us are glad that you'll begin teaching us how to do it—after you've taught us what it is. (We're also pleased with your parenthetical remark: "If you forget, after a while, that by Psychotherapy we don't mean simply psychotherapy, then I will be far from dismayed, for I won't deny that deep down I believe its methods and guidelines apply to all forms of psychotherapy that are good.")

First we learn what it isn't: namely, what is commonly referred to as analytically oriented psychotherapy, and amounts to a diluted and attenuated psychoanalysis with substantial infusions of support, reassurance, and advice. Quite the contrary: instead of an adulterated psychoanalysis, Psychotherapy might be regarded as perhaps an even purer form of it. That's a bold claim, and Susan wonders how we can make it (even with the caveat "perhaps") when we have abandoned the "fundamental rule." Don't analysts regard free association, as well as the couch, as essential?

I, too, find the claim a bit rash, despite the fact that we rely on the interpretive mode of intervention along with many of the conceptions of psychoanalytic clinical theory; we pay attention to phenomena that analysts attend to, such as intrapsychic conflicts, resistances, transference, daydreams, and night dreams. Our chief differences from psychoanalysis stem mainly from our thoroughgoing nondirectiveness, which for one thing prevents us from directing our patients to use the couch and free associate. But if they want to, that's fine; they aren't instructed or advised to, that's all.

27

Moreover, a course of Psychotherapy can be indistinguishable from a course of psychoanalysis, insofar as our patients may slip naturally into the free association mode, their conflicts and fantasies may be brought to the surface, their symptoms and habits subjected to analysis, a transference neurosis may burgeon and be resolved. There is nothing in Psychotherapy that prevents this, and there are features of the method that can facilitate its happening. The critical difference is that we, as therapists, don't make it happen.

Since we do nothing to prevent it, and inasmuch as key features of our format are consonant with its happening, it can and does happen. It depends largely on the patients (their purposes and personalities, for instance) and on the circumstances of therapy (the frequency of sessions, say), how closely a course of Psychotherapy will approximate a psychoanalysis, or if it will instead take on features of other forms of traditional psychotherapy, such as those that can be labeled humanist. For while it maintains the formal structure of psychoanalysis, Psychotherapy borrows from nondirective and existentialist psychotherapy their concepts of freedom and caring and their goals of self-determination and authentic selfness.

Our principles are antithetical to those of many behaviorists and some interpersonalists. Instead of any manipulation of a patient's behavior (by means of learning and conditioning, or exercises and games), our method requires of us a systematic avoidance of any direct influence. We don't give our patients any instruction, advice, counsel, or guidance, and neither do we judge or evaluate them. Our overriding goal is to provide patients with a unique kind of experience in examining and expressing the contents of their mind.

To support and promote their freedom of self-expression and self-experience, we have to behave in ways that hold to a minimum all forms of direction and control. This means that we can't relate to them as teacher or mentor, and of course not as friend. Our role is that of an interested and caring but impartial observer and commentator. We listen actively, we supervise the therapeutic process actively, and we help them understand their experiences by articulating and interpreting them. But we take pains throughout to keep from influencing their experiences and shaping their behavior, and this requires of us a significant neutrality which in turn mandates a substantial degree of impersonality and impassivity.

Like most forms of psychotherapy whose heritage is psychoanalysis, Psychotherapy deals with patients' private experiences (or if we prefer, their phenomenological ones)—their mind, in other words. Psychotherapy doesn't altogether ignore their actions, it just doesn't pay much attention to them (as you put it: "We deal mainly with our patients' mind, and leave the rest to human nature").

"I will not tell you what to do; I'll try never to suggest, or even imply, what decisions you might make or how you should behave." That's a fundamental limitation we impose on ourselves and make clear to our patients. This doesn't mean we don't care about actions. "I will try to help you understand your actions, and I may sometimes help clarify the reasons for your decisions, but what you do and how you decide will be up to you."

Psychotherapy is contemplative. Action is thought about and not taken, behavioral events are examined at a distance. This not only reflects a key feature of its distinctiveness but contributes substantially to its effectiveness. Dealing with actual events—in the form of direction and advice in respect to actions, for instance—would not only vitiate Psychotherapy's distinctiveness, it would undermine its effectiveness in effecting significant changes in patients' behavior. The term *undermine* is probably too strong here, but we must cling to the conviction that Psychotherapy's dynamics and goals require a rigorous neutrality that can be maintained only when we abstain from trying to influence our patients' behavior and action.

That it places stringent restrictions on us and on our participation in the treatment, is perhaps Psychotherapy's most distinctive feature. These restrictions may strike us, you warn, as prohibitive (they already have—we're sure they would many seasoned practitioners as well), but our reasons for submitting to them can be summed up in the concept of uniqueness. In a nutshell: we want our treatment to be unique. We want our patients to have a unique experience: that's why we want it to be unique. Psychotherapy places a high priority on uniqueness; it does so in order to provide patients with a profound experience in a unique kind of process.

Our theory of therapy prevents us from engaging them in anything like an encounter. Our relationship remains formal and in the background. And while the transactions that transpire in our therapy often have to do with nonintellectual aspects of their behavior, the transactions themselves transpire in verbal and cognitive terms. When they feel warmly toward us, our patients aren't at liberty to embrace us; when they are angry at us, they aren't free to hit us; when they attempt to provoke us into an emotional state, we won't permit ourselves the emotion (at least we don't reveal it to them). Not that we ever discourage them from experiencing feelings during sessions; they may laugh and weep, exult and despair, feel desire, rage, and the rest. But the format does impose a constraint both on the intensity of their feelings as well as on the mode of their expression. Verbalization remains the chief currency of expression and this throws a cognitive cast over things.

Moreover, while patients are not discouraged from experiencing emotions and feelings, there is an undercurrent in the therapy that flows in the direction of cognitive control over them. The larger goal, while it isn't to stifle or inhibit emotions and feelings, is to gain a measure of control over them. What exactly this means, to "gain control," we'll have to examine as we go along. But we might bear in mind that it often leads paradoxically to a release of affects, to a disinhibition or a freeing of emotions and feelings from an undue grip of cognitions.

Now to our definition of Psychotherapy, with which Susan and I are not unanimously happy. I am into definitions, naturally, but she is impatient with them. (She teases me with the story of the child who was traumatized when a teacher read to the class from her essay, "Father came home yesterday with a cliché on his face." The dictionary defined it as a "tired expression.") I find our definition fascinating, in that it pivots on the patient, puts the therapist in a formally subservient position, and neatly finesses against their relationship. As you write:

Every psychotherapy can be defined by specifying two sets of intentions and behaviors, those of the therapist and those of the patient, and many definitions of psychotherapy pivot on the interaction of these two sets of intentions and behaviors. Given, however, that the interaction of such sets can only be defined in terms that are different from those of each set, inasmuch as the interaction cannot be described at the same level of abstraction as its two components, those definitions tend to be vague and formalistic. Therefore I prefer a definition that makes no reference to any interactional process, and restricts itself to a two-part formulation, where one part specifies the intentions and behaviors that describe the therapist, and the other rests on the concept of the "therapeutic process," which denotes the experience that psychotherapy affords the patient. Such a two-part definition has the advantage that we can nest one of the parts within the other, so that the intentions and behaviors of the therapist can then be construed in terms of their chief function—namely, the facilitation and promotion of the therapeutic process.

A nested two-part definition is intriguing but our dismissal of the "relationship" seems a bit cavalier. When people enter into a relationship, they have something which has properties that may be difficult to define but this doesn't make it "vague and formalistic." There's nothing vague about our relationship, for example, and the one that Susan and I have is far from formal. To be sure, the one between therapist and patient may well be formal, if that's their choice, but surely you don't mean to claim that it has to be vague. I would have thought you'd insist that it ought to be as clear and unambiguous as possible. Susan rises to your defense by reminding me that it's the definition of psychotherapy that tends to become vague and formalistic when it pivots on the relationship (she isn't sure why, though, and your remark about its occupying a different level of discourse is puzzling to her).

Our definition requires us to articulate the intentions and behaviors of the therapist. Because they are functionally organized around a ruling construct, the therapeutic process, that's what has to be defined formally. Our definition of the therapeutic process will comprise at least three propositions. (1) It is an intrapsychic and mental process, as distinct from an interpersonal transaction or a behavioral event. (2) It is a process of comprehending, gaining clarity, and discovering, as distinct from learning and forming habits. (3) It doesn't encompass everything that happens in therapy, it's the main event but not the sum total. Each proposition needs to be fleshed out, and you promise to do it later. For the time being you say this:

> The therapeutic process refers to our patients' work as they express and explore themselves. It consists of recounting and revealing, reflecting and introspecting, reminiscing and recollecting. The focus is likely to be on the inner reality of affects and emotions, impulses and wishes, needs and conflicts, attitudes, beliefs, and values. Often there is an emphasis on experiencing individuality and autonomy, as well as on a sense of volition. The process is grounded in the complementary acts of understanding and being understood; it's an activity of self-inquiry that strives to gain clarity and discover.

Very thorough, but isn't the concept overworked? Is it a good idea to subsume all of these acts and experiences in a single construct? An omnibus definition, in my opinion, can be a cop-out and I think we might do better by subsuming these patient activities under the rubric of a "core event." Don't you think there is one? Susan thinks there is but she can't decide whether it might be the introspecting or the remembering, the gaining of clarity or of insight; it could even be analyzing and resolving the transference neurosis. My choice would be the self-inquiry as reflected in recounting and revealing, to which I would add some uncovering and discovering. But whatever "it" is, can't we identify it and propose that it's the core event?

Regarding our pleas for theory, you have taken them to heart. Once upon a time, you say, you'd gladly have fulfilled them. In fact, you would have included a fourth proposition in our formal definition of the therapeutic process, and it would read: "It is founded on the psychoanalytic conception of ego autonomy."

You trained, after all, at an orthodox institute. So you took it for granted that analysis was supposed to promote your patients' ego autonomy. You preferred to call it *freedom*—from neurosis, in the broadest sense of the term. Phenomenologically it was freedom from ego alien experiences and compulsions. Anyway, that goal shaped much of your technique; all of the guidelines had some bearing on your patients acquiring greater autonomy. You believed they benefitted from the therapy to the extent that they secured autonomy from, and therefore control over, the forces that operated upon their ego, both from within as well as from without.

Ego was the core of personality, consisting of the self-image and "executive functions." It was also the phenomenological self that all of us come to recognize as our autonomous sense of "me-ness." A central assumption (it's more like a theorem) was that ego is embedded in a matrix of forces that originated from within the personality. They consist of ideas, memories, feelings, action tendencies, and needs—in states of conflict and ambivalency—that are never in perfect harmony with the core me-ness; upon reaching a degree of dissonance, they are referred to as ego alien. Ego is also subject to the demands of reality that aren't ever in perfect harmony either, and when that dissonance becomes excessive we speak of maladaptiveness. The task of mediating and harmonizing these relatively independent configurations of processes and forces— which can be conceptualized as id, superego, and reality—was ego's chief function. Add to this the hypothesis that ego, too, had substantial claims on behavior, and we have a picture of a complicated and dynamic counterpoint, which is what ego autonomy, and its essential relativity, denoted. The fundamental goal of analysis, and also the way to picture the analytic process, is the gradual freeing of ego from the grip of both inner and outer compulsions. More accurately, the goal is to restore and secure an optimal balance between the great agencies that govern and regulate behavior.

All of that is what you used to believe, until you caught yourself taking it too seriously and slighting the way it reflected an intractable attitude toward the relationship between theory and practice. It seemed to provide a good rationale but often felt more like a rationalization, of a kind that when you observed it in patients counted as an intellectualization. This was in the 1970s, when patients suffered from "alienation" and had to have an "encounter." But alienation can be from oneself, too, and you believed that the chief difference between encounter-type and analytic-type therapies lay in the priority accorded to these two alienations. You subscribed to the assumption that your patients' alienation from themselves took precedence and, having resolved it in therapy, the alienation from others was bound to be resolved outside. You were oversimplifying autonomy.

You were also sweeping under the rug misgivings you had concerning ego. It's a reification, but that didn't bother you; it simply meant it was a problem solver, a stopgap measure (a heuristic concept). What did, however, bother you is that it's a stopgap heuristic problem solver only for a mechanistic theory of psychology, and a mentalistic theory really doesn't need one. But . . . .

You cut yourself off here and remind us that our theory lesson is on hold! In this you are showing a side of yourself that I have assured Susan you didn't have, namely a tendency to make tantalizing, if not also provocative, remarks. We're beginning to suspect that it's a pedagogical tactic of yours. Is it also a therapeutic one? Do you make such remarks to your patients to pique their interest and give them an incentive to continue the ordeal of therapy? In any case, we are finding it frustrating, and need no additional incentives (Susan is intrigued by your sketch of ego autonomy).

But you do agree that Psychotherapy must have some theoretical basis. It has to have (at some point) a connection (of some sort) with psychology, if not also with psychopathology. You grudgingly grant this. Then what kind of psychology must it be? You (provisionally) put it this way:

> It is a psychology that is rooted in everyday human experience, a psychology we develop as we grow up in a society and a culture, and a psychology that has developed and grown from the dawn

of human existence. It's an empirical psychology, in the fullest and simplest sense of the term, and our heritage is filled with it. It relies on "theoretical" propositions like these:

- If someone insults me, I feel hurt and my feelings are hurt.
- If someone hurts me or my feelings, I want to hurt them.
- If I'm caught in an act that I deem shameful, I feel ashamed.
- If I do a wrongful deed, something I regard as bad to do, I feel guilty and remorseful and bad about myself.

These are some of the "laws" of our psychology. We need to be loved, valued, cared for, feel safe, secure, and free from worry and anxiety. Isn't this true enough? And isn't it also true that when we aren't loved, valued, cared for, and the rest, we are disposed to developing neurotic characteristics and can benefit from psychotherapy? It isn't a sophisticated psychology, and we aren't so unsophisticated. But why can't we bend our sophistication to the enterprise of psychotherapy, and develop sophisticated theories of therapy, without much further sophistication of psychological theory? Do we need a fully elaborated theory of psychology, and of psychopathology, in order to have a good theory of psychotherapy?

So our next lesson will be dedicated to our sophisticated theory of Psychotherapy.

SIX

NONDIRECTIVENESS, NEUTRALITY, AND PSYCHOTHERAPY AS UNIQUE

Before I don the mantle of parrot-pupil (I'm glad you approve of the way I'm wearing it), I need to quibble with your use of the word *unique.* I looked it up and found "1. being the only one; SOLE; 2. being without a like or equal; 3. distinctively characteristic; PECULIAR; 4. UNUSUAL." Only sense 3 fits our needs, and *distinctive* is closer to what we mean (it has the advantage of admitting of comparison and modification, and also the right antonyms: *common, ordinary, expected, familiar, conventional*). Now to today's lesson.

In your view, no school of therapy can be described with any degree of practical generality, for when it comes to actual methods and techniques there are big differences among its members. With that in mind, we can locate Psychotherapy within the family of methods that belong to the psychoanalytic school—and yes, we know how proud and quarrelsome a family it is, how striven with defections, offshoots, and intermarriages. Still, appearances notwithstanding, the spirit of individuality has prevailed, and because analysts have preferred to write about their theory and their patients, it has gone unremarked that their techniques have evolved and diverged.

Candidates at analytic institutes, from their contacts with teachers and supervisors, have long known the differences that prevail in the ways that analysts, even orthodox ones, conduct analysis. Some have given up the silent posture in favor of a more active involvement in the analytic process, making freer use of questions and other interviewing techniques. Some analysts no longer pursue every sign of transference and resistance, but do so only when the resistance or transference assumes the proportions of an impasse;

and there are further divergences that make for significant differences. Nevertheless, most forms of psychoanalysis share an underlying spirit and attitude, and so does Psychotherapy. Take our nondirectiveness: it faithfully follows the spirit of classical analytic practice, though not the letter of contemporary practice. Many analysts have abandoned, or at least substantially attenuated, the traditional posture of neutrality and they therefore believe that it is no longer necessary to be nondirective. The blank screen—which provides a template for patients to project their imagos and form their transferences—was the traditional rationale for neutrality. It grew controversial, and its rejection ostensibly pulled the rug from under neutrality. This, in turn, removed the rationale for nondirectiveness. If, however, nondirectiveness is taken to be fundamental (as we are enjoined to take it), and if it is based on a different rationale (as we will base it), then neutrality is restored to its rightful place (on the rug) as a necessary consequence of nondirectiveness—which, in turn, is a necessary consequence of our fundamental goal of providing patients with a maximum of freedom in order to experience an optimal therapeutic process.

The two concepts differ in their referents. Some therapy matters are best framed in terms of neutrality, others in terms of nondirectiveness, and each has its distinctive limits and boundaries that are based on considerations of feasibility. The plain and obvious fact is: whether due to the constraints of reality or based on the dictates of clinical judgment, we can never be completely nondirective and neither can we be completely neutral. But this doesn't mean that we shouldn't be as nondirective and neutral as possible, and that the degree to which we are successful or otherwise won't make a significant and substantial difference.

We can bear in mind that the "fundamental rule" is directive only insofar as it mandates a speaking of one's mind. The analyst's interventions are meant to maximize the patient's freedom from inhibitions against full and free expression; they are supposed to weaken the roadblocks to freely associating by identifying and analyzing them. Whatever else such interventions might concretely consist of, they are not directives. In Psychotherapy only the basic instruction is different. This doesn't mean we're more directive.

But analysts have modified the "fundamental rule" in recognition of the fact that free association is both an occasional act and a difficult one. Furthermore, it would have been more accurate to describe it as a stream of consciousness rather than a process of association, for the latter requires a stimulus to associate to (a dream, for example, can be associated to; more precisely, a particular dream image or idea can be). Anyway, many analysts have reduced free associating to the status of an option and softened its requirements. "What's on your mind" has replaced "everything that comes to mind," "if you like" has replaced "tell me," and the matter is treated quite casually. You, however, have dispensed with the rule entirely, and for two reasons: (1) it fosters a passive posture on your patients' part, and you would rather they took an active one; (2) it gives them a task they can fail to accomplish, and you would rather not expose them to that possibility.

Saying everything that comes to mind (as distinct from babbling) can take on the properties of a task and result in failure. Your first analytic patient started his second session by saying, "I found it tough to free associate during the first session, and I think it's going to take me some time to get the hang of it. So I've decided instead to talk about my childhood today. Is that all right?" (You said, "It's up to you"—and worried what your supervisor was going to say.) In your own analysis you often cheated by pretending that you were free associating when you had in fact rehearsed the session on the subway. That made you feel guilty and you resented having to feel it. (Then your supervisor mentioned that the ability to free associate could be taken as a criterion for termination, and you felt better.)

For a while you experimented with no instruction. After business matters were settled, you simply said, "You can begin now." That worked fine except for those patients who wanted to know what it was they could begin. You had a patient who even asked, "What's the procedure here?" You were tempted to respond, "There is no procedure here,"[4] but felt that it would have been not only provocative but untrue. So instead of giving an instruction only to those patients who asked for one, you found one that could be given to all patients: "You can talk about the things you want to talk about. It's up to you. When I have something useful to say, I will say it."

As you wrote in your first letter, it is minimally directive, more a notification than an instruction. In today's letter you stress that its task requirements are negligible and by giving it we define ourselves as one who sets no tasks—limits yes, flexible boundaries too, but nothing that amounts to a task that the patient can fail at.

Even if this is an overstatement and we do detect a task, this task, unlike the one set by the "fundamental rule," has the important characteristic of being incapable of evaluation—at least for us, the ones who set it. What can it mean, from our vantage point, to succeed at it or fail? We've told our patients to talk about the things they want to talk about, and we cannot judge them for talking about things they feel they "should" talk about. We want to construe "want" broadly to include all manners of choice, because it reduces the task requirements to a minimum.

You had a patient, a lawyer, who clarified this point. At the start of his second session, he asked whether he was supposed to lie on the couch. Instead of answering directly or repeating the basic instruction, you took the opportunity to tell him that you planned to give him no advice, and you emphasized that this included advice about how he should behave in therapy. When he heard the reply he snapped his fingers. During the subsequent sessions he occasionally snapped his fingers, usually after you had made a remark, and you didn't learn what the gesture meant until after the trial period, when he explained that the gesture meant you'd made an error—and he reviewed them. Your response to his query about the couch was an error because he was not asking for advice (in fact,

---

[4]Hellmuth Kaiser recommends this answer in a fascinating disquisition, "The Universal Symptom of the Psychoneuroses: A Search for the Conditions of Effective Psychotherapy," that can be found in *Effective Psychotherapy: The Contribution of Hellmuth Kaiser*, ed. L. B. Fierman (New York: Free Press, 1965), pp. 14–171.

he added, if you had breathed a word of advice during any of the sessions he wouldn't have continued with you). His question had been, "Is there also a rule about the use of the couch?" (being a lawyer, he needed to know the rules). So your response was immaterial, though it did imply that there were no rules beyond the basic instruction.

But let me be lawyerly and raise a question: "When they stay silent aren't our patients violating the basic instruction?" Susan says no, strictly speaking, but in practice, she admits, it isn't easy to imagine therapy in the face of utter silence. Still, short of silences that are utter (and that's for our clinical judgment to determine), Susan argues that the basic instruction also allows for the decision not to speak and tell. Therefore, when they are silent our patients are not failing at anything. Not from our vantage point, they aren't.

From their vantage point, however, they may in fact be failing. To the extent that patients construe the basic instruction as having set them the task of deciding what to talk about, they might well take their silence as a sign of failure (Susan brushes this aside with the assertion that it's something we and they can work on therapeutically, but I think she is being high-handed).

You do emphasize that our patients' freedom from constraint is limited to verbalization; the basic instruction doesn't say that the patient can behave however he or she likes. So I would think that the following rendition was more precise, albeit also more obsessional: "There are no rules governing your behavior here beyond the condition that it be mental. You are free to speak your mind and express your thoughts and feelings however you want, but you aren't free to put them into action."

When we initiate Psychotherapy, we can presume that we've set no task and that nothing we do will necessarily implicate us in making judgments of success and failure. This frees us from taking an evaluative role and protects our patients' freedom and autonomy. We can regard this nonevaluative stance as an integral aspect of our therapy's distinctiveness; it reflects a significant difference from the underlying orientation of most forms of traditional therapy.

In your view, every psychotherapy can aim to provide patients with a unique experience. The rationales and techniques of Psychotherapy, in any case, are rooted in the idea of uniqueness. Everything about it aspires to be unique. Its conditions are unlike any others that patients are likely to know; the kind of relationship they have with us is likely to be unlike those they have with others; the freedom they have is of a kind and degree they aren't likely to enjoy in other situations; the kind of autonomy they can exercise, the degree of freedom they can experience, and the exploration and self-inquiry they can engage in, are just not found in other settings.

Therapy works best, or so you promise us, when its uniqueness is taken seriously and not thought of the way we think of a doctor's "bedside manner." Good medical practice is to establish a working rapport and behave in a caring and warm way. When they ask how a patient is feeling, and they take the time to listen to their patients, doctors aren't practicing psychotherapy, they are practicing medicine; and when they give explanations and emotional support, they are being good doctors, not good psychotherapists.

To be sure, we might choose to begin a therapy session the same way, and we may choose to give our patients explanations and emotional support. But we do these things in the context of a format that is different from medical doctoring. For just as we aren't practicing surgery when we remove a splinter, we aren't doing psychotherapy when we relate to a patient in a caring way. Psychotherapy can and should be done in a systematic and disciplined way, and approached as if it were unique. (Now there's a sentence where *unique* actually works!)

Our techniques are therefore predicated on more don't's than do's. These don't's, in turn, are predicated largely on ways that our behavior differs from the behavior of other service givers and we don't do what they do. Here's a paraphrase of how you put it:

  • Unlike the physician, we do not diagnose and then administer treatments; we offer no nostrums and palliatives to assuage pain and suffering, and neither do we invoke a "trust father" attitude, with all the authority, faith, and suggestion that it elicits.

- Unlike the scientist, we do not apply standards of evidence to our patient's report; we don't maintain an attitude of skepticism; and we don't offer a technology for problem solving and for ameliorating maladaptive behavior.
- Unlike the teacher, we do not instruct and train; we give no reinforcements and neither do we provide incentives; we don't impart a methodology for self-improvement, and don't rely on the teacher-pupil relationship.
- Unlike the priest, we do not invoke a higher order of truth, and we don't offer the security of a social institution or group in which membership can be gained by making psychological changes.
- We *do* provide our patients with the opportunity to have a distinctive and unique psychological experience, one they may not have by themselves or with other professionals; and that distinctive and unique experience we call the *therapeutic process.*

But I'll sum up my summary of your overview with your summing up of it.

Psychotherapy entails the untrammeled exploration of our patients' minds. Its central goal is that they progressively free themselves from the tyranny of inner compulsion and conflict; and this freeing up is achieved within the therapy through the therapeutic experience itself. For it is during the sessions that patients learn how to be free. They speak to us as freely as they can, they exercise their volitional powers as fully as they are able, they strive for recognition and for authenticity, for clarity and for understanding—and they get better!

SEVEN

BUSINESS AND THE BASIC
INSTRUCTION EXERCISE

Your teachers taught you (as ours have taught us) that everything is grist for the therapeutic mill, the tenet of psychic determinism mandated an analysis of all behaviors, especially those that occurred in sessions. Your patients have taught you otherwise: all behaviors are not equal and neither are all motives, and for Psychotherapy to work well they must be treated differently. This is reflected in the distinction that you draw between *narrative* and *business*.

When you write us the theory letter, you will examine the concept of narrative. In the meantime we're using the term for its contrast with business, and we're starting with business for two reasons: it's where every psychotherapy starts; ours is so nondirective, and so unstructured too, that we have to take pains to make sure that its format is as unambiguous as possible. So critical is it that our patients know—and understand, comprehend, grasp, fathom, and get the hang of—the formal requirements, if not also appreciate and accept them, that our first order of business has to be *business*.

The term is a bit abrasive but seems to fit our needs quite well (my dictionary defines it as "purposeful activity, role, function; an immediate task of objective, mission; a personal concern; a serious activity requiring time and effort and usually the avoidance of distraction"). You make a big point of the fact that when the therapy is Psychotherapy, we have to broaden our definition of business so that it can encompass a wide range of issues, and then we need to make sure its boundaries are elastic enough so that they can be stretched to conform to all of the working requirements that may pertain to us, in particular, as well as to particular patients. As you write:

Business includes everything that we and our patients regard as relevant to the requisite conditions of the therapy. If we believe that more than one session a week is required, that counts as business; but it can also count as business if we have difficulty hearing them because they speak too softly, or we find it hard to listen because they gesticulate and pace the floor. Similarly, if patients believe three sessions a week will be impractical, it counts as business; but so can their conviction that a fifty-minute session isn't long enough, or that we must give them advice and feedback. If they are distracted by the way we dress, or if a picture hanging on the wall disturbs them, we *can* choose to construe the matter as business. For I believe the potential value of a broad and flexible definition of business is so great as to justify the technical guideline: *When in doubt, count it as business.* This is especially important when we are working within the framework of a therapy as nondirective as ours. When we're working on business matters we must be as direct as possible.

Narrative is an unfortunate term, too. It refers of course to everything patients talk about, and in that sense narrate, but patients do more than talk. A term like *psychological event,* if it weren't so clumsy, would, in my opinion, be more accurate. Susan prefers to speak of *therapeutic* (by which she means analytic) *experience,* but it's just as clumsy. In any case, narrative will have to include everything that is left over after we've subtracted business. For it makes a certain sense to construe all of the events that occur in therapy as either business or narrative, or, since no practical matter is ever devoid of psychological significance, as blends of the two.

The distinction makes good intuitive sense, and we accept your claim that it is a crucial distinction to make in that it tells us when to interview a patient and when not to. In your words:

> So long as we face an issue that belongs to business, we cannot be reluctant to investigate it, and interviewing will often be the only way. This will entail our asking direct questions, which is

dissonant with our otherwise nondirective stance. We can make it clear that only when such practical issues arise will we ask such questions. We can tell our patients that our need to have the answers is restricted to such matters, and we should respond forthrightly to their answers. Being direct and being directive can be sharply distinguished. Telling them that we need a piece of information (or some time to think about a request they've made) is one thing, it's another to deflect them, or buy the time, with counterquestions and interpretations.

Next you warn us that sustaining the distinction between business and narrative takes technique, for which purpose you have composed a set of exercises. Before giving them to us, you emphasize that the very viability of a dynamic form of psychotherapy, especially one that is as nondirective as ours, can depend greatly on this guideline: *"Whenever the material is narrative, we must eschew the interviewing mode; whenever it is business we must eschew the interpretive mode."* Therefore you need to make sure that we understand the difference between the two modes—and it's not nearly as simple as it sounds. As you construe it, it's a complicated issue (and to me, at this juncture at least, a puzzling one), so we'll have to study it as we go along. By way of introduction, you offer us a brief (and for me, too cursory) explication.

The interviewing mode pivots on a sharing of viewpoints whose purpose is giving and getting information deemed necessary for the business at hand. The interviewer solicits the information and gives the interviewee the needed information. That is clear enough; it's when we contrast it with the interpreting mode that things get muddy, for that mode isn't defined by substituting "explanations" for "viewpoints." We cannot claim that an interpreter gives explanations instead of information, because an interpretation needn't be an explanation at all, it can merely be an articulation of what's on the patient's mind. Our definition of an interpretation is going to be so broad as to include remarks like "you think that I know how old you are" when the remark elucidates a narrative and can be prefaced with "if I understand what you are saying" or "in other words."

Where the interviewing mode centers on information, the interpreting mode centers on understanding. We can hardly say "if I understand you correctly, you are forty," it would have to be "if I heard you correctly, you said you're forty." By its very nature, an interpretation is a speculation, even when it amounts to an obvious and gratuitous one. We could of course say "my hunch is that you are forty," but that would be speculation as to a fact about the patient, not about something the patient said and which was part of his or her mental and psychological experience. When we say anything about a patient's mental and psychological experience, we are in the business of interpreting. But. . . .

The nature and function of interpretations is a major subject for us, and we will have to study it thoroughly, after we have attended to business. So let's go back to our guideline.

Our rationale for it centers on what is arguably the most difficult concept, and also the most controversial, in all of contemporary psychotherapy: neutrality. Therefore you will have more to say on the subject (a great deal more, you warn). In the meantime we will have to settle for saying that business matters cannot be approached with the same degree of neutrality that we can apply to matters of narrative; personal preferences are inevitably implicated, and to maintain neutrality about them strains our patients' credulity in insidious ways. As we intend to maximize it and keep it from becoming ambiguous, we must restrict our neutrality to matters that are unequivocally narrative, and never mix business with narrative.

You go on to tell us that your clinical experience has persuaded you that neutrality is viable and reasonable only when it is confined to the patient's narrative, or as you put it, "neutrality can only be protected by limiting it to narrative." The best way to achieve this goal is to broaden our definition of business, and prevent the distinction between business and narrative from becoming blurred.

Fine, then why don't we say something about it to our patients and tell them about our intention to be neutral? It seems to me that it counts eminently as business and therefore we can clarify and explain the matter carefully, because whether they accept it (or believe it) or not, our patients should know that we intend to be neutral with respect to their narrative. You agree, but only to a point. You would rather wait and see whether—and more significantly, how—the issue is raised by them. Chances are it will be, if not sooner then later, and we can work more effectively with the issue if we do it on their terms. Neutrality has subtle shades of meaning, as well as a variety of potential significances; it can be construed in many different ways. Therefore, on balance, we're better off letting our patients broach it.

When they first hear it, they might react to the basic instruction with incredulity, wondering if there weren't certain topics that are appropriate for starting therapy. Even after hearing our reply ("I prefer you told me the things you want to tell me"), it's easy to imagine them perplexed, having taken it for granted that a therapist would suggest topics and ask leading questions. If this occurred we could now explain our nondirective stance and tell them that we intend to work without any preconceived ideas about what might be best for them to talk about. But if they don't raise the issue, neither do we. Moreover, even if it has been raised and discussed, we must not presume for a moment that it was settled.

Let's say, then, that our patient (and we will call our patient "P" in all of our exercises and examples) proceeds to speak about something, either because he (and let's make every one of our Ps a "he") had planned the topic beforehand or judges it to be appropriate for therapy. This doesn't mean that P believes that we are neutral about it, much less that we should be. If we assumed that he's grasped the full import of our nondirectiveness, we will most likely turn out to have been mistaken. The more prudent assumption is that P believes that he will be provided with direction and guidance, at certain times and in certain ways. Typically, this belief surfaces in the form of an expectation during later sessions, when he feels that his problems have been documented and that his life history has been recounted. But if it emerges right away, as soon as the basic instruction is given, say, then we have a chance to deal with it— and we must be very clear as well as very careful.

The Basic Instruction Exercise

It's the first session; we have given the basic instruction; P says, "It's altogether up to me to decide what I should talk about here?" and we say, "Yes." He persists with, "And it doesn't matter what I talk about?" We say, "What matters is what you want to talk about," and now P says:

> But you're the therapist. Surely you must know what would be most useful for me to talk about!

How do we continue? What is our most useful response?

The problem we face is whether to stay with the basic instruction, by reiterating and perhaps amplifying it, or whether to address the challenging incredulity. The "natural" thing to do is the latter. We'd make a remark to the effect that P is feeling incredulous and perhaps also challenging us. We could say, "You're finding it hard to believe, aren't you, that I'm leaving it up to you to decide what to talk about here?" We could even say, "You're finding it so hard to believe that I'm leaving it up to you to decide what to talk about here that you are challenging me on it." However, we have been fully forewarned that such remarks are interpretations and thereby treat the incredulity and challenge as narrative.

Nevertheless, Susan thinks that the time is right for a transition from business to narrative, and that these interpretations are called for. P seems to have understood the basic instruction; his question conveys disbelief more than puzzlement. When we hear the skepticism, and the overtones of mockery, in "but you're the therapist," we are keeping our promise to listen and understand.

My inclination would be to stay with the basic instruction (but maybe only because I figure it's what you want me to do) and use the opportunity to amplify it. So I might say, "I will be able to say more useful things when you talk about what you want to talk about." Susan faults this on the grounds that it's less an amplification than a distortion; it alters the basic instruction by implying that my non-directiveness serves my needs, not P's, in that its purpose is to help me to understand him. Not only is it not true but P could argue that this purpose is better satisfied by his answering my leading questions and speaking about topics that I recommended.

Then how about my saying something to the effect of, "I don't know what would be useful for you to talk about," it's a direct and businesslike response. The problem is it sounds strange to my ears, and would probably sound even stranger to P's. Perhaps I can settle for, "Anything you decide to talk about will be useful," and then, when P says, "But can't you advise me as to what's most relevant?" I can say, "Yes, but I'd prefer to give you no advice as to what to do or say either here in therapy or outside of it."

Susan accepts this solution. She would add, "I'm not sure, however, that I understand what you meant by 'most relevant'." P might then say, "Well, you said that anything I talked about would be useful, but I can't help believing that there are certain things that will be more useful than others," and she would say, "Your thought is that everything can't be equally useful." P then says, "Exactly! That just makes no sense to me"—and since it made sense to Susan, and this can be taken for granted, she doesn't have to respond. She can listen to how P resolves the problem. Will he continue the challenge, and in what form? Will he acquiesce to her nondirective stance, and in what form will he do that? In any event, Susan thinks this is good because she hasn't done anything to defuse his incredulity.

But what about the challenge? It seems to me that she shifted the focus away from it, and in that way has taken the heat off herself. I think she would have to focus on the challenge and interpret it as follows:

S   I gather you believe it's going to matter what you choose to talk about here, and that I should know what you need to choose, because I've had experience with therapy.

P   Yes. What else can I believe?

S   Then let me take it a step further. Perhaps you're thinking that I do know what things you should talk about, only I refuse to tell you what they are. This is making you feel outraged, perhaps because you feel it's unfair of me.

P   Of course! What the hell else am I supposed to feel?

S   I didn't mean to imply you had no reason to feel outraged,
     and neither did I say you shouldn't believe that I knew
     what you should choose to talk about. The reason I'm
     pointing out your thoughts and feelings is because I'm
     trying to understand them. It's the main thing I'll be doing
     in therapy.

P   Okay, I get it. But I still think that you are playing games
     with me.

And however P continues, therapy is off to a good start. You would
probably disagree. There is too much defensive disclaiming, and P's
final remark provides good grounds for critiquing S's performance.

Then let's see how you play the exercise. P's outburst could reflect outrage or it could reflect desperation, you don't know; he
could be challenging, or he could be importuning, you don't know.
And in a certain sense, you don't care, because you aren't going to
"deal with it" in any case; you are going to remain in the business
mode and continue to explicate the basic instruction. You therefore choose the simplest rejoinder that you can think of, which is:
"I still prefer to leave it up to you, because I believe it will be best
for your therapy if you choose what to talk about." This is certainly
straightforward, clear, and businesslike.

Now we turn to your first variation on the exercise, in which the
focus of P's challenge and incredulity is changed. Instead of "but
you're the therapist," he says:

> But what good will it do me? I mean, if I just talk and talk—
> what good is that!

How do we respond? Well, since P is now leveling his challenge
more squarely at our method, a reiteration of the basic instruction
is not going to be responsive, while saying, "All the good in the
world!" would be responsive but also provocative.

Susan would love to treat P's remark as a rhetorical question,
and opt for a silent response, but the exercise implicitly demands a

nonsilent one. So what could she say about P's "just talk and talk"? She hesitates to say, "But it won't just be talk and talk," because P will ask her to please explain what kind of talk it's going to be, and then what will she say? Neither does she like the prospect of asking him to explain what he meant by it, because it's pretty clear already, so the question would come across as either disingenuous or challenging, and probably as both.

She and I debated this variation for an hour and ended up nonplussed; we couldn't find the right answer. Then we read your solution and felt exonerated. It's no wonder we failed, you had not yet taught us about the trial period. When P asks what good is therapy and how is it going to help him, he is raising a question that is best answered by defining the beginning sessions as a trial run.

To be sure, the beginning sessions are, in any case, a trial (in both senses of the term?). P is under no obligation to continue. When you write us in detail about the beginning stage of therapy, you will examine the matter of a "contract," and also have more to say about the trial period. In the meantime you write this:

> Although sometimes raising more problems than they solve, trial periods are usually useful and sometimes necessary. Expecting patients to commit themselves to an unfamiliar form of therapy, as well as to a therapist whom they know only by credentials and perhaps recommendation, is expecting a great deal. A trial period can help them decide whether to make the commitment. Notice that it leaves matters "up to them" and defines treatment strongly as a choice, something they want.

The solution, then, is to suggest that P regard the beginning sessions as a trial period ("It might help you decide whether this way of working makes sense to you"), and if he rejects the suggestion, we go ahead and treat the problem no differently than if he had mentioned difficulties with the schedule or the fee.

In our second variation, P pauses (after we've said, "What matters is that it's what you want to talk about") and then says:

Won't you at least tell me what I should want to talk about?
Surely, it has to make a big difference what I talk about!

Well, for starters, we could point out the non sequitur, provided
we weren't too anxious to hear it. It's easy to spot it in writing but
it isn't going to be so easy in practice. (This is of course going to
be true for all of our exercises, and it's unavoidable.) Even so, I
don't think I'd want to point it out to P and get into a logical dispute. It's clear enough that he believes he needs to be told what to
talk about because it's bound to make a significant difference. In
my opinion, the best thing to do is address each part separately because we can give a qualified yes to one and a qualified no to the
other: "Yes, I could tell you what to talk about, but I prefer not to,"
and, "No, it probably won't make as big a difference as you think,
though it might make some." Susan agrees.

We disagree, however, on the best way to do it. Since P is challenging us, and being somewhat clever about it, Susan's inclination would be to call him on it. "What do you mean by 'at least'?"
she would ask because he is in effect undercutting the basic instruction. I think this might amount to a counterchallenge ("Hey,
it's no small thing you're asking for!") and could provoke an
argument. Similarly, "How can I know what you want to talk
about?" (which she offers as an alternative) strikes me as a counterchallenge that can come across as both contentious and defensive. I think we're better off simply saying, "I prefer not to tell
you what to talk about," but Susan says this is simply nonrespon-
sive.

Then how about saying, "Only you can decide what makes a
difference"? It's responsive enough, except that it sounds strange
and dogmatic to both of us, and will probably sound that way to P.
("Really!" he responds, "How come?") Susan suggests the variation "only you can decide what's important," which is less strange
but no less dogmatic. Moreover, it injects the idea of "important,"
and we're sure you won't allow us to do that. We assume that it
was for a good reason that we didn't instruct P to talk about "important" things.

So what's the right answer? You play the variation this way: first you respond to P's question (you must be responsive because this, after all, is business) with, "Yes, it can make a difference, but it's hard to say in advance." Then you continue with, "Nevertheless, in my experience (or in this form of therapy), what makes a difference is that you choose what to talk about." In this way you've kept the issue at the level of business and treated it pragmatically, thereby minimizing the possibility of dispute. If P wonders why it's hard to say in advance, you will fall back on "in my experience."

Next we're to imagine our P turning up the volume with:

> Do you mean to say you don't care what I talk about, whether I decide to talk about useful things or not? Surely it's going to make a difference to my well-being if I don't waste my time here!

This, now, is strong stuff, and taxes our imagination—if not also our patience with business as usual. (Maybe it taxed your patience, too, because you neglected to give us your solution.)

Despite the fact that P is incredulous and outraged, we must give him no interpretations to that effect; we must try our best to keep from approaching the matter therapeutically. P is providing us with plenty of narrative here but the business component has to be given all the priority. We are not neutral with respect to our mode of treatment, and we reserve the interpretative stance for matters we can remain neutral about—matters of narrative.

Therefore I'm sure you will condemn my inclination to be "understanding," as follows: "I understand that you find this incredible. It's not what you expected, and it seems like such an extreme position that you are feeling outraged by it." This, you'll have to concede, was a considerate thing to say, for it both empathizes with P's feeling and also explains it. Unfortunately, it contaminates my businesslike stance, which must remain direct, practical, and devoid of interpretation. To Susan's ears it also sounded patronizing.

She again thinks the moment is right for a shift from business
to narrative, to allow us to be empathic. So she would put it this
way: "I do appreciate the awkward position this puts you into. I
can understand your finding it hard to believe that I'd leave it altogether up to you to choose what to talk about" (and she would love
to continue with, "I wonder if it doesn't feel to you as if I don't
care," but this is another interpretation so she'll hold her tongue).

All right, now it's our turn. Here's an exercise that Susan and I
have concocted for you. We call it "Tell Me What to Talk About."
It's the second or third session and P says:

> I couldn't sleep last night thinking about what I'd talk
> about this morning. It just kept me awake, and I don't
> want that to happen before each of my sessions. I'm sure
> it isn't going to keep happening, but until it stops and
> until I get more comfortable here, it would be very
> helpful if you told me what I should talk about so that I
> don't have to think about it beforehand. Is that okay with
> you?

How would you respond?

EIGHT

TWO EXERCISES

Your comments on our performance of your exercise, as well as on yours of ours, can be summed up in a guideline that might read: *"Anything that pertains to the basic instruction, no matter how tangentially it pertains to the basic instruction, counts as business and must be approached in a businesslike way: sans dispute, sans suasion, and sans interpretation."* Our rationale is threefold: (1) we want to avoid the disputes and suasions; (2) we have to protect our interpretations from being corrupted and squandered ("they are our chief resource"); (3) the overriding purpose of the basic instruction is to establish our therapy's structure and format in a clear and unambiguous way.

Our handling of the exercise impressed you. It's tough to resist a patient's challenges and blandishments, especially when therapy is so young, and it isn't easy to amplify the basic instruction without distorting it. When P said, "You're the therapist, you know what would be useful for me to talk about," he was appropriating "useful," which is what *our* talking is supposed to be—and it's the treatment that will be more *useful.* So instead of ever saying that patients will benefit from talking about things they want to talk about, we should always say their therapy will benefit from it.

We're going to examine the transition from business to narrative when we study timing. But you mention that this is too soon anyway to make the transition—later on in therapy, all right, but never this early. Our chief task at this earliest stage is to launch the therapy in the best way possible, which means that when a business matter is at issue we must scrupulously stick to it as long as we can and resist the temptation to interpret. Any interpretation we make, no matter how valid, is too likely to be premature.

Anyhow, we ended up with a solution that you approve of. Susan's version is good, whereas my impulse to address P's challenge is reactive and risky. When patients challenge us or our therapy we are prone to feel challenged and defensive, and such feelings are apt to interfere with our work. We are better off keeping them from governing our response. At the very least, we should refrain from making any interpretations when we are emotionally aroused.

Next you discuss our solutions to the final variation, focusing on Susan's impulse to say, "It feels to you as if I don't care." It's a good impulse and she needn't have held her tongue. Yes, the remark is an interpretation, but P was saying "Don't you care?" and thereby raising a question that has profound ramifications in respect to our neutrality. Is it tantamount to indifference and does it mean that we don't care? Such a vital question is this, and so much is at stake in the context of our nondirectiveness, that we should seize any and all opportunities to address it even if it has to entail breaking the rule.

A good way to play this exercise is to address, as Susan does, the issue of caring. Her beginning remark—"I appreciate the awkward position this puts you in"—can be dispensed with; like mine, it's a supportive gesture that P might find patronizing. Instead it can go something like this: "I understand that my leaving it up to you to decide what to talk about leads you to infer that I don't care, but I do; I care that you talk about the things you want to talk about. It's my belief, you see, that your therapy is likely to go better if you do so—and I care that your therapy goes well." In other words, when we are accused of not caring, we can tell our patients that we do so—though it's their therapy we care directly about and thereby indirectly do we care about them.

The same is true for a range of questions that pertain to the way we work and that count as business. For instance, if P says, "Did you hear what I said before about my dinner with Andre?" (and we did hear it), we should say, "Yes, I think I did." We should not say, "What makes you think I didn't?" and neither should we say anything like, "I wonder if you are feeling ignored by me." Remarks like these turn therapy into a contest and a game.

For the exercise that Susan and I made up, in which P can't sleep nights for obsessing about what to talk about during the session and therefore asks us to relieve him of the task, you offer us a solution that has five steps. The first is to comply with the request, for we have no other good option. Telling P that we'd prefer not to comply would be redundant because he already knows it, and refusing might put him in an untenable position and his therapy at risk.

Moreover, he isn't really asking for too much, a circumscribed suspension of our nondirectiveness (he isn't asking us to tell him whether to get married). When therapy is this young, such modifications, so long as they are defined as temporary ones, are far from fatal. After all, even in the normal course of events we might have started the therapy with a series of diagnostic interviews.

So your five steps are: (1) comply, and do it first in order to be responsive; (2) establish its temporariness, and establish it very clearly; (3) make sure we aren't dealing with topics P feels he *should* talk about but rather with ones he *wants* to discuss; (4) find out what sorts of things he has in mind to talk about, the topics he's been thinking about, for chances are that we will be able to choose one and not have to introduce any of our own; (5) select a topic. Throughout each of these steps we will not be evasive and deflecting and/or "therapeutic." Therefore, the interview will pretty much have to go as you've presented it to us. (I am marking our running comments, questions, and critical analysis with an asterisk.)

The Correct Solution

P   I couldn't sleep last night. . . . It would be helpful if you told me what to talk about. . . . Is that okay with you?

Us   Yes, I can suggest some topics for you. And if I understand you correctly, you have in mind that this is a temporary measure, and you are aware that I wouldn't want to do it on a regular basis.*

   *We take pains to spell out the temporariness clearly, and formulating it in terms of P having it in mind is tactful.

P   Yes. I hope that won't be necessary.*

      *We note that he is not making a promise. Might we com-
      ment on this, or would that be tactless?

Us   I don't think it will be.* Now, you say you've been
      thinking about things to talk about here. Please tell me
      what they are.

      *Whoa! What kind of remark is this? Are we making a prom-
      ise? Isn't this a flagrant piece of reassurance? How exactly
      do we justify this remark?

P   Well, there's my childhood, and things about my growing
      up; like the birth of my sister and my mother's illness
      because of it. Then there's my social isolation and inabil-
      ity to make friends. And there are the problems I'm having
      keeping up with my schoolwork. It was these problems
      that made me come here.*

      *P gives us a chance to make inquiries and we will pass it
      up. We are going to stick to business and deal with the mun-
      dane question of should versus want.

Us   And when you think about these things when you're going
      to sleep, you are trying to decide which one of them to
      talk about here. Is it perhaps a question of deciding which
      of them you should talk about?

P   No. You said I should talk about the things I wanted to talk
      about. I just can't decide which one I want to talk about.*

      *So we are assured that *should* is not directly involved. It
      would have been easy to continue if that were not the case.
      Nevertheless, you made sure P included a should in his re-
      ply, so that we can clarify the matter.

Us   I didn't mean to say* that you should talk about the things
      you want to talk about; I meant to say you can.

      *We do not say, "I didn't say," and we never do. Saying, "I
      didn't mean to," or, "I didn't intend to," is all that's ever nec-
      essary and all that's ever tactful.

P   Oh, I'm sorry.* That's what you did say. But it's typical of
      me to feel that I should be doing things, instead of

wanting to do them. I don't want to be thinking about
what to talk about here, not when I'm trying to fall asleep.
But I seem to have no control over it; I can't help doing it,
and that's the problem.**

*We'll store this apology away in our memory and not at-
tend to it now (by wondering aloud what it means and
whether P feels chastized). Chances are he'll do it again, and
probably often, so we aren't losing an opportunity.

**Again we are handed some good narrative to work with,
and again we will steadfastly keep from attending to it—we
will scrupulously stick to business.

Us If you knew which one to talk about, you wouldn't have to
obsess about it. . . .

P And I'd go to sleep.

Us So if I were to say you can talk about any of them, and it
doesn't matter which one, that wouldn't be any help,
because you already understand that anything you'd
choose to talk about would be all right.*

*This maneuvering back to the basic instruction might strike
the layperson as a bit opportunistic.

P Yes. I know that. As far as you're concerned, it's up to me
to decide what to talk about, and you are not going to
criticize my decision. It's my obsessionality and uncertainty that's the problem. Decisions have always been
difficult for me.

Us So if I made some of them for you, it would relieve
you.*

*Once again we've steadfastly stayed with the practical is-
sue by pointedly refusing to discuss P's problems. He's practically been begging us to take an interest in them!

P I think it would. I'm not altogether sure, but it's bound to
be of some help.*

*P is hedging his bets and offering us a chance to back off
from our promise to comply with his request. Why then do
we turn down the offer? Why not explore the matter a bit

further? There are apparently two reasons. One is, P might
well have been construing our interviewing questions as an
effort on our part to talk him out of his request, and we need
to counter that impression. The other is, we run the risk of
making a premature transition from business to narrative
before the business issue has been settled—and we don't
want it to be settled on the basis of any interpretation we
make.

Us   Then I will do it.* Let me suggest that you talk about the
      problems you are having currently.

      *And we will try to do it as minimally as possible. There-
      fore we're going to choose his current problems because that
      seems more neutral and less arbitrary than choosing, say, his
      childhood experiences.

P   My social isolation and my school problems are the main
      ones.*

      *And since these are the problems that brought him into
      therapy, the choice is easy and we needn't obsess about it too
      much.

Us   Perhaps, then, you might begin with your school prob-
      lems.

We turn now to the exercise that you gave us for today's lesson.
We thought ours was tough but yours is a lulu. The narrative is so
rich with psychological significance, it was clearly designed for
the purpose of practicing our ability to withstand the pull of the
interpretive mode, not to mention the confrontational one, and tax
our frustration tolerance.

The Father Exercise

It's the second session, the basic instruction had been given in the
first one, and P says:

    I am going to be talking a lot about my father here. He's my
    main problem. I figured it would help if you saw him. I am

too involved with him to see him objectively, and you will get a distorted picture of him from me. So I called him up yesterday and asked him would he be willing to see you, and he said he would. He can come pretty much any time you want. When would be a good time for you?

It would have been reassuring had you promised us this was not going to happen—ever. But it conceivably could happen, and then what will we do? Well, for starters, panic. Then make every mistake in the book. But since we're getting it in writing (thank God we're practicing, not performing!) there's no reason to be flustered; we have the time to be calm and considerate.

It was thoughtful of you to mention that in practice (when we're performing, that is) we can usually buy some time by simply telling our patients that we need to think about the matter they've raised. You advise us to do it when we are taken aback, or caught short, and we judge that silence is not an appropriate response. We can train ourselves in saying, "Before I respond, and I'll do it later (or next session), I would like some time to think about this."

But we had all the time we needed and still couldn't figure out how to do the exercise right. Susan took the position that under no condition is she going to meet with P's father. The therapy will be fatally flawed if she does. Whenever he talks about his father, P will expect her objective and professional opinion of him. I, on the other hand, am flexible to a fault: I will meet with the man if I have to. After all, isn't every therapy "flawed"? (You said so in your second letter, when you were advocating compromise in order to avoid extreme positions, and again in the current letter when you go ahead and comply with P's request for topics.) Moreover, what's my option other than referring P to a more experienced therapist?

To be sure, Psychotherapy might not be the treatment of choice for P. You once mentioned that some symptomatic conditions can benefit more from other forms of therapy and that not all patients are suitable for ours. You promised at the time to write us about this, and we're hoping that it will be soon because it's a question that has already come up several times in our discussions.

Back to the father exercise. Despite the fact that we know we have to treat the matter as business and conduct a little interview, and we know the interview has to be an edifying one and not an interpretive one, Susan and I have decided to show you what we would have done if we didn't know that. Had you given us this exercise three letters ago, this is how we might have done it. In other words, instead of doing it right, we're going to show you how we would do it wrong—and since we know that it's wrong, it follows that we'd know how to do it right, right? Anyway, Susan thinks the right way may emerge as a result of discarding all the wrong ways. This is apparently the way you compose counterpoint, you don't do the do's so much as you avoid doing the don't's (and haven't you written that our technique is grounded in don't's?).

Mistake 1

S   What do you mean you're "too involved" with him?

P   Why do you ask? Are you unclear what it means, or is this just your indirect way of getting me to talk about it?
     Listen, I told you last time I moved out of home because I couldn't stand his meddling and nagging. But now we talk on the phone every day, so I'm just as hassled by him.

S   How come you have daily phone calls? Are they really necessary?

P   I couldn't stop talking to him altogether, could I? Is that what you think I should have done?

S   It's one thing to stop talking to him altogether, it's another to talk to him every single day.

P   It was his idea, and the only way he'd let me move out.

S   In other words you had no other choice, he forced you to do it.

P   And you think I'm wrong to think so, eh? But this just proves that you can't possibly imagine what he's like—and that's exactly why you have to see him for yourself.

Mistake 2

Me You think that I need to have an objective picture of him, and you believe that I won't be able to get it from you?

P Yes, that's exactly what I think and what I believe. I'm much too involved with him.

Me So you believe that being involved with someone prevents a person from having an undistorted picture of them.

P I can't see how I'd believe anything else. I have strong feelings and conflicts. And not just about my father.

Me You have strong feelings and conflicts about your mother, too?

P They're not nearly as strong as my feelings about my father. But if she weren't dead I'd have her come to see you, also.

Me What about your three brothers? [They can't also be dead!]

Mistake 3

S This therapy is for you. And what's important here are your feelings about your father.

P No fooling! You thought I wanted you to treat him?

S You said "at least once." That means more than just getting a picture of him, it seems to me.

P Don't worry, it'll take more than just once to get the picture. He's a complicated man.

S You don't think that if you tried you could do him justice?

P Maybe Philip Roth could, but I'm just an accountant. No, you're going to have to see him for yourself. Otherwise you'll be in the same boat as me.

S And it's a leaky boat, I gather.

P Hey, how did you know? I used to be a bed-wetter. And I still am, in a way—my feelings leak out like I was a sieve.

Mistake 4

Me It isn't really necessary for me to have all the facts.

P   You just need all the feelings?

Me I didn't say that. I said the true facts aren't necessary.

P   How should I have known? I've never been in therapy.

Me Did I say you should have? Look, I understand you feel perplexed. You've never been in therapy, so naturally you believe that it's important to get at the truth here.

P   It's a relief to hear it's natural. But isn't it also important to get at the truth here?

Me Yes, if it's the psychological truth.

P   What the hell is that?

Mistake 5

S   You made the arrangement without first talking to me about it and finding out whether I would agree to see him.

P   Sure. But why do you scold me for it? I'll pay you for the session. What's the problem?

S   It's not the fee. The problem is your assumption that it would be appropriate for your therapy that I meet with him.

P   Oh, that's what you're scolding me for! In fact, I'm assuming more than that; I'm assuming it's absolutely necessary for my therapy. I don't think I would have started therapy if I thought you'd refuse to meet with him.

S   Look here, I'm not refusing to meet with him. I am just trying to understand your assumption that it's necessary.

P   Believe me, it is. He is beyond description and there's no way you'll get a picture of him without seeing for yourself.

S   And you're assuming it's important that I get that picture.

P   Look here, if it was someone who wasn't so complicated, and who I wasn't so involved with. I'm not talking about my brothers or even my mother. My father is very special.

S   So it's especially important to you that I see him.

P   Right! I hope you won't say no.

S   I won't. [We can't!] Let me consult my calender.

Mistake 6

Me   We can discuss that later. First we have to talk about the plan itself. I don't normally see my patients' relatives.

P   Why not?

Me   Because I couldn't separate their picture of them from mine.

P   I see. Why don't you want a separate picture of your own?

Me   It's better for you to examine the one that you have.

P   But my picture is all screwed up. It's necessary for me to straighten it out, and I can't see how you're going to help me do this if you have no idea what he's really like.

Me   I can appreciate the point. But were I to see him, I wouldn't get a picture of the way he behaves toward you—he'd be behaving toward me, after all.

P   I see. So you don't think it's a good idea. Then I'll call him up and call it off. No problem.

Did we cover all the errors? But afterwards we pooled our resources, we tried to play the exercise correctly and figure out a solution that avoided any and all errors, and here's what we came up with:

The Solution

Us   I will answer your question in a moment. First I want to discuss your plan, in order to see whether it's feasible.

P   Why not? What's the problem?

Us   Well, it might be better if I didn't meet with your father. It isn't my practice to do that, you see.

Continuation 1

P   Oh, but I didn't know that.

Us   So you spoke to him, without finding out what I thought of the plan, because you believed that I would think it was okay.

P   Yes. I should have waited till I spoke to you about it.

Us   I didn't mean to imply that you should have waited. But since you decided not to, I want to ask whether it will be a problem for you, telling him that I think it may not be a good idea.

Continuation 1a

P   Oh, no, not at all! He won't make a fuss about it—he hates to leave the house.

Us   Then I think it would be better if I didn't see him.

Continuation 1b

P   No way! And not just a problem. He'll kill me. You don't know my father. There's no way I can call him off now. Look here, I just want you to see him, not treat him.

Us   I understand. Then I will see him. Let me consult my calender.

Continuation 2

P   How come?

Us   Because it may not be necessary for me to have a picture of him that's different from yours.

Continuation 2a

P   How should I have known that? I've never been in therapy. I thought you needed to have an objective picture.

Us   I didn't mean to say that you should have known. And I do understand that you think I need an objective picture. But therapy works better if we both work with the same picture.

P   I see. Then you think it isn't such a good idea.

Us   Yes, I think it might be better if I didn't meet with him.

Continuation 2b

P   Why not? Look, there's no way I can give an objective picture of him. Maybe Philip Roth could, but I'm just an accountant. No, you're going to have to see him for yourself. Otherwise you'll be in the same boat as me.

Us   It's necessary for me to have an objective picture, I gather.

P   Absolutely. I have such strong feelings and conflicts—and not just about my father, either.

Us   But your feelings and conflicts are very strong about him.

P   He hassles me like nobody else does. When I finally persuaded him to let me move to my own place, it was only on condition that I phone him every day. So I'm just as hassled by him now.

Us   Moving to your own place wasn't the solution, then.

P   No—and I hope that therapy is.

Us   [We do, too!]

NINE

EPISTEMOLOGICAL CAVE, ROLE DEFINITION, AND THE FATHER EXERCISE

We enjoyed our *mistakes*, too, but making them was unnerving. It's reassuring to know that not only is a flawless performance impossible but the effort to achieve it can make things worse. Being disciplined isn't the same as being perfectionistic, and the homily that we learn from our mistakes happens to be a truism in our profession—and not just for those of us who are students. Anyway, it is less important to keep from making mistakes than to spot them, for we can usually rectify things even if it means owning up. When the circumstances prevent us from saying that we said it wrong, not the way we intended to, we can always say, "I want to take back what I said, because it was a mistake."

And there's no need to apologize. It's quite sufficient to say we were mistaken. An apology, when it isn't merely a verbal gesture, is a plea for forgiveness. When our patients apologize to us, we will want to interpret, if not to them then to ourselves, its full meaning: "You have done something wrong, if not bad, and you are asking me to forgive, if not exonerate, you for it." Would we ever want to say that to them about us?

Today's lesson centers on the father exercise, and examines two issues that stem from it. The first concerns what might be dubbed our "epistemological cave," inasmuch as it is based on the fact that our knowledge of our patients' world has to be restricted to what they choose to tell us about it. The second concerns our role definition, how to establish it clearly and unambiguously, and keep it free from contamination.

Your performance of the father exercise is reproduced herein, together with running commentaries, some of which you will recognize as your own. The questions, critiques, and complaints are, of course, ours.

A Correct Rendition of the Father Exercise

U I will answer after I've looked at my calender. Before I do it, I want to discuss the plan because I think it may not be best for your therapy for me to meet with your father.*

> *We don't discuss P's presumption that we would agree to meet his father. That would be a diversion at this point, and also difficult to do without injecting a note of censure. Besides, the presumption cannot be treated as business. Perhaps it can be examined, qua narrative, after the practical matter is settled.

P Why not? What's the problem?

U The kind of therapy that we're going to be doing works best when you talk about the things you want to talk about, and this means that I know only those things. So the way I get to know your father, or anyone else you speak about, is from what you say and feel about them.

P You mean to say you're just going to take my word for it? So when I tell you the man's unreasonable you're going to think that he really is unreasonable?

U Actually, I'm going to try and not think about the way he really is. Instead I'm going to try to think only about your view of him.*

> *This difficult and important point may have to be spelled out a bit more.

P But that's manifestly impossible! How can you possibly keep from thinking about the way he really, objectively, is?*

> *Treating it as a rhetorical question could be tactless, so we are going to answer.

U Yes, I agree. It's not going to be possible for me to do that completely. I'm bound to form a picture of my own, and have some ideas about the way he really is. But I will try not to let them influence me very much. I will try my best to work with your picture and your ideas. In my experience, you see, it's not only unnecessary for me to have a picture that's different from yours, it can be better for the therapy if I don't have one.

P   If you say so, okay. But before I pursue that issue let me ask you this: What if I told you he was ten feet tall and weighed eight hundred pounds, you would simply believe me?*

      *Yes, it's conceivable that a patient would actually interrupt himself to ask this. But it's obvious that you are being pedagogical with us, and the ensuing dialogue could just as easily have been rendered in prose.

U   No, I couldn't believe that, because I know it's incredible.* I might wonder whether you're intending to exaggerate for my sake, and I might say so to you.** Short of that, I'd have to tell you it was not credible to me. If you told me he was seven feet tall and weighed five hundred pounds, I might perhaps find it unusual but I'd have no reason to doubt it.

      *Moreover, P knows it. Nevertheless, this raises the question of how much can we be expected to know, and what role does our personal knowledge play in Psychotherapy.

      **But this is an interpretation, so you might not.

P   Would you actually tell me that you thought it was unusual?

U   Perhaps yes, but probably not. I'd rely on my judgment.*

      *Here's the hoary hedge! We might cast it formally as, *"When in doubt, defer to clinical judgment."*

P   Okay, but what if I was just lying?

U   I would have no way of knowing it.

P   Wouldn't you suspect it?

U   I might. But I try hard never to suspect it, just as I try hard never to pass judgment on you and on what you talk

about. You see, it would be of no benefit for your therapy
if I took any kind of skeptical and judgmental attitude
toward you.*

*We are saying, "I don't diagnose!" More precisely: we're
claiming that we try to keep our diagnostic impressions from
playing a role in our work, which seems to me a difficult
claim to defend, much less maintain.

P   What if I was a pathological liar?* Are you saying that it
would be of no benefit for my therapy for you to know
it?**

*P is shrewd! He keeps finding the tough questions.

**He would probably say "benefit for me and for my well-
being," but our response would be the same.

U   Independently of your telling me, I take it.*

*This may strike the layperson as a stalling tactic, but it's
important to keep matters crystal clear in therapy.

P   Yes. I'm talking about your figuring out that I'm a liar by
hearing me tell you incredible kinds of things.*

*In other words, are we not diagnosticians? Are we not
going to observe P and diagnose him on the basis of our
observations? Even if we believed that it was desirable to
not do it, which is a big even-if, can we possibly keep from
doing it?

U   That might amount to a sort of passing judgment on you
of the kind that I try to eschew.

P   And you'd never even suspect it?

U   Even if I did, I would not share my suspicions with you,
unless—and this is, of course, an important unless—I
thought you were putting yourself in danger by your lying.
If I judged that you might be seriously hurting yourself, or
hurting someone else seriously, then I would certainly
speak up.*

*Beautiful! You've succeeded in introducing (a bit oppor-
tunistically, but this is such a vital issue that we forgive you
for it) the problem of where we draw the line between

being neutral and being irresponsible. However, this is an issue that we have to postpone for later, so P won't pursue it here. Instead we'll have him pause and then return to the exercise.

P   [pause] Okay, let's get back to my father. I'm still puzzled by this: my picture of him is distorted and my ideas about him are all screwed up, and that's my problem in a nutshell. How am I going to straighten things out? How, for example, am I going to find out whether he really is unreasonable or not?*

> *This needn't be regarded as a business question (and therefore responded to with a didactic lecture on the way Psychotherapy works). It can be taken as an expression of his mystification, and regarded as narrative. But even if we do take it as narrative, we wouldn't want to interpret the mystification because the business matter has not yet been settled. Therefore, since silence might be provocative (i.e., tactless), we will respond in the business mode and raise the idea of a trial period.

U   One way for me to answer your question is to suggest that you try it out and see whether it helps you with your picture and ideas about your father. I'm suggesting that you can regard our beginning sessions as a kind of trial period.

P   Oh, so you're telling me to wait and see! That's fair enough. Only tell me, what do I do about my father? He's all geared up to meet you; he's champing at the bit.*

> *We might say, "Call him and tell him that I don't think it's a good idea," but we obviously couldn't. Anyway, P isn't asking us for advice, he's challenging us. In either case, we need to avoid an interpretation.

U   You expect him to make it hard for you to postpone* the decision, I take it.**

> *Not "cancel" because we said that we prefer not to meet with his father, we haven't said we refuse to.

> **But what kind of remark is this—an interpretation, no? Did you slip here because you felt challenged?

P   It sure is! I don't know if I can pull it off. I wish I'd waited until I spoke to you before calling him up and proposing the plan. That's what I should have done, isn't it?*

> *There is clearly no reason to say yes, but there's also no reason not to take advantage of every opportunity to shore up our nondirectiveness. Therefore. . . .

U   When it comes to things you did and things you do, as well as things that you're planning to do, I would prefer to make no comments that would suggest any advice or criticism.*

> *If P had said, "That's what I should have done," without adding, "Isn't it?" we could still have made this remark, prefacing it with, "I can tell you what I would have said." It's good technique to do this; it treats a piece of narrative as a piece of business.

P   But look here, you advised me to give therapy a try. What's the difference between that advice and this advice?

U   That advice had to do with our therapy. I don't think it was much different than suggesting that you talk about the things you want to talk about here.*

> *This statement merits study (by us, not necessarily by P). We are establishing the narrow limits of our directiveness and reducing the basic instruction to the status of advice. But aren't we getting too argumentative and legalistic with P? Isn't this likely to be too intellectual and abstract for him? So what if we're logically consistent with our own viewpoint, what difference does it make to him? Why point out to him how consistent we are? He may as well say, "I'm impressed, you are logically consistent, good for you!"

P   Okay, but advice is still advice.

U   Yes. And for the most part, I'm going to try and avoid giving you any kind of advice, particularly when it comes to things you do outside of here. That applies, of course, to how you decide to deal with your father.*

> *Are we not steering too actively? (I don't think so, but Susan wonders.) It's one thing to supervise the therapeutic process,

it's another to steer it. (I countered by reminding her that we're engaged in business, not in therapy.)

P   I see. [pause]*

*The exchange has become a battle of wits, and this pause signifies (to me) that P is feeling defeated.

P   Listen, I know I shouldn't have told him about a meeting before finding out if it was okay with you. It just never occurred to me it wouldn't be okay with you. It seemed like a reasonable idea—and frankly it still does.* But I've never been in therapy, so how should I have known different?** [pause]***

*We note the accusation—we're being "unreasonable"—and we store it away in our memory. (Susan disagrees, but I think it's P who is feeling accused.)

**The businesslike reply, "I didn't mean to imply you should have," would be ambiguous here because nothing we said comes close to implying he should have known.

***We remain silent here, which is also ambiguous because it suggests that we are treating the question as rhetorical (i.e., as narrative). Our other option is to interpret his sense of being unfairly faulted, and inasmuch as the business issue hasn't been settled, we are loath to do that.

P   I'm really in a big jam. I really don't know if I can get myself out of it. [pause]*

*If this pause turned into a silence we'd have the option of letting it ride or of saying, "What are you thinking?" They are our only options.

P   I could call him up and tell him you don't want to meet him. Is it all right with you if I do that?

U   I'd rather not say, one way or the other.* I want to leave it up to you how you handle the problem with your father, without telling you what my personal feelings might be. You see, I believe it's important that my personal ideas and feelings should never play a part in your therapy.**

*I personally think this is insensitive, if not unfair, and would exasperate P. I would say, "It's up to you," even though it implied "it's all right with me." I might even say it explicitly; it's the least I could do to be helpful.

**We take the opportunity to make this important point again. Even though it might divert P from the issue at hand, it's worth laying some groundwork and establishing some format, particularly when a business matter is being discussed. If he now digressed into this issue, we'd have to find a way to direct him back to the matter at hand.

P   But even if I laid the blame on you, it wouldn't work. He's going to be very unreasonable, like always, and make my life miserable. [pause] I can't see how I'm going to get out of this jam.

We may be at a point of impasse. Suppose P now becomes distraught and his eyes well with tears, we have two options: (1) we can calmly hold our ground and show some faith and courage; (2) we can help him out of his jam by offering to meet with his father. A strong case can be made for each, and both run the risk of jeopardizing the therapy but in different ways. The first may jeopardize the therapy itself, while the second may jeopardize its integrity.

P could force our hand by making it clear that his therapy depended on it. If he were to say, "I can't see myself calling him off, the consequences will be too dire; I don't think I can continue seeing you if I have to do it," then our options would be reduced to either aborting the therapy or agreeing to see the father. Short of his making matters that clear, we can only rely on clinical judgment to decide how seriously therapy is now at risk.

If we judged that the impasse was serious, and decided against aborting the therapy, and therefore acquiesced to the meeting, we would have to specify, clearly and carefully, the conditions under which we are agreeing to meet with his father. There are three.

1. When it's clear to P that we're doing it for practical reasons alone, which means it was necessary to do it in order that therapy actually take place. This would have to be spelled out: "I want to

make it clear that the reason I'm agreeing to meet with your father is that I want you to continue in therapy."

2. When it's clear to P that we do not intend to form an objective picture of his father, and what picture we do form will play no part in therapy: "I will try not to form an opinion and picture of him. I won't share with you whatever opinion and picture I do form. Not only will I keep it to myself but I will try not to let it influence my work with you."

3. When we spell out the guidelines for the meeting itself, which will include: (a) P's presence at the meeting—under no condition will we meet with the father alone; (b) the length of the meeting—we will want to make it as short as possible; (c) a discussion of the questions that we will ask the father, and of the way we will try to answer the father's questions.

Here's a condition that you would include in 3, which Susan and I find surprising and intriguing: when you meet with P and his father, you will expect them to talk to you but not to each other. In fact, you will make it a ground rule that they direct all of their remarks to you. The rationale for this technical measure is twofold: (1) you do not want to witness any interaction between them, because you want to retain as limited a view of how things actually happen between them as possible; (2) you don't want any interaction to take place because it may cast you into the role of arbitrator, and you must retain your neutrality. (You mention parenthetically that you use this ground rule, for the beginning sessions at least, when you do couples therapy, for not only don't you want to play the role of arbitrator, you don't want to imply that you are diagnosing the relationship that you're observing. Another reason is that you want each partner to listen to the other, and perhaps hear things they have never really heard before. But your main rationale is predicated on eschewing the role of diagnostician.)

What surprises us most, though, is that our efforts to define ourselves as a psychotherapist, pure and simple, are so concerted that they rule out playing the role of psychologist. In fact, they practically rule out our knowing anything about reality. We are experts in conducting therapy, so far as our patients are concerned, and that is all the expertise we need to claim. For not only does our knowledge of the world play no vital role in therapy but it can compromise our impersonality, which in turn can attenuate our neutrality. This is obviously a big issue, and we will only scratch its surface in this lesson.

Let's begin this way: What if it happened that I was not just a psychologist but also a computer maven and my prospective patient (who happens to be studying computer science) knew it? He might well ask for some computer advice and I'd have to refuse it. That's clear enough. But what's the difference, you ask rhetorically, if he asks for psychological advice? Inasmuch as the rhetorical answer is clear enough, too, we have to raise the next question: Of what value is it, then, to define ourselves as psychologists (or psychiatrists, or social workers, or whatever our credentials happen to allow)?

I'll play devil's advocate and answer the question. My patient is not in therapy for his computer problems, so my expertise in that area is both accidental and immaterial. He is, however, in therapy for his psychological problems, and it's no accident that I am a psychologist, and neither is it obviously immaterial that I'm a student of the psyche. So if he is examining his emotions, say, and decides to apply the James-Lange theory to them and wants me to tell him whether his version of it is correct, why can't I? After all, he has good reason to expect that I might know the theory (whereas he has no reason to expect that I know anything about computers). I would feel funny saying something like, "Yes, I do know the theory, but I would prefer not to correct your version of it"—though not nearly as funny as saying that I never heard of it.

Susan says it's more likely that my patient will ask if I believe that when he dreams about the Empire State Building, he's dreaming about a big penis—"And isn't that Freud's theory?" She would respond with, "Yes, I'm familiar with the theory, but a useful way to work with your dreams is to explore your ideas about them and your associations to them." But I can imagine him now saying, "Oh, so you believe in the theory of associationism!"—and we're back where we started from. Anyway, your rejoinder is:

Opening a dialogue with patients on matters of psychological theory runs the risk of casting me in the role of an authority on psychology, an expert on human behavior, and that is a role I'd rather not play. Psychotherapy rarely requires it of me, and Psychotherapy proceeds best when I don't cover anything other than the conducting of therapy with the mantle of authority. Now, lest this claim seem implausible to you, I hasten to add that it's not that I pretend to know nothing about psychology or that I have no pragmatic, theoretical, and even scientific knowledge about human behavior. I merely try to avoid taking the position that I know more than my patients know. They, too, have a theory of behavior; they, too, have both pragmatic wisdom and an operating theory, and they might also know the science. What I try to do is keep from teaching them mine. The didactic mode has a limited utility in therapy because its function is usually to provide reassurance and in that respect it overlaps with intellectualization, having the additional disadvantage of being mine instead of theirs. Therefore, I regard it as generally prudent to avoid any steps that would invoke, or seem to invoke, my knowledge of psychology in general—as distinct from my patients' psychology in particular.

Let's let the matter rest there for the time being. It will come up again when we study the issue of our impersonality.

TEN

INQUIRING, SILENCE, AND "WHAT ARE YOU THINKING?"

Patients come late to sessions and sometimes miss them. These events may count as business but can be fraught with psychological significance. Do they therefore count as narrative? Strictly speaking, no. But since we've decided that narrative equals everything that's left over when business is subtracted, our definition of narrative would have to include such events. Accordingly, and according to our rule, we cannot and should not treat them simultaneously as narrative and business, for business and narrative must be treated differently. This is because, for one thing, it is often outright necessary, and, for another, the very integrity of the therapy can depend on it. (Don't you tire of making this point?) The aim of business, after all, is to improve the therapy not the patient.

To practice this problem (or is it a dilemma?) you've given us an exercise in which P (our generic patient) has been punctual to date and today he is fifteen minutes late; we have no ideas about the lateness and no reason to believe it has any psychological significance, but we suspect that it might because P makes no mention of his lateness; instead he begins the session with a fifteen second pause, as he has each of his sessions, and then begins recounting an event of the day before: "I bumped into my old friend Harry in the library yesterday, and. . . ." We have three options.

Option 1 is to interrupt and inquire about the lateness. ("Before you talk about what happened in the library, I want to ask you about your having come late today.") Option 2 is to interrupt and inquire about the fact that the lateness went unmentioned. ("Before you talk about what happened in the library, I want to ask you about your having come late; I'm wondering how come you have not mentioned it.") Option 3 is to say nothing and listen to what happened in the library.

We followed your suggestion to discuss the options before reading what you have written about them. I took the position that options 1 and 2 are good, Susan argued that only option 3 is.

We agreed that option 1 treats the matter as pure business and imposes the topic; it says in effect, "I want us to discuss your lateness." Treating it as narrative, by making a confronting interpretation like, "Are you not aware of the fact that you've come late today?" is risky because chances are poor that P will reply, "Yes, I was actually not aware of the fact," and chances are good that our remark will simply have amounted to a scolding.

In either case, however, we have to be clear about two points: (1) coming late to sessions (and missing them) is something that matters in P's case, and (2) P may not be aware of the fact. So we must be prepared to continue by saying something like, "The reason I want to discuss the lateness is that I think it's necessary, for the integrity and effectiveness of the therapy, that you not come late to sessions, and I wasn't sure you knew it." The crucial proviso is: we need a basis for believing that not coming late to his sessions is in fact necessary for the effectiveness and integrity of P's therapy. Susan and I arrived at a consensus on this.

It isn't the way you approach the issue in your letter, where you formulate it in terms of resistance. A reason for rejecting option 1 is that we have no reason to believe that the lateness is psychologically significant and it's too likely the topic will be fruitless. P might well respond by saying something like, "I was delayed at work for ten minutes, and then the subway stopped in the tunnel for ten minutes." Will we now want to pursue the matter further? Will we now ask him to please explain why he doesn't make adequate allowance, or how come he lets himself be delayed at work? No, we don't want to do any of that. We'd run the danger of casting ourselves into an inquisitorial role, and we'd also be fishing for significance.

The fact that the discussion we instigate with our question is too likely to be fruitless is our main consideration in rejecting option 1. But there's a further one, and here's where your resistance comes in. Let's suppose, you say, after hearing P's explanation we choose not to pursue the matter any further, and since we have no reason to think that the lateness had much significance, we accept it as fortuitous. We must now contend with the likelihood that P will find our having asked the question far from fortuitous. Say, after giving his explanation he asks why we asked. We are now obliged to respond, and our response might take this form: "I wondered if your lateness might mean that you're having avoidant feelings about coming here" (this, after all, is our reason for having asked—lateness is a classical form of resistance). And we have little choice but to introduce this note, for once we've chosen to inquire into this (or indeed, any) matter, we must be prepared to answer the question, spoken or unspoken, "Why do you ask?" The answer we chose is rich with unwanted implications ("Coming late to these sessions is a bad thing to do") and with imposed issues ("You have avoidant feelings about coming here"). These are your main reasons for avoiding option 1.

I can think of a reason for not avoiding it and a rationale for choosing it. I have in mind what you wrote when emphasizing how wide a range could be encompassed by our broad definition of business. You included distraction. So my reason is: the matter is on my mind and it is distracting me; it is interfering with my work and consequently counts as business. This rationale can be articulated as follows: "I am thinking about your lateness, and it is distracting me. This distractedness may interfere with my ability to listen to the account you are going to give. So I am treating the matter as business exclusively for my sake, in the sense that it will help me devote myself to listening to you with a clear mind."

Susan doesn't like it. She thinks my rationale is forced and self-serving. Why should I be that distracted by P's lateness? Am I feeling irritated by it, put out, rejected? If so, isn't it my problem, not his? After all, there are going to be many distractions for us when we conduct therapy: surely, we aren't going to burden our patients with the task of undistracting us. Shouldn't we be able to listen while still keeping the lateness in the back of our mind?

Susan is adamant about this. She thinks the only justification for treating the matter as business, and choosing option 1, is two-fold: (1) we have a reason to wonder whether P knows that not coming on time interferes with his therapy; (2) we have a reason to believe that coming late will in fact interfere with his therapy.

Both of us think the matter should be treated as business the first time it happens, for we have no way of knowing whether it's going to happen again, perhaps often. If we failed to address it the first time, when P is late a second time and we choose to address it, he may well wonder why now ("I've come late before and you didn't comment on it, what's different about today's lateness?"). We think option 1 is good only when the lateness is new and we have some basis for believing that P knows that coming late may be problem-atic. If it turns out that he believes it's no big deal, and curtailing an occasional session by ten or fifteen minutes is perfectly all right, then this becomes a quite different matter.

(And how would you handle this situation? It seems to us you'd have no option other than being perfectly permissive. If P regards latecoming as no particular problem, do we have any basis for dis-agreeing with him? Can we say for sure it would be better if he always came on time?)

Susan and I failed to agree on option 2. Here it isn't the lateness that's at issue but the fact that P neglected to talk about it. Susan believes that an omission like this should never be regarded as busi-ness. After all, the basic instruction grants P the full freedom of talking about whatever he wants to, and directing him to address a topic violates that freedom. Our only justification for ever impos-ing a topic is when the topic is a piece of business. In what sense, then, can his failure to talk about the lateness be regarded as ger-mane to the format and structure of therapy?

You've already pointed out that many therapists believe that everything is grist for the therapeutic mill, that every opportunity should be taken to deepen and broaden patients' self-inquiry and exploration in order to help them achieve insight—and you dis-agree. We can pick and choose, you believe. In principle, every-thing is grist, yes, but in fact not everything is good grist; there are important considerations that separate the wheat from the chaff, and it's rarely a good idea to "go fishing for significance."

Take the slip of the tongue. Now, there's an event few therapists will let slip past, for it provides a potentially invaluable insight into the dynamics of a patient's unconscious. And yet, the insight may not be worth it—at least not when it is weighed against the potential implications for our role definition. We must have good reason to believe that the result will be worth it. As you put it, "I have found from experience that fishing for significance is rarely worth it—unless I can smell the catch."

You'd agree, then, with Susan that option 2 isn't good. It falls in the same category as a slip of the tongue. Just as we won't say, "Please give some thought to your slip of the tongue," we won't say, "Please examine your reasons for not mentioning the lateness." We must have good reasons for resorting to such dissonant directives, and rarely do we have any that are good enough.

Again, however, might not my justification be distraction? Even if I had no idea what the lateness might mean for P, I'd be wondering how come he made no mention of it; I'd find this odd and therefore would be preoccupied with it. Is he deliberately keeping me in the dark? Why would he want to do that? Moreover, during the rest of the session I'd be listening hard for some allusion to the lateness and the darkness surrounding it, and this is apt to interfere with my paying attention to everything he was recounting.

Susan thinks it shouldn't, and neither do you. The issue will be on my mind but it needn't be a significant distraction. Issues will, after all, always be on my mind. Neither is there too sharp a distinction between listening *to* and listening *for*; we necessarily do some of both. For one thing, it isn't possible to listen free of ideas and hypotheses; no one is a tabula rasa; everyone has schemas that filter and organize data; perception is never wholly passive and fully veridical. As a consequence, I have to learn to listen well despite the fact that I have things on my mind—and sometimes they will serve a valuable function there. There will be times when having something in mind can help me listen better, because it will turn out to have been on the patient's mind, too.

Since listening is a major topic for us, we are reserving it for a future lesson. Still, you make some relevant comments in the course of examining option 3, which is the course you would follow. You make no bones of the fact that it's due mainly to the unattractiveness of the other options that you choose it. But it will frequently be the case, you remind us (again!) that our decisions are based on negative considerations, on proscriptions instead of prescriptions, even though we're inventive enough to fabricate for ourselves rationales that obscure the fact.

Choosing option 3 does, however, raise some tough questions. Are we colluding with P in sweeping the matter under the rug? Is our silence not implying that the latecoming, not to mention his silence about it, is of no import? Susan doesn't think so but I do. I think silence is always a significant communication, and in psychotherapy I would think it's an especially significant one. This particular silence can convey a certain gingerliness, or perhaps a worry that the topic is too hot to handle. I would worry that P knows that he's evading the issue, and will notice that I, too, am evading it—and wonder why. Do I want to define myself as the one who colludes in a defensive measure that is so central to Psychotherapy?

Your response is: we needn't necessarily evade it, we can prudently postpone it (Susan and I smirked simultaneously at this, and came up with the shrewd interpretation that our pending theory letter is much on your mind). Option 3, in your view, can count as a postponement, inasmuch as we will bear in mind the lateness, and the darkness surrounding it, and we may soon find ourselves in the position of referring to them.

You give us a for instance. Say P, in the library yesterday, had a conversation with Harry about therapy, and he voiced some feelings about being in therapy, feelings that he didn't realize he had. This could provide a basis for explaining his lateness and we might be able to point it out to him to good effect. Or suppose he talks during the session about his conflicts over telling us everything, and suppose Harry is an old friend with whom he shares his secrets. The encounter may have thrown him into a conflict of loyalties (with all manner of oedipal overtones), and it may be the reason he chose not to tell why he was late. When we address this, with an interpretation, say, we show P that we have not swept the issue under the rug, we have been saving it for good therapeutic purposes. I agree that this is a strong point and justifies the postponement and the tolerating of the distraction, and so does Susan.

Next you ask us to suppose that P had not begun the session the way he did, but instead he remained silent for a few moments, and let's suppose that this is not his usual habit. Is option 3 still the option of choice? In your opinion it is. During the initial silence we will probably be thinking about the lateness, and it's a fair assumption that so will P. Some question may arise. Is he reflecting on how it feels to have come late? Is he wondering whether we'll ask why he came late? Is he thinking we're irritated with him, or disappointed in him? Each of these possibilities represents a topic of potential significance, and we can get to examine them by simply asking him, "What are you thinking?" This is a more neutral probe than options 1 and 2, and. . . .

Since you've already overused your delaying tactics with us, instead of promising to teach us the uses and misuses of "What are you thinking?" in a future lesson, you interrupt this one to do it. (I have recast your remarks into the form of an extended dialogue between you and us.)

An Interview on Silence and "What Are You Thinking?"

U   When P falls silent we have the option of asking, "What are you thinking?"

Us   It's a flagrant directive and yet a good option?

U   It's a big exception.

Us   Please explain.

U   The gap in verbalization that occurs when P is silent isn't the same as a gap in information when he's speaking, and while there's a surface similarity between the directives, "Tell me the fact you omitted from your narrative," and, "Tell me the thought you had during your silence," there is also a fundamental difference. The former runs the risk of imposing a new topic, the latter doesn't.

Us   If we had asked, "Why are you silent?" that could amount to an imposition insofar as it's quite likely he wasn't thinking about the reason for his silence.

U   Yes, and it's important to notice that it isn't the directive I'm referring to. "What are you thinking?" is significantly different from "Why are you silent?" Moreover, even when he answers, "Nothing—I wasn't thinking of anything," we haven't changed the subject or imposed a topic.

Us   We have if he feels impelled to consider why he was silent.

U   But it wasn't our question. And this has to be made clear.

Us   So if he responded as if we had asked the why question, we would take pains to make it clear that we hadn't intended it.

U   Furthermore, asking him to verbalize his thoughts is quite different from asking him to provide an omitted fact or feeling. We aren't directing him to speak about anything new and different, something he wasn't already thinking about.

Us   But if he was silent because he didn't want to speak his thoughts, aren't we violating the basic instruction by asking for them? He might respond, "Look here, you said I was free to speak about whatever I wanted, and I'm assuming that included the freedom to remain silent. I was thinking about something I don't want to talk about. Are you directing me to speak about it anyway?"

U   Even if he didn't articulate the issue so clearly, the first thing I'd make clear is that he was free to remain silent if he wanted to, and I didn't mean to imply that his silence was not all right. Then I'd explain my reasons for having broken his silence as follows: "I had no way of knowing you were thinking about something you didn't want to talk about. I thought you might have slipped into a reverie, and perhaps you were having difficulty overcoming the inertia of the silence itself. I figured it might be useful to help you overcome that inertia by asking for your thoughts." Notice, please, how my explanation avoids the message, "I am interested in your unspoken thoughts."

Us But it fails to avoid the implication that reverielike states aren't useful, and raises the question of why it is useful to have the inertia of silence overcome.

U My answer is based on the premise that the therapeutic process is enhanced by verbalization, that self-inquiry is facilitated when P is not only thinking but also verbalizing his thoughts, mainly because he is then in the position to listen to himself. Other things being equal, self-observation is usually enhanced by observing oneself in action, and for most people, most of the time, verbalizing their thoughts improves their ability to observe those thoughts. So if I judged that P was no exception, or this particular silence wasn't exceptional, I would base my answer on that rationale, and say: "Overcoming a silence's inertia is useful because speaking your thoughts may benefit therapy." Notice again how the explanation avoids implying that my participation is at issue.

Us There's no compelling reason to formulate it that way, is there? Couldn't we take the position that the second part of the basic instruction requires him to speak in order that we could listen?

U Of course. But that point is so self-evident that I'd be inclined to emphasize the first rationale.

Me But that rationale can be adapted to fit a variety of different directives. If I had reason to believe that the therapeutic process could benefit from the interpretation of dreams, for instance, the rationale could justify the directive to bring them in. And suppose P was speaking

I. H. Paul

about a symptom and focusing only on its current status, and suppose I had reason to believe it might be useful for him to explore its historical origins, why not notify him of that conviction in the form of a directive? Or conversely, if he were speaking only about its genesis, why not say, "Talk about the way the symptom happens now, because that might be useful"?

U   In other words, if promoting the process was our only goal, why should we be prevented from following the most expeditious course of action across a variety of different areas—"What's wrong with interviewing?"

Me   And the basic instruction hasn't ruled it out! So far as P is concerned, were I to give those directives, he'd have no reason to conclude that I had departed from its conditions—especially since the directives restrict themselves to therapy's procedure. Mind you, I haven't forgotten that you mentioned the need to find an appropriate time to amplify on the matter. After we've judged that P was suitable for Psychotherapy, we look for an opportunity to notify him that we will "try" not to give any kind of advice, and we're supposed to clearly specify that this means advice pertaining not only to behavior outside therapy but also in it. He will likely understand why I refrain from advising him on courses of action to follow in his daily life, and the matter is easily explained in terms of my wishing to remain objective, but he might be puzzled, if not worse, about the restriction on advice as to how he should proceed in therapy, saying, "I can see why you wouldn't want to tell me whether I should change my major, or invest in the stockmarket, or even go out with women. But that's quite different from telling me what to talk about here, isn't it?" I have some expertise in this area, I ought to be able to give some useful advice.

U   I've already examined the large answer to this question as well as the specific one, "In my experience, the most useful thing for you to speak about is what you want to." If you continued to press the question, I could make the

distinction between short-term and long-term considerations. I could concede that a directive might be useful in
the short run but contend that it might impede the long-
range goals of therapy.

Me   And the long-range ones have all the priority, I take it.

U   In general, yes. But there's no need to minimize the
potential usefulness of certain directives. If P feels at a
loss about what to talk about and says it would be useful
for the moment if he got some directive from me, he may
be right; it might be useful. But the question I'd ask
myself is whether it would be useful only in the short run,
and therefore shortsighted, to fulfill his request, because it
might impede the optimal development of the therapeutic
process in the long run.

Me   Does it mean our sole obligation is to the long-range goal
and under no circumstances do we support short-term
benefits?

U   Not at all. All what's required of us is an awareness of
these options, that they can be antithetical to each, and it
might be more useful to P if we helped him explore why
he feels at a loss over what to talk about and feels a need
for direction, or why he doesn't bring in his dreams, or
why he never speaks about the history of his symptoms.
That's the option that has to be kept open, and it requires a
readiness on our part to frustrate his need of directives.

Me   But these considerations don't apply equally or fully to the
silence-breaking directive, "What are you thinking?"

U   Insofar as the short-term benefits don't necessarily conflict
with the long-term ones, this may be an exceptional case.
So when P falls into a silence and needs our help to end it,
I don't recommend frustrating that need. We can make an
effort to distinguish between meditative or reverielike
silences on the one hand, and resistive silences on the
other. We can try to figure out the nature and function of
each silence, and depending on our understanding of it,
choose to interrupt a silence with a directive or with an

interpretation. Or we may decide, of course, not to
interrupt it at all.

Me Okay, so much for P's silence. Let's return to option 3,
which concerns mine. I want us to suppose that P was
embarrassed by his lateness, so much so that he chose not
to mention it. Let's suppose further that he projects his
feelings onto me, inferring that I, too, was embarrassed by
it and for that reason I remained silent while he proceeded
to tell about his meeting with Harry. Can't I argue that the
reason for avoiding option 3 is to show him that I have no
feelings about his having come late and therefore I don't
evade it? And by mentioning it, wouldn't I be showing
him that I regard such incidents as latecoming to be of
potential interest and significance?

U   Such demonstrations are likely to be of limited value
and the point will have been made at some cost to the
therapeutic process. You see, Simon, if he is projecting,
the most useful action you can take is interpretive; if he
is assuming that you don't care, you can deal with that
assumption not only by declaration ("Look, I do care!"),
but by interpretation ("You're assuming that I don't
care").

S   Moreover—if I may be permitted to join in—you can
often expect to be able to make the same point in a way
that does have value insofar as it supports and promotes
the therapeutic process. Suppose you had chosen to
remain silent; you may soon be able to observe the
consequences of that choice. If P now begins to think and
feel that you don't care about him, then you may well
conclude that this is his reaction to your silence. Supposing, after a pause later in the session, he says, "I don't
know why—it's weird—but I can't shake the feeling that
you are not interested in what I am talking about today.
For some reason it seems to me you don't care." You can
now say to him, "I have an idea about what may be
bothering you: you came late today; it's the first time you
ever did; and I didn't ask you how come."

Me "That makes sense; I did wonder why you didn't ask."

S "And perhaps you took it as a sign that I don't care."

Me And now he will of course say something like, "Whenever I came home from school my mother would always start in with the questions—what happened in school? Did I have a good lunch? Was I a good boy?" Perfect! Not only have I shown him that the evasion was his, not mine, and that such events as latecoming can serve the interests of useful therapeutic work, but I've helped him gain understanding of a significant piece of action.

U And you've dealt with him sensitively and patiently, without censure or direction—in other words, with good technique.

ELEVEN

CONFRONTATIONAL AND NONCONFRONTATIONAL INTERPRETATIONS

Today we're imagining P as someone who comes to his sessions with a topic prepared in advance and has never spoken about the habit. He begins this session with a typical remark: "I was thinking, as I came here, about my difficulties getting to know people. I went to a party Saturday and had a bad time trying to make conversation with this very interesting man." We now predict, with dead certainty, that the session will consist of a circumstantial account of a party, along with a systematic examination of difficulties getting to know people, and will have all the earmarks of a rehearsed recitation. Suppose we took the view that P might benefit from breaking the habit and occasionally allowing himself a measure of spontaneity by permitting the topic to emerge without forethought. Putting this view into practice is the subject of our lesson.

For starters, we could inform P of our opinion by simply saying, "I believe that your therapy might benefit if you refrained, at times, from preparing what to talk about." This amounts to treating the issue as business. I believe we are justified in doing so, Susan doesn't.

My rationale centers on the third of our stipulations for patients that you mentioned in your first letter (you called them "qualifications"): P is expected to talk openly and freely. Susan says I am stretching it; the basic instruction makes no mention of this stipulation, and contradicts it in a certain way; P is free to be unfree, in the sense of planning his sessions in advance. She is also loath to opening the door to requests on his part for advice on how to be a "good patient." You agree with her, but on different grounds. "We may believe that it would be more useful for therapy—and consequently beneficial for him—for the habit to be understood than for it to be simply abolished," you say. "The advice could result in forestalling that understanding."

I'm outvoted; we are ruling out the business option. Our goal is to draw P's attention to his habit so that it can become the topic of his exploration, our task is to study the merits and demerits of the various ways of achieving it, and we start with a straightforward one:

> I'm interrupting you in order to draw your attention to something that may be useful to think about. You were thinking about this topic before you came today. Now, it seems to me that this is what you do before each session.

An interpretation of this kind is known as a confrontation. It draws a patient's attention to his or her behavior ("holding up the mirror," as it is put metaphorically). When judiciously used it can be a valuable technique, but it can be dissonant in Psychotherapy insofar as it imposes a topic. To argue that it isn't an imposition because it was the patient (the patient's behavior, strictly speaking) who introduced the topic, is something of a sophistry. Still, confrontational interpretations may be effective and at times also necessary. Therefore we're going to examine the four responses that P could potentially make to ours: they are acceptance, rejection, counterconfrontation, and perplexity. (His actual response might be an amalgam of several of these possibilities but we have no option other than to examine them separately.)

The first response, acceptance, may be exemplified by P saying something like this:

> It's true, and I can see why you're pointing it out to me. I agree that it could be important for me to consider it, because it is something I always do. I think about what I will talk about here and make sure to have it worked out in advance. I don't know why I have to, and sometimes it makes me feel uneasy—kind of guilty. It's as if I were doing something wrong, or even bad. It's a strange feeling. I've been

> meaning to talk about it but somehow I always put it off. I
> wonder why.

This is the ideal response; it fulfills our fondest hope; it's the reason we ventured the confrontation. To expect it, however, is likely to be wishful thinking. It also smacks of compliance on P's part, and should alert us to potential transference implications.

If P chooses to reject our confrontation, he might do it this way:

> No, I don't do it at all. What I meant when I said I was
> thinking about it before I came was that it occurred to me
> as I walked in. But I wasn't thinking about it before
> that—and I do not usually do that kind of thing.

This response is acceptable, in my view, for unless we have good reason to believe that P is evading the issue, we can put the matter aside—and this can be useful insofar as it removes a distraction from our mind and will help us listen attentively to what happened Saturday evening. (I am still hung up on the subject of distraction.)

Susan disagrees. The implications of rejection are bound to be significant, particularly since we had a good basis for making the interpretation. Is P lying or being disingenuous? Wouldn't we think so? A certain trust has been undermined; P has distrusted our observation, and we've been put in the position of distrusting his veracity. That's what Susan thinks. I think he is probably being evasive rather than untruthful—and evasion is a respectable defense mechanism.

You seem to agree with me, though you don't specify on what grounds. Instead you take the opportunity to deliver a little lecture on the merits of our occasionally being wrong and inadvertently giving invalid interpretations. What are those merits? Not only do we not want to foster the role definition (or is it a transference issue?) of the omniscient one, and not only do we prefer a role definition as the one who *tries* to understand instead of the one who *does,* but an invalid interpretation, provided that its form is good, can be useful for the therapeutic process. The key proviso is good form, and for a confronting type of interpretation to be mistaken (and the same holds for an articulation of a patient's feelings) is likely to be more significant than for other types of interpretation because the patient isn't in a good position to disagree with it. P's third response may be called a counterconfrontation.

> So what if it is so? Why do you choose today of all days to bring it up? If it's what I've been doing since the start of therapy, you've had opportunity to draw it to my attention. Why do you do it now when I'm about to speak of something that's important to me?

On this response we're in full agreement: it's the one we would welcome least, for our only honest rejoinder might be something to the effect of "enough is enough!"—and even with all the tact we can muster, this would carry with it implications both of advice and of criticism, if not also some personal irritation. If we get this kind of counterconfrontation we may have little choice but to focus on P's feeling of outrage, and follow it up with the interpretation that he is being guarded, and we'd rather not do that because it can too easily amount to a counterconfrontation of our own.

Consider this awful illustration. We have said, "You are feeling outraged, aren't you?" and P responded, "I resent your interrupting. I don't understand why you choose now to do it." Now we give this interpretation: "It seems to me that if it were only a matter of not understanding, then you might feel puzzled. But you are resentful and outraged. So I wonder whether you're also reacting to what I said, and you'd rather not have to consider your habit of preparing in advance." Two successive confrontations to follow up our original one—that's a feat! What can we now expect, P will back down with a sheepish, "I guess you're right"? That unlikely outcome will merely mean we've won the contest.

Confrontations have a way of provoking impasses; patients might grow more argumentative; they might intellectualize and obfuscate; they might retreat into stubborn silence. It is pointless, if not worse, for us to pursue them with further interpretations in the face of these defenses. For one thing, those interpretations are apt to be taken as criticisms and scoldings. We must never lose sight of the fact that our interventions—be they interpretations or confrontations or simple observations—are useful only when they are acceptable to, if not welcomed by, patients, either at a certain level of their consciousness or to a part of their personality. Otherwise, they have no good way to deal with the interventions.

The same is true for P's fourth potential response, perplexity.

> What do you mean? Of course I think in advance about what I'm going to talk about here. Isn't it the right thing to do? But if it were, then you would not be interrupting to draw it to my attention. So I'm puzzled. I assumed that everybody did it before a therapy session. Don't they? Is it a bad thing to do?

We can draw P's attention to his perplexity and mystification, and we might add that his reaction may be defensive. But this, too, runs the risk of bringing things to impasse, and for us to ever respond, "What makes you think I said it was a bad thing to do?" is only to have compounded defensiveness with more of the same. So we may have little choice but to fall back on the procedural instruction that we had in mind in the first place.

In the exercise that we're working with there was no request on P's part for any guidance in the matter. In fact, the issue of spontaneity is far from his mind. Our only available option, therefore, and despite all of our wants, expectations, and hopes, is to listen carefully and wait patiently for a chance to make an appropriate interpretation. For in view of the fact that we are too unsure how P will respond to a confrontation, and in view of the likelihood that the confrontation will quickly require us to make an interpretation, we can well decide to go the route of interpretation to begin with. And this, let us imagine, is the one that formulates in our mind:

> I think you are feeling vulnerable here. You are worried lest anything come to your mind spontaneously that might be upsetting to you, or even frightening. Or perhaps you are feeling that it's somehow dangerous here because I might say

something to you that would upset or hurt you. And for
these reasons you need to come to your sessions with
something all worked out and prepared in advance, which
you can fill up the whole session describing and talking
about. This ensures that there will be little opportunity for
me to say much about it. Or, if not that, then having something worked out may be a way of preventing something
from coming spontaneously to your mind here, something
that you'd have little control over because it would come
as a surprise, and that could be frightening.

But we'd never dream of saying all that!—for a variety of technical (we could call them commonsense) reasons, of which two can
be singled out. (1) The interpretation imposes a number of altogether fresh topics, and if P has not already alluded to any feelings
of vulnerability, then the interpretation is a major imposition. (2)
There is far too much in it. Even granting that it may all be quite
valid, what is P to do with it? Is he to choose from among the four
or five distinguishable ideas the one that he is prepared to deal with?

The interpretation violates the technical principle of parsimony
to the point of caricature. It has at least four major parts to it, and
we have delivered them all. What we should do, instead, is decide
which one of them has the priority, or the greatest relevancy. Not
which part is most valid, since we're assuming that all of it is,
but which part is most timely. Is it the feeling of vulnerability, of
fright, the unexpected thought, the unexpected interpretation, or
is the fear of loss of control the most relevant aspect?

So, if we decide in favor of an interpretation over a confrontation, we have to simplify and articulate the interpretation in our
mind and then wait for a suitable opportunity or opening so that
the imposition (after all, we are introducing a topic) can be kept
minimal. We won't interrupt at the beginning of the session, and
we will listen to P's account in two ways: attend to the manifest
content, listening to understand and to remember it; listen for some
content that we might be able to connect with or associate to an
aspect of the interpretation in an appropriate way. The latter might
occur when P says, "I knew I was going to have a miserable time

at the party on Saturday." Sensing an opening, we might, in a half-questioning way, say, "You knew it in advance?"

"Yes. Parties like that have always filled me with dread."

"And I take it that you think a lot about them beforehand."

This remark is pivotal. In a sense, we're making the opening with a conjecture, but it is neither too farfetched nor without tact. If P now says no and then wonders aloud why we made the remark, we can casually deflect it with a comment such as, "I figured you did that." Admittedly it's lame, but we have to resist the temptation of joining the issue at this point by responding, "Because it seems to me that it's what you do before your sessions." That may be way too premature.

But let's imagine we were right, and P responded, "I certainly do that. While I was getting dressed for the party I kept imagining that I was going to have to make conversation with some stranger."

We could now focus on the theme as follows: "And you imagine in detail how such a conversation might go, I gather."

"Not always in so much detail," responds P. "But I think about what I say and what he says, and things like that. This is something I've always done. Like when I used to go on dates when I was young, I used to figure out in advance things to talk about. Otherwise it would be deadly."

If we sensed that he was returning to his rehearsed account, we might encourage him to continue exploring the habit itself and focus on the question of why he feels the need to prepare. We might raise the question of the habit's utility, suggesting perhaps that it's less useful than he believes. Or else we could move directly into the interpretation—"I believe that this is similar to what you do here; you tend to come to your sessions with something figured out in advance to talk about"—and the topic has now been raised.

It has not been imposed unless P experienced it as such. He might accept the idea as altogether related to the topic he brought in, in which case there's been no violation of his autonomy. "Yes, I guess it's true," he responds. "I don't know why I should do it here too. After all, it's not as if I felt the same way talking to you here as I do about talking to a stranger at a party."

We are now in good position to implement one of our interpretations. Not that we should necessarily do it; there may be value in some forebearance and tact. It may be sufficient to dwell on the contradiction he's expressing and allow him a chance to develop the theme of the interpretation himself.

But what if he does experience an imposition and denies that there was any connection between the topic he brought in and the therapy itself? "But that is altogether different," he responds. "It doesn't strike me as similar at all. I'm not nervous about coming here like I am about going to a party. And the reason I think about what I should talk about here is because it's the most efficient way to benefit from these sessions."

Now we must choose our words very carefully. "I understand," we could say. "But I'm wondering whether it might not benefit you to examine that assumption. After all, you did have a dreadful time at the party even though you rehearsed for it beforehand. So perhaps the advance preparation doesn't help you."

Notice which assumption we chose to address. We have chosen to retreat, in a way, from the therapy theme and turn toward P's original topic. This is a technical measure serving the interest of clinical tact. He may not be ready to deal with his advance preparations for the session, and we must remain sensitive to that readiness. Thus, after having mentioned it, we can shift back to his topic. ("Our patients should never be backed into a corner," you write sternly. "Our patients should always sense that they have freedom of movement, if not to maneuver. In this way they don't feel coerced into considering something they don't want to consider at the moment.")

The main point is this: P is free to continue talking about his habit of preparing for parties ("It's true. I always have a dreadful time at parties despite the advance preparations"), and he is free to examine his habit of preparing for sessions ("It may not help for the parties, but I think it does help for the sessions—because if I didn't do it, I would sit here with nothing to say"). In either event, we are fully engaged in the implementation of our intentions, and that's what technique means.

TWELVE

NEUTRALITY WITH RESPECT TO CONTENT

First you ask us to examine the ramifications of a particular confrontation, then, after we've done it, you ask us to question its premise and consider whether drawing P's attention to his lack of spontaneity isn't an infringement on our neutrality. This could count as a dirty trick if it weren't so patently designed to segue smoothly into the topic of "neutrality with respect to content."

Well, as it turns out, we had already questioned that premise. Susan did it before we did the exercise, and we argued about it for an hour (and I didn't mention it because it would have been a distraction from my unadulterated rendition of your lesson—besides, I got the better of the argument). She wondered why you'd want us to draw P's attention to his habit of preparing for sessions, regarding this as something we had to be neutral about. I argued that she was stretching the concept of neutrality. How could we remain neutral in respect to the very work of therapy? Are we not going to side with P against his neurosis? Aren't we going to be partial to his ego in its struggles against his id and superego? We want him to be free of debilitating anxiety and inhibitions, don't we?

My point is this: if we aren't neutral about such intrapsychic matters, then we can hardly be neutral in respect to the ways of dealing with them. I find it hard to imagine being impartial when it's his neurosis that P is struggling with. Not only do I have to take his side, so to speak, I also have to make it clear to him that I'm doing it. Therefore, if he needs to know that being spontaneous can be helpful in this struggle, my neutrality is not germane.

Susan believes he'll have to discover these things himself and she's confident he will. She steadily worries about teaching patients to be "a good patient," and argues that we only invite compliance when we suggest that they recount their dreams, examine their childhood, talk about their sex life, or be spontaneous.

You seem to side with both of us. You remind us that the basic instruction promises that we will abstain from giving any advice as to what might be beneficial to explore and examine. Therefore, if patients never talk about their childhood, their dreams, their sex life, we cannot suggest that they do it. You refer to this aspect of neutrality as "neutrality with respect to content," and you write:

> Every therapist has convictions about the fruitfulness of topics (commonly called material). Based on an amalgam of theory and clinical experience, those convictions are likely to encompass a range of topics. We may believe that our patients stand to benefit from an exploration of their development; we may believe that a balance is best struck between the past and present, between the intrapsychic and interpersonal, between affective and cognitive; we may believe that night dreams and daydreams are valuable for uncovering conflicts and memories. This list can be extended. Psychotherapy doesn't require us to abandon those convictions. The basic instruction doesn't imply that we foreswore them. Just because we want P to choose his own topics doesn't mean we have no preconceptions.

What then is required of us in respect to such convictions? We should hold them in abeyance, you say. We have to keep them from attenuating our nondirectiveness. Therefore, not only don't we inform our patients about them, but:

> We try our best to keep them from influencing P's choice of topics in such a way as to maximize the occurrence of the types of material we believe will be most beneficial—and that is no easy achievement. The ways in which we can shape and steer narrative are so manifold and subtle, and it is so unrealistic to expect that our interpretations won't reflect a selective bias, that the achievement can only be regarded as an ideal goal.

In other words, perfect neutrality may be a theoretical fiction, worth striving for but impossible to attain, but we can still achieve a degree of neutrality that is sufficient to the task. We simply face a conflict of interests; on the one side stands our conviction about the differential fruitfulness of topics, on the other, our conviction about the profound ramifications of allowing patients to talk about what they want to. We can resolve this conflict by making a choice, but we can attenuate the choice by construing the two convictions as nested within a larger one: in order to yield its beneficial results, a topic must freely be chosen, the choice must not be made under the aegis of an externally imposed task. To support that larger conviction, we accept this working hypothesis:

> Whether it is the weather or his childhood, the baseball strike or his marriage, whatever topic P chooses to talk about will reflect something authentic, meaningful, and salient for him; the choice will prove relevant in the short run, if not also valid in the long run. Therefore not only will it serve the therapeutic process, but P also stands to benefit from exploring it.

We can construe the choice as reflecting a wish and an intention, perhaps a hierarchically ordered set of them, and when P speaks about the weather, and when he speaks about his childhood, we do the same thing: try to understand the choice he's made.

But look here, isn't it true that speaking about the weather might reflect his wish to test us, if not also an intention to sabotage the therapy? Is this no different from talking about his childhood? Your answer is: "In respect to the way we work with narrative: yes. Whatever the wish, whatever the intention and expectation, we listen in order to understand, and when we think we've understood, and judge it useful to share that understanding with the patient, we offer an interpretation." Yes, but what does *useful* mean in this context? Surely it has to be useful (if not crucial) to interpret P's intention to sabotage the therapy; this is, after all, a major resistance, and I don't see how we could be neutral with respect to it. The same cannot be said about the topic of his childhood.

Susan says it can. P's wish to provide us with history, and his intention to thereby expedite the therapy, can be construed as resistance, for short-circuiting the therapy can be a form of sabotage. She admits that it's rather less blatant and substantially more subtle than the weather, and this will probably make a huge practical difference for the ways we can articulate our understanding and help P understand the meanings and purposes of his choice of topic. But otherwise it needn't make any significant difference.

To be fair to Susan, it was only for the sake of our argument that she assumed P's reason for beginning with his childhood embodied a resistance. It could also be based on a desire for a psychoanalysis and the belief that it's the appropriate way to begin one. The same applies to free associating, recounting dreams, and the rest. So she would not challenge such decisions, she'd want only to understand them, and direct an interpretation at them only if she had reason to believe they were subserving a resistance. In other words, our convictions about the differential fruitfulness of topics must be held in abeyance until the therapy is in jeopardy. That's her reading of your lesson. She constructed a scenario to illustrate the point.

P   I've been talking exclusively about my childhood here, and I'm wondering how come.

Us   It's puzzling to you because it feels as if you're talking about your childhood for some ulterior motive.

P   Well, I haven't said a thing about my marriage or my work, which are both very troubling; they're the reason I came into therapy in the first place. But here I am giving you all the details of my early development. I feel funny about it.

Us   I think you may be feeling that you're doing it for a reason.

P   What reason do you have in mind?

Us   To get the therapy over with as quickly as possible.

So I countered with this one:

P   Since you are being neutral with respect to content, I have decided to speak exclusively about the weather.

Us I take it you're doing it in order to test the limits.

P   Correct. I want to find out whether you intend to allow me to sabotage the therapy if that is my choice.

Us I can spare you the time and trouble by telling you that I have no other choice.

P   That's too bad—not so much for you as for me, because this leaves me with no other choice than to quit therapy.

Us Oh, but in that case I am permitted to stop being neutral, because your therapy is now in jeopardy.

P   But you knew it already when I said "sabotage the therapy." You did, then, have another choice. Didn't you have this choice without my telling you about my intention? Wasn't it sufficient that you believed I had the intention?

And that's my point! To be sure, if P says, "Do you want me to talk about my childhood?" my response is, "I want you to talk about whatever you want to" (and if it was, "Should I talk about it?" I would simply say, "If you want to," or, "It's up to you"). But he might respond, "I know that. I'm asking whether you think it might be beneficial to me if I told you my dreams. Look, it isn't a personal question; I'm asking for your professional opinion." Isn't the question now a business question? Can't I regard it as a matter of the therapy's format and procedure? Can't I say, "Yes, in my experience (or in this type of psychotherapy), it might be beneficial"? I see no reason why not, but Susan thinks we should stand firm and say something like:

> I prefer not to answer the question and tell you what you should talk about. I prefer to leave it up to you. You see, I

> believe that you're more likely to benefit from these
> sessions if you choose freely and decide what to talk
> about without any guidance from me.

That's pretty severe, isn't it? Doesn't it construe the basic instruction too stringently? Isn't there a middle ground? (I can virtually
see you writing, "There always is. Extreme positions should always be avoided in an enterprise as complicated and dynamic, not
to overlook human, as psychotherapy.")

In any case, you seem to suggest a middle ground with your
characteristic "it depends." It depends on our having a basis for
expecting that the remark will be taken as a notification and not as
a directive. Even then, however, we must take pains to point out
that we're not intending to advise. Admittedly, things can become
quite subtle.

And here your position veers away from Susan's, although it
doesn't exactly veer toward mine. You draw a neat but subtle distinction between what we want and what we expect. When P says,
"Do you want me to come at four o'clock?" we may say yes, but
strictly speaking we aren't saying, "I want you to come at four,"
what we're saying is, "I expect you to come then." There's a difference here. I agree that it can be a significant one. It's too abstruse for
Susan's tastes, though, and she thinks it would be for P too.

You go on to point out that being neutral doesn't mean that we
don't have expectations. We expect patients to pay the fee but we
don't, strictly speaking, want them to. We also expect them to
express their feelings in verbal and nonverbal forms but never in
action. If they are angry at us, they are free to say so; they aren't
free to strike us physically. Similarly, we don't want them to obey
the basic instruction, we merely expect them to. But when it comes
to taking sides, to judging and evaluating, and the rest, then we're
dealing not with our expectations but with our wants.

I explained it to Susan this way: in ordinary parlance, whenever
it makes good grammatical sense to say *expect*, we can usually say
want, but the reverse isn't necessarily the case. "I want you to tell
me the things you choose" works, but "I expect you to tell me the

things you choose" doesn't. "I want you to speak about your feelings and not act them out" is not as correct as "I expect you to refrain from striking me physically." And we can hardly say, "I expect you to speak openly and freely, if not also spontaneously," we have to say, "I want—I desire—you to do it," which rules it out.

Accordingly, whenever we cannot use "I expect," and must use "I want" and "I desire," we are in the terrain of neutrality. Thus, "I expect you to restrict yourself to telling, and I expect you to refrain from doing" is okay (even though *want* can easily be substituted for *expect* without changing the meaning), and the matter can be construed as business. However, when *expect* is inapt, as in "I expect you to recount your dreams, or expect you to speak about your childhood," and we have no choice but to use *want* or *desire*, then chances are good that the matter cannot be construed as business.

Susan gets the point but finds it mind-boggling and doesn't see how it could be a useful guideline. Try explaining it to a patient who isn't into word games and see how far it gets us!

Then let's go back to our unspontaneous P, and let me raise a few questions. You had us believe that he could benefit from breaking his habit and occasionally being spontaneous. This reflects, you now say, a certain bias on our part, coupled with an intention to modify his behavior; it is therefore problematic. My contention is this: we aren't dealing with wants or expectations, we're in the realm of opinions and beliefs. If I happen to believe that P will benefit from being spontaneous, why can't I treat it as business?

Being spontaneous, it seems to me, can be regarded as not so significantly different from being on time to sessions. If I take this position and deem it necessary, or even just desirable, for him, I can simply tell him, can't I? I hope you appreciate that I'm not advocating a reliance on the therapeutic process to bring about the change in his behavior; I'm assiduously avoiding using any interpretations; I know they mustn't ever be used for the purpose of modifying a patient's behavior. (You wrote it again in this letter! You warn us that you'll be writing it again, so vital is this point for Psychotherapy.)

But is this properly a business issue? Should we expect P to be spontaneous? Your answer is a "yes-but-no." It's one thing to hope or expect, it's another to want. You don't think we should ever want patients to tell their dreams, though we can certainly hope that they will. If we actually want it we should go ahead and ask for it, but if we merely hope for it we must wait patiently for it to happen.

Suppose P doesn't ask whether we want him to tell his dreams; instead he says, "I know you've instructed me to talk about the things I want to talk about; that's what you want me to do. But I want to know whether, in your professional opinion, dreams can be therapeutically beneficial." It seems to me that I can say yes with impunity. For even if worst comes to worst and he says, "So I should tell my dreams, eh?" I can say, "That's up to you. I meant only to give my professional opinion." And if he persists with, "It seems to me that you wouldn't have told me this unless you felt that I should," I can say, "I appreciate that may be true, to an extent, but I still want to leave it up to you as much as I possibly can."

Or suppose I had a couch in my office and P says, "I see you have a couch in here, should I lie on it?" When I say it's up to him, he continues as follows:

P   But you wouldn't have one if you didn't think it was good for your patients to use it. And I've heard that it can be helpful for therapy. Don't you think so?

Me   Yes, I do think it can be helpful.

P   So you want me to use it, then?

Me   You want me to help you make the decision, I take it.

P   Yes, I guess I do. I don't know whether I want to lie on the couch or not. But I will do it if you suggest it.

Me   I would rather not. As I've already said, I prefer to give you no advice or direction.

P   I understand, and I can appreciate your reasons. But your having said that it can be helpful makes it harder for me to decide not to do it, because then I would be putting up a

barrier against the therapy right away. In other words, I
really don't have complete freedom of choice now.

Me Yes, I do appreciate that. But you still have some, and I
would rather not restrict it further by telling you what I
think you should do. I may tell you what I think might be
helpful, but it's still not quite the same as telling you what
to do. I know there's only a fine distinction between the
two, but it's one that I'd like to preserve.

Susan isn't persuaded. The distinction is too fine for her taste,
and she thinks it would also be for P's. She would respond to his
"Don't you think so?" by saying that some patients find it helpful
to lie on the couch, others prefer to sit up. If he asks whether it
might be helpful for him, she'll say she has no way of knowing.

If I were P I'd bristle at this. Is it all a matter of what some of
her patients "find helpful" and others "prefer"? After all, some of
them who found it helpful might also have preferred not to use it.
That she has no way of knowing for sure whether it will be helpful
for me is so obvious a point as to be gratuitous. Why can't she tell
me that it might? That's the reason it's there, isn't it? She can say
that it can be helpful, but whether it will be for me is something
only I can determine. Can't she?

THIRTEEN

NEUTRALITY
AND IMPERSONALITY

You have no quarrel with my handling of P's requests for a professional opinion, and Susan's stance is somewhat too stringent. Along the lines of her approach, you would make sure to say that you had no way of knowing whether the couch was going to be helpful for P. You'd say this first because it might be all he really wanted to know. In any event, however, you would avoid, and assiduously, any reference to what "some patients" find helpful, because you want to steer completely clear of any and all normative formulations. It simply is not a good idea to compare and contrast a patient with other patients, or for that matter with other people. Not only don't we want to foster any sense of competition but we want to avoid ever indicating what may or may not be, from our point of view, "normal." This is an important ingredient in our neutrality.

Patients often raise the question of their normality by asking are their actions, thoughts, feelings, and wishes normal. "I'm asking for your professional opinion," is usually added or implied. Do we now don our mantle of expertise (as psychologist, social worker, psychiatrist, or whatever our credentials allow) and give our opinion? No, the only mantle of expertise we should be willing to don is that of psychotherapist. It is this expertise that will be of direct benefit to our patients, especially when they are engaged in a form of therapy that is as nondirective as Psychotherapy is. All other areas of expertise are usually irrelevant and can be considered personal.

Today's lesson ranges over the topic of neutrality and therefore examines the issue of impersonality. Why the "therefore"? Because our chief reason for wanting to be impersonal is that we need to be neutral, and our basic reason for needing to be neutral (in case we've forgotten) is that we've chosen to be nondirective.

I say "ranges" because your letter, to put it nicely, is discursive ("rambling" might be more accurate). I am therefore taking liberties with it that might strike you as unseemly. You'll see what I mean when you read the following paragraph.

Based both on your writings and on what I know about you personally, I can confidently assert the following. You are not a cold fish, a detached person, and neither are you aloof and unapproachable. You aren't callous and unfeeling or grim. You are reserved and a bit phlegmatic, but also compassionate. I'm convinced that your patients see all of this in you, yet they also know that you are being neutral.

At the outset of therapy they might find you a bit stiff and somewhat distant because you don't reach out to them and show much warmth and concern. You are cordial but not friendly, sympathetic but not sentimental, you're businesslike. But they soon learn how intensely you pay attention and listen to what they say, and how careful and tactful you are in what you say. You also show them some warmth and enthusiasm, but throughout the entire course of therapy you remain as neutral and as impersonal as you can possibly be—and there is no contradiction in any of this. Only a misconstrual of the concept of neutrality would find any contradiction here.

Neutrality is a difficult concept and also a controversial one. We therapists tend to be unneutral when it comes to the question of our neutrality; we become passionate, if not indignant, when the subject is broached. Who, after all, wants to be considered a detached, cold therapist? Moreover, it isn't enough to deny that neutrality mandates detachment and coldness; we have to offer sound and compelling reasons to justify our neutrality, and then face the difficult task of specifying its nature and determining its limits.

Does being neutral mean we don't care? No, for we aren't impartial when it comes to the integrity of the therapeutic process. We care deeply about it, and inasmuch as the therapy is of utmost importance to our patients, we thereby care about them. Do they realize this? Most patients come to appreciate the value of this

distinction and recognize that our neutrality serves a vital function in their therapy.

We have many ways of showing them that our neutrality is not
an indifference. These range from the ways we deal with business
matters that matter to them, to the ways we show them that we've
understood their thoughts and feelings. The way we time and formulate our interpretations, not to overlook the very intensity of our
interpretive approach, mitigates against both the substance and
appearance of indifference, particularly inasmuch as the interpretations imply no passing of judgment, no criticism or personal
evaluation.

Now we turn to your argument that neutrality mandates impersonality, and the lesson grows Talmudic in its ins and outs and hair-
splitting. Instead of summarizing your obsessional ruminations and
interspersing my obsessional doubts, I have cast them in the form
of two dialogues: one between me and Susan, in which she takes
the hard line and I defend a soft one, the second between both of
us and you, which allows us to present your arguments verbatim.

Susan and Me

Me   Are we not going to tell P how old we are?

S   It depends on whether we regard it as business. Our
       approximate age shows, of course, but there can be a
       range of uncertainty.

Me   Okay, so say he wants to narrow it, he asks for my exact
       time and place of birth.

S   For what reason?

Me   Let's say he wants—no, he needs to run my horoscope
       because he believes in astrology and it's important for him
       to know my sign. He regards it as a qualification, a
       credential. Doesn't it thereby count as business?

S   You don't believe in astrology, I take it.

Me You don't take it, you know it! But what difference does
    that make? I can't be the exclusive judge of what counts as
    business. The determination has to be one that is mutually
    arrived at.

S   Sure. But this means it's not altogether up to him, either.
    You needn't automatically accede to his definition. You
    can tell him that you believe your astrological sign won't
    affect your ability to serve as his therapist. This, after all,
    isn't your personal opinion, it's your professional one.

Me Yes and no. It's a professional opinion that overlaps with a
    personal one. It bespeaks a personal position vis-à-vis
    astrology, doesn't it? He might have started with the
    statement, "I'm a strong believer in astrology," and then
    said, "What's your position on it?" I would not want to
    answer that question.

S   Why not?

Me Oh, you know why not. You just want me to spell it out.

S   No interpretations, please, just answer the question!

Me Okay. Because if he knows that I don't believe in astrol-
    ogy, he's not going to feel so free to talk about the subject,
    for whenever he does, he's bound to feel that I am judging
    him.

S   You could tell him that you don't believe in astrology but
    you believe you can be neutral and nonjudgmental about
    it.

Me That would strain his credulity.

S   Perhaps. But what alternative do you have? If you be-
    lieved in astrology and told him, you'd be implying that
    you would have told him if you didn't. This would expose
    you to a host of questions about your personal beliefs and
    opinions. For example in P's case, your personal position
    in respect to homosexuality might be raised. That, after
    all, is likely to matter to him, too. Once you open the
    door, it isn't going to be easy to shut it.

Me A door that opens easily can be shut easily. I'm leery of arguments that hinge on not giving away inches. Besides, I don't think we should be concerned about letting ourselves be "manipulated" by our patients. Not only is it self-serving, I'd rather we defined ourselves as flexible and not rigid.

S How about consistent?

Me But there are things about myself that I cannot conceal or that I voluntarily choose to reveal. I can't hide the fact that I'm a man but I can keep my sexual orientation from showing. And say I tell him I'm heterosexual—out of respect for his having construed it to be a professional credential for him— what if he says he needs to know whether I have a girl friend, too?

S Tell him that you prefer to define this as a personal question. Doesn't it strain credulity to construe it as a credential? After all, you'd do the same, I hope, if he next asked you whether you're in love with her. It isn't very hard to draw the line.

Me So let me pick a harder line. Say he asks me whether I've seen a particular movie. And he wants to know because he had some emotional reactions to it that he planned to explore during the session. "I could devote more time to them if I didn't have to describe the movie to you, so it will serve a useful purpose if you told me whether you've seen it." Wouldn't it?

S In the short run, yes. Whether it would be useful in the long run, I would question. Your having chosen to see this movie—and for the sake of argument, let's suppose it was an X-rated homoerotic one—could say something about you personally.

Me My not having gone to see it can say something as well.

S My point exactly. So it counts as a personal question.

Me So I'm going to tell him it's none of his business.

S   Words to that effect. What's your problem?

Me   He's going to say, "If you don't tell me whether you know the movie, I'm going to listen hard to your remarks for signs of it. That's going to be very distracting, and not only to me, because you're going to have to choose your words carefully to keep from tipping your hand." And he's right. I'm going to have to work very hard to keep the information from showing.

S   Nobody said Psychotherapy was easy.

Me   Nobody said it has to be this hard, either. Anyway, do you want me to draw a line in the sand on this issue? Is whether I've seen a movie, or is my exact time and place of birth, so personal, and therefore so germane to my neutrality that you believe it is necessary to risk the therapy over it?

Both of Us and Uncle

Us   Okay, but the big question is twofold. (1) How impersonal should we be? and (2) How impersonal can we be? Let's start with why we should want to be impersonal in the first place.

U   I see no way round the conclusion that, as we intend never to pass judgment on P, evaluate him, and be a source of reinforcements, we have no choice. For if he knows I'm a pacifist, how can he be persuaded that I'm not judging him when he advocates war? If he knows that I believe in the sanctity of marriage, how can he behave adulterously without fearing my valuation? And if I've told him that my tastes in music range from the Renaissance to the baroque, he might have to defend a love of Tchaikovsky.

Us   But we can stay neutral despite anything he may know about us personally. We do, after all, have opinions and attitudes and values: he knows that. Doesn't our task remain the same whether or not he knows what they are?

U   From our vantage point, yes, but not from his. Of what use is it for him to know personal things about us? Won't knowing them complicate his task of accepting our neutrality and working securely within it? Moreover, Psychotherapy doesn't require us to be personal. For inasmuch as the relationship that we have with P plays no significant role, there's no therapeutic purpose served by our being personal. Psychotherapy requires of us a degree of warmth, a measure of enthusiasm, along with a great deal of empathy, sensitivity, and an ability to listen. But this isn't personal.

Me   Sure, but only according to that definition of "personal."

U   However it is defined, impersonality is a feature of Psychotherapy that I would expect you to challenge, especially when I spell out the extent to which I might strive for it. For I don't stop necessarily at refusing to divulge whether I am happily married, I might choose not to tell P whether I am married at all. And I might refuse to divulge whether I had seen that movie because it could amount to having revealed something personal about myself, and therefore I might choose not to.

Me   Your intention to remain impersonal can extend that far, but judging from the words you stressed, I gather it doesn't have to.

U   There are distinctions and caveats. Insofar as it pertained to my knowledge alone, my having seen a movie differs from my marital bliss. And my store of information may be personal but it can have implications for my neutrality that differ from other aspects of my personality. If he asks whether I've seen *Citizen Kane,* or do I know Mahler's Ninth Symphony, I might tell him.

S   Even if you thought it might be a loaded question?

U   By "loaded" I take it you mean the extent to which its intention is to learn something about me personally. Yes, I might tell him even if I thought it was. Otherwise I'd be back in the business of evaluating and judging, namely,

"I'll tell you only after I've satisfied myself that your need for the information is legitimate."

Me So we can draw the line at knowledge by excluding it from the domain of "personal," and that resolves the problem.

U   Unfortunately, no. We need to draw a distinction between those of our personality features that have a direct bearing on our ability to understand P and those that don't. His personal questions, especially at the beginning, are usually directed at our professional experience and credentials. Are we competent is the underlying question. Often they are also directed at our personal experiences and our personal credentials. Are we compatible is the question. They might reflect a concern over whether his life-style will be comprehensible to us. "Do you have children?" "Are you Catholic?" "Do you know much music theory?" P might regard these to be specialized areas with which we have to be familiar.

Me If he was having problems with his children, P might believe that a parent was likely to understand him better than someone who was childless; if he is a devout Catholic, he might believe that only a devout Catholic could comprehend his feelings and experiences; if he's a composer with work problems, he may want us to know music theory. These are legitimate questions.

U   Up to a point they can be answered in a way that preserves sufficient impersonality. If he thinks a childless, non-Catholic, unmusical therapist isn't likely to understand his problems, I can acknowledge his belief and explore it. I can do it without taking a position on the belief itself. But I must keep in mind that my being a parent doesn't ensure my ability to understand his particular problems, my not being Catholic might have little bearing on my ability to really understand his religious experiences, and even if I knew a good deal about music theory, it might not suffice. So finding out those personal facts about me won't serve the purpose P had in mind.

Us   Then how do we satisfy that purpose?

U   A trial period is often the optimal way. But in cases where
     aspects of special competency aren't likely to become
     significant until later on in therapy, I might choose not to
     rely on the trial period and instead invite P to interview
     me.

S   Interview you? Even if it amounted to a kind of examina-
     tion, could you take it without compromising your
     neutrality?

U   Why not? If I tell him I know the problems of parenthood,
     I'm familiar with Catholicism, and knowledgeable about
     counterpoint, I haven't told him anything so personal.
     Even specifying the extent of my knowledge won't cross
     the line. "Yes, I know Fux's rules," is significantly
     different from saying, "I studied counterpoint for two
     years at McGill's Conservatory." It's the difference
     between what I know and how I came to know it. Both are
     personal, but the former belongs to the domain of my
     factual knowledge, and that much I can share with him.
     The same is true for, "I know the problems of parent-
     hood," in contrast to, "I know them because I have two
     children of my own," and, "I'm not Catholic but I grew up
     with Catholic friends."

Me   So we draw the line at our factual knowledge. We define
     "personal" in a way that limits it to our opinions, senti-
     ments, and tastes. And the reason we exclude them is
     because those aspects of our personality are irrelevant to
     our effectiveness as therapist for an average expectable P;
     they need not interfere with our ability to understand him
     or with our capacity to supervise his therapeutic process.
     But the same isn't true for our factual knowledge. Our
     ability to understand can be significantly impaired if we
     aren't sufficiently informed about aspects of his experi-
     ences.

U   So up to a point what we happen to know might matter,
     and that point depends on P. If he has a psychological

problem with counterpoint and needs to explore it in detail and depth, we may need to understand counterpoint. To the extent that we don't, we will have to ask him for clarification.

S   But in itself this needn't be a handicap for him. For he can benefit, can he not, during the course of his explanations, by discovering things he'd been taking for granted?

U   That's a good argument but a weak one. The possibility remains that our grounding in music is so lacking that his explanations won't suffice, and that possibility has to be taken seriously.

S   But aren't you overstating the problem to make the point? The illustration, after all, is very specialized.

U   I chose it because counterpoint is a subject that few non-musicians are likely to know much about. The average therapist can expect to have a fund of common knowledge (whatever is fit to print in the *New York Times*, say) but will be uninformed about many topics that are known to the average P. This doesn't obviate the fact that what we know can matter, and in a way that has to do with neutrality because the problem, alas, isn't fully resolved by drawing the line at knowledge.

Us   We hope you're not going to tell us that distinguishing between a familiarity with the writings of Philip Roth, say, and an opinion of those writings won't satisfy the demands of neutrality!

U   I have no choice. Knowledge is selective; it reflects values and interests. We can no longer expect to know every-thing—not even everything in the *Times*—so our choices are revealing. If P knows that I've read *Portnoy's Complaint* but not *Airport*, knows that I recognize John Cage but not John Lennon, he has learned some things about my literary and musical tastes. That I "happen to" know a thing, or not, does say something personal about me. I see no way around this. All we can do is weigh each of his personal questions to estimate whether the balance is on the side of getting personal information for the sake of ensuring a level of understanding or whether it's more on the side of learning personal things for other purposes.

S   Can't we translate the question into, "You're asking me whether I understand"? Since I ask him for clarification anyway, instead of answering the question, can't I tell him that I'll ask whenever I haven't understood?

U   Sure. But this can't apply across the board, and there will be occasions on which he'll need to know in advance whether you will be understanding him.

Me   Okay, so let's just go ahead and tell him we're familiar with the book, or movie, and run the risk of a "flaw" in our neutrality! The same "flaw," after all, will undoubtedly develop when he speaks on a subject in a way that presumes our familiarity with it and we don't ask for clarification.

U   Which boils down to the hard fact that feasibility sets limits, and those that are based on what we choose to divulge are bound to be arbitrary. To refrain from telling P whether I am married is one thing, but don't I wear a wedding ring? How about the way I dress and decorate my office? Isn't my personality reflected in a wide range of nonverbal behaviors?

Us   What about the argument that we therapists must come to know our "stimulus properties"?

U   It isn't germane here. Every therapist must take pains to know them, the one who doesn't strive for impersonality no less than we ourselves.

S   Then let's keep them minimal and nondescript. Doff the wedding ring, dress and decorate conventionally.

Me   There are limits. Furthermore, if P wanted to learn about us, there are ways—look us up in the professional directories, for instance—so why not spare him the trouble. Isn't it artificial to make him do it? It just tests his resourcefulness and shifts the burden of feasibility onto his shoulders.

I. H. Paul

And let's suppose he puts it this way: "I have a need to know whether you're married, and I don't care to understand it or make it go away. If you refuse to tell me, I'll go to the library and look you up. So your refusal will cost me time and effort."

U I might judge it unfeasible, ultimatum or no, not to comply, because the practical implications and side effects for him would be too far-reaching. That, of course, is largely a matter of judgment, and it's going to depend on who P is and the stage and state the therapy is in. But it can be formulated in terms of feasibility.

Me So, with respect to the movie example, P might say, "If you don't tell me whether you've seen it, I'll listen carefully to your remarks to discern whether you're familiar with the movie. I don't care to understand why, but I'm going to do it. I'll be preoccupied with your remarks. And even if you are able to choose your words so carefully, which will constrain you, I'll be distracted. So it would keep from being a distraction if you simply satisfied my need to know whether you saw it."

U Even if he didn't articulate all those factors, I might judge that feasibility, from his vantage point, required me to tell him whether I had seen the movie. In fact, I can envisage circumstances in which I'd tell him even if he hadn't asked. Say he was describing the movie in a way he wouldn't if he knew I'd seen it: I can imagine interrupting with, "I gather you're describing the movie to me because you don't want to ask whether I've seen it or not."

Us Hello! Why would you ever do that?

U To raise the issue of his reluctance to ask me personal questions. But my intention is to address the question of feasibility in a businesslike way. In the end it comes down to a matter of clinical judgment. The fact that it reveals something personal about us notwithstanding, there's no a priori way to decide whether we should divulge information or not.

Us   And isn't there a point beyond which the minimal requirements of neutrality have been breached, when P knows too
much about us and therefore will be unable to work
effectively enough within the format of our method?

U   Yes, and that point, too, is a matter of clinical judgment.
Just as neutrality is a relative achievement, so is impersonality.

Us   Which doesn't justify abandoning all attempts at it.
Having granted that the line has to be artificial isn't the
same as contending that it's futile to draw it.

U   Moreover, we can share the problem with P; we can
explain our position to him, concede that there's a substantial arbitrariness to the degree of our impersonality, and
promise him that we'll rely on our judgment to keep the
arbitrariness to a minimum.

Us   So the line, in your opinion, can feasibly and sensibly be
drawn at what we divulge verbally—provided we exercise
good judgment in each instance rather than follow a rule.

U   And also provided we draw a distinction between being
impersonal and being without personality.

Us   "Without personality"? What on earth does that mean?

U   I'm referring to the minimal, nondescript and conventional
appearance that you mentioned. I see no merit in it. Not
only would it take an effort which is bound to show, it
would fall short of any useful standard. Moreover, the
requirements of neutrality, as distinct from those called for
by the "blank screen" theory, do not call for it. Neutrality's
requirements are fully satisfied by maintaining a nonselective
position. They are satisfied not by our being without personality, but by using our personality in nondiscriminating and
nonselective ways.

Us   And what on earth does that mean?

U   If you are warm and demonstrative, it's part of your personality, then you can behave in a warmly demonstrative

way toward P without at the same time having violated your neutrality. This is the critical point: you remain warmly demonstrative throughout, without significant regard to what P is saying and how he is feeling. If he is sad or elated, if he is feeling vindictive or victorious, if he is angry at you, you still remain warm and demonstrative. You avoid, or at least minimize, variations that are reactive.

Us   But that's asking for a lot! That kind of nonreactiveness has to be difficult, if not quite impossible.

U   Only if the level is high, to begin with, and also low. You may have to temper it, that's all. The same applies to other expressive aspects of your personality: if you are an enthusiastic person, you need to try and maintain the same degree of enthusiasm throughout, and too much of it can make the task more difficult.

Us   You chose those illustrations deliberately, we gather. You've mentioned several times that Psychotherapy requires of us a degree of warmth and enthusiasm.

U   Yes, these qualities can be beneficial to the therapeutic process and I see no reason why they necessarily vitiate our neutrality.

Us   But isn't there bound to be a difference between our neutrality and our impersonality in the degree to which they strain P's sense of credulity? Despite our efforts to maintain neutrality, despite the care we take to time and formulate our interventions so that they are nonjudgmental, P. may find it hard, if not impossible, to fully believe it. He will cling to the conviction that we are valuating and criticizing him, only hiding the fact.

U   That is often the case. Even if he appreciates the profound benefits he derives from having such reactions hidden from him—and most patients do come to appreciate it— he may be unable to avoid being distracted by thoughts about what our reactions must be. Deliberate impersonality, however, is quite different. For one thing, it isn't so hard to achieve, not at the level of divulging personal information, at least. Also, the fact that we have a personal life, with convictions, opinions, tastes, and values, is never in question, and P will accept the fact that it's going to be kept from him. He may balk at it; he may recognize no special benefit for it and therefore protest it. But it's been my experience that the relevant issue is special competency and a compatibility, and once that issue has been resolved, P comes to appreciate, and also value, the benefits of our impersonality.

For inherent in the dynamics of Psychotherapy is the fact that our impersonality comes to serve a vital function for our patients. Their not knowing us in a personal way provides them with a profound freedom in therapy. They are free to admit every shameful secret, every humiliating experience, every embarrassment and degradation, without running the risk of incurring criticism and deprecation. The same applies to "good" experiences, feelings of pride and victory, for instance; they, too, can become inhibited from full expression when another person's interests are at play. Impersonality must therefore be maintained as an integral aspect of our basic position. If the optimally functioning therapeutic process depends on freedom and autonomy, then we must remain neutral and impersonal, both.

FOURTEEN

ON CARING

On Friday, while writing your neutrality letter, you had the nagging sense of a memory lurking in a corner of your mind. That night you had a dream in which you were seated at a large table around which were children eating from big bowls of fruit. The children were also throwing fruit at one another, and you realized that it was a summer camp, for there was a counselor on the far side of the table, a bearded man, in his thirties perhaps, wearing a silk, embroidered shawl. He was sucking on a yellow fruit and smiling benignly as he silently surveyed the kids throwing fruit; the fruit that he was sucking on, you realized, was a lemon. You woke up, startled, and now knew what had been lurking in your mind while you were writing the neutrality letter. So on Sunday you sat down and wrote it out. The explanation of the dream is adequately given in the lesson, which consists of a memory that you recount to us in story form.

On Caring

A case was being presented in group supervision, at the psychoanalytic institute where I was a student, under the tutelage of a wise and experienced, if acerbic, analyst. The patient's wife had had major surgery the evening before the session being reported, and our student-therapist began the session by asking him how it had gone and how his wife was feeling. Our teacher's reaction to this was a disapproving shrug and a grimace that silently but clearly said, "What for did you do it?"

"I asked how his wife was," explained the puzzled student, as if our teacher hadn't heard her.

"To what purpose?" he asked.

"Because I cared," was the rejoinder.

"You had reason to suspect he didn't know it, I take it."

"No, I didn't actually. I asked because I cared." Then she added, a bit defensively, "And what's the harm in showing him that I did?"

"Perhaps none," conceded the clinician, wearing his lemon-sucking grimace. Then he added, a bit offensively, "Since when do we justify our remarks on the grounds that they do no harm?"

At this point others joined in. "Most of us would have asked," one of us remarked. "Give me a reason, please," said our teacher. "One is the implications of not asking," said another, and when the teacher said, "And those implications are what?" the student said, "To begin this session like any other session ignores the fact that a very important event has preceded it."

"Its importance I do not minimize," said the teacher, "and it certainly must not be ignored. But"—raising a finger and widening his eyes—"to not inquire into it is to ignore it? If the patient will begin the session in a way that appears to ignore it, then will we not draw his attention to this remarkable fact?"

No one answered, so he went on. "If it was my patient and he began speaking of something that appeared to be unrelated to the operation and his wife, I would soon be making a remark that conveyed to him I was wondering how come."

"But before you can get around to it," protested one of the bolder and rasher students, "the patient may react by thinking you're a heartless son-of-a-bitch."

The clinician took this in stride and his face kept its sour expression. "Yes, it might have that consequence." Then he scanned the table so the tactless student wouldn't feel obliged to field this question: "And what would that mean?"

Someone ventured, "It would mean that you've provoked an unnecessary and time-wasting resistance."

"If it did provoke such a reaction, such a resistance, I would hardly judge it to have been unnecessary and time-wasting. Quite the contrary, it could be the important thing to work on during the session. You are assuming, are you not, that it was altogether rational for him to construe my failure to inquire into his wife's welfare as evidence that I did not care about her. But why, tell me, is it less rational to construe it as my waiting for him to speak of her condition?"

"Because in his social world people who care ask, they don't wait."

"And therapy is part of his social world? We greet him with 'How are you feeling today'? And if we do not, it means that we don't care how he is feeling? Say he's insomniac—we begin sessions by asking whether he slept well the night before? More than conveying to him that we care, we would be directing him to think about the way he slept."

"But," cried the student who had made the comment, "our patient has had an extraordinary event happen. His wife had an operation and may now be moribund if not dead. It just doesn't happen every day."

"And the issue of directiveness can hardly be involved," added another, "for he can hardly be thinking of anything else."

Again our teacher was unruffled. "That is more than likely true. But what if it happens not to be? Would that not be very interesting? And very vital? And what is the danger of waiting a few moments to find it out?"

There was a pause while we searched for a danger. Then someone said, "One is that it may cause him to think that we've forgotten about the operation," and got an appreciative nod.

"Yes, it may well be that the reason he needs for us to inquire is that he needs a proof that we have remembered. This is natural in therapy, and one of the ways we care about our patients is we remember what they tell us. When, at the beginning of this discussion, I asked was there a reason to suspect that our patient thought we didn't care, one of the things I had in mind was this question of remembering. Fine, then let us assume it. Let's say there was some reason to suspect that he was wondering if we remembered his wife's operation was the evening before. What meanings and ramifications can this have?"

"That we don't take his problems seriously, we dismiss them between sessions, is one possible ramification."

"He'll wonder if we pay enough attention to the things he tells us. And this can raise the question, Are we being distracted by our own problems, or even worse, by the problems of other patients about whom we care more?"

"Another possibility is that we are filled with such dread by his problem that we defend by evasion and repression."

We were rewarded with an approving nod. "That is an interesting list, and I am sure you could expand it. Notice, however, that it does not yet include the possibility that we are simply uncaring people. But even if it is included the same conclusion must be drawn: all of these meanings and these implications can be of vital consequence for the therapy, and consequently for the patient's welfare.

"And here now is my rationale for not making the opening inquiry: none of them has a chance to emerge into the foreground if we have taken steps to keep them in the background. If we have not found out whether or not he needs for us to ask, we will not have found out if he is wondering have we forgotten, and we have lost the opportunity to expose any of the meanings and ramifications in our list. It is our obligation to allow for the possibility for a significant reason that he cannot bring himself to volunteer the information about his wife. For if there is one, then it is our job to find it out and to help him examine it. That, after all, will benefit him far more than anything else we can actually do.

"Look, is there any doubt that our asking the question will affect neither his nor his wife's welfare in any way? How can there be? On the other hand, however, our failure to ask it can potentially benefit him directly, and indirectly therefore also his wife, enormously."

There was a pregnant pause at this point. Then our teacher intoned: "During times of crisis you may have to temporarily abandon your analytic posture. If your patient is in some trouble and you can help with some information and advice, or reassurance and support, then you may want to do it. If the wife developed, say, an edema as a consequence of the operation and he is worried about it, and you happen to know it is little cause for concern, then you may want to tell him to set his mind at ease. But at the beginning of the session we are discussing there is no way to know whether there is a crisis, so there can be little harm in waiting to find it out. Bear in mind that the operation might have been a complete success and he finds it difficult to tell you that. The key question, if so, is why, and if you have not allowed him to experience this difficulty, if you simply ask about the operation, then the question will evaporate—for the time being, at least—and you care too much about him to let that happen."

The discussion should have rested there but our rash and tact-less peer felt unsatisfied and apparently desperate. What he cried out in protest made the rest of us wince. I'll include it, neverthe-less, for I like the response and it's a fine way to end this parable.

"But it was a trivial thing, to say, 'How is your wife?'!"

"A good and excellent reason to not say it! I thank you for saying it. Trivialities and social amenities not only serve no prac-tical or therapeutic purpose in our therapy, each one of them de-tracts from the practical and therapeutic value that we can have to our patients. Each one of them robs our patients of a potential benefit to be derived from their therapy. It is precisely because we *care* for our patients that we preserve our analytic position as much as we humanly can. What better way is there for us to *care* than to strive our utmost to *understand*? To understand another person, and to nurture and to foster his understanding of himself, is also to care deeply about him. No?"

FIFTEEN
ON THEORY

The theory letter arrived safely. Your apologies for its discursiveness and prolixity were brushed aside; we read it as you asked us to, as a work-in-progress. What kind of work-in-progress we're not sure; it's part lecture, part polemic, and part rumination. Instead of paraphrasing and critiquing it, we decided to edit it, format it, give it a title and some suitable subheadings, and—publish it. We hope you don't disapprove.

What Kind of Theory, and How Much of It, Does Psychotherapy Need?

After giving synoptic, if not dogmatic, answers to the question, I will discuss them with the help of three cases: the case of Meno, specifically Meno's slave; the case of Anna O, specifically Bertha Pappenheim; and a case of successful treatment that I once heard at a convention of psychoanalysts.

Psychotherapy needs a theory that is empirical in the broadest sense of the term, a theory that respects appearances and is willing to take events at their face value: a clinical theory in the fullest sense of the term. It's a theory that restricts itself to half of the classical epistemological question, How *do* we know? and bypasses the other half, How *can* we know? Psychotherapy doesn't need an ontology in the form of a theory that postulates realms (such as the unconscious) and that relies on the predicate "exists" (as in "memories exist in the unconscious"). Ours should be a theory that is satisfied with a description of its events and phenomena, and has no compulsion to construe them as manifestations.

We need a theory whose core concept is an act, or an experience, rather than an entity or an existence, but I will have difficulty naming it. I propose that the principal event of Psychotherapy can adequately be explained by saying that our patients engage in this difficult-to-name act-experience, and that this is what is therapeutic. I will not speculate on why it is therapeutic; instead I am going to argue that such speculation is not only unnecessary, it can be a diversion.

I am also going to contend that a theory of what ails them—a psychopathology—can be a diversion too. Psychotherapy benefits a wide variety of patients, it isn't a specific remedy; it belongs in the category of healing rather than curing, and is more akin to convalescence than to surgery.

The question of how much theory we need is a pragmatic one and a matter of clinical judgment. In my view, we tend to theorize more than we need to, and with too little regard for utility and parsimony. We do, of course, need theory; there's a sense in which we cannot avoid it; but we don't need a theory that encompasses all of human experience and behavior. It can be limited to the format of our therapy, on the one hand, and to the core therapeutic experience on the other.

On Empiricism

Empiricism doesn't mandate a belief in facts as "raw data." As Susan suggests, our facts can be construed as small theories and our theories (so long as they are "true," that is) as big facts. Our cognitions, after all, are pervaded with theorizing and our phenomenal world is dense with meaning. All of us, not just those of us who occasionally make theory, theorize all the time. We can make a concerted effort to keep our theories small, which means keeping their level of abstraction low and their distance of denotation short.

Empiricism means having faith in the powers of observation and taking a clinical approach to theory making. When we say "it's just a theory," we mean less to denigrate theory than to keep it in a proper perspective, a clinical one. If facts are small theories and theories are big facts, we want our theories to devolve into smaller facts; we want them to become small enough for us to see their factualness and grasp their meaning. We want our explanations to be apprehensive, rather than comprehensive, and have the lucidity of facts.

By small I mean concise. A big theory may encompass too many facts and gives them too global a meaning because every fact carries a meaning which can be accounted for by a theory, and if every fact is made into a theory then we have too many theories, while if too many facts are brought together to fit into one theory it becomes vague and procrustean. To be sure, when we slice our pie too thin it isn't very nourishing, but I believe we should guard against gluttony.

We work with facts that are mental in nature. This doesn't require us to abandon an empirical posture, provided that we keep from inferring the existence of unobservable mental realms and don't construe mental facts as manifestations of them (epiphenomena). We can cling to the conviction that our facts are fully observable and describable, and that our task is to do it—and then trust that our theory will reveal the meanings that are immanent in them.

For example: we observe a moving billiard ball contacting a stationary one which immediately mimics its movement and we see a cause and effect; we observe a child kicking his legs and screaming, "No, no!" and we see a temper tantrum. These are facts we're seeing, not inferences we're making; they are small theories. We can make them smaller by recognizing that they are composed of smaller ones. This allows us to entertain alternative theories which take into account other facts: the balls may be controlled by a contrivance and the child might be playacting. Being a "trained observer" (a good clinician) entails holding our theory in abeyance and entertaining alternative ones, and this requires us to look for further facts.

Being a trained observer also entails a sense of wonderment about facts and a skepticism about theories. Facts can be opaque in respect to their meaning. "I wonder what it means," we say. "It can mean different things, depending on context and perspective. What facts can I find to improve my observation and thereby improve my theory?" We don't reverse the sequence and ask, "How can I improve my theory (i.e., make it bigger) and thereby increase my powers of observation?" That's what defines us as empiricists: we bet on smaller facts (smaller theories) to make them better, rather than on larger theories (bigger facts) to make them comprehensive. It probably boils down to a matter of taste and strategy but it does influence the cogency and effectiveness of our work (a priest, and a mathematician too, does better with one approach, we do better with the other).

What kind of answer will satisfy us when we ask why psychotherapy works? Traditionally, empiricists (following Newton's success with prisms) have believed that analysis into parts is the way to answer the why question: we isolate the phenomenon's constituents and examine how they interact (e.g., "Experience is a product of sensations that interrelate according to the laws of association," and we inquire no further into any why's). But we have an alternative that is just as empirical. It's a field theoretical approach asking about the properties and dynamics of psychotherapy, its conditions and forms. To do this, we must first identify the core event and agree on its phenomenology. We can then regard the core experience of therapy as an autochthonous event (a fact), and go ahead to study its forms, vicissitudes, and developmental history, and thereby get to understand it. When we've exhausted our study we'll know what it is. By knowing how it works we'll know why it works (determining whether it works is of course another matter, and it's clearly an empirical one).

The word *disclosure* comes close to describing the essence of the core event but it isn't satisfactory. The meaning I want for the word may become clearer as I write about it, but I'll mention that disclosure needn't be to another person, disclosing to oneself is crucial. And I'm not referring only to a sharing of secrets, or speaking aloud something that was never spoken aloud. The watermark of the event is the feeling of surprise that comes with an experience of having discovered something or having understood it. I will capitalize the word *Disclosure* to signify this particular sense of it.

The Case of Meno

Imagine a patient, Meno's slave, an uneducated barbarian, suffering from an ignorance of Pythagorus' theorem and seeking therapy for it. Socrates, a prominent Athenian idealist, gives him a course of therapy and it's a smashing success. It consists of drawing diagrams and posing questions about them, the answers to which lead to a discovery of the theorem—and the patient is cured of his ignorance.

Let's take liberties with the facts and imagine Socrates stumbling serendipitously on his method and now needing a theory to explain it. He hypothesizes that Meno already knew the theorem, it was in his mind; the therapy consisted of education: a leading of the patient to an uncovering of the solution, which entails a recollection of it. This peculiar hypothesis is based on Socrates' theory, his epistemology, which in turn is based on his ontology, idealism. There are two theories. One is that knowledge exists in the mind, it has only to be uncovered, or discovered, and a way to achieve it is education. This is the theory of therapy; unable to arrive at the solution by other means, the Socratic dialogue is the appropriate therapy. The second theory is a theory of knowledge, the Theory of Forms. The two theories may be regarded as occupying adjacent levels of discourse, but I'm not sure that this is the correct way to construe them. In any case, they are idealistic as distinct from empirical.

It serves my purposes to say that there is no place in the theory for the relationship between Socrates and Meno because it isn't relevant to an understanding of the therapy. Socrates did one thing, Meno did another; it is inapt and unnecessary to theorize about their relationship. The apt-necessary theory is a theory of knowledge, and how much of it we need is a matter of judgment. Do we need the general theory, the ontology? Socrates did (he had bigger fish to fry), but do we?

Meno suffered from the ignorance of a piece of mathematics; so did Pythagoras before he cured himself. Everyone is in the same boat. We are dealing with ideas. They are mental things. They exist in the mind, are the theory, and need only be made conscious for them to be known by the mind. Making conscious is only a matter of method, whether you call it education or reasoning or technique. To be sure, there's craft to it, but it requires no ontology, only an epistemology (i.e., a psychological theory) to provide a set of practical principles and guidelines.

Notice also that the findings do not strongly support Socrates' theory. Meno probably didn't feel that he had recollected the theorem, or even uncovered it. That wasn't his experience. He would probably have agreed that he had figured it out; with the help he got, he had reasoned and thereby discovered it.

And is Socrates' method crucial? No, it merely makes the treatment more efficient. Meno could have spoken about triangles—and it needn't have been aloud—and eventually he'd get to the theorem (wasn't this the way Pythagorus did it?). Education-by-teacher is an expediency; the therapist is an enabler and in no other sense participates in the process, which is mental and autonomous. When we have elucidated the process we will have understood his behavior and our theory will imply his role.

It suits my purposes to imagine Socrates stumbling serendipitously on the method, discovering that he can teach Pythagorus' theorem (and any mathematics or abstract thinking) by posing a series of questions. He then elaborates a theory of knowledge and this, in turn, leads him to a theory of existence. While we're at it, let's also say he goes ahead and founds a school of pedagogy based on the method, and establishes an institute to train and indoctrinate teachers. Their treatment method is the dialogue and their theory is the Theory of Forms. This is what happened for Freud; psychoanalysis begins with a serendipitous discovery which is elaborated into a theory of psychology and a metapsychology. The theorizing is Socratic in spirit, rather than Aristotelian, idealistic more than empirical.

The Case of Anna O

Bertha Pappenheim is an educated woman suffering with hysteria and a patient of the prominent Viennese physician, Joseph Breuer. He has been treating her with hypnosis and she persuades him to let her use it in a novel way: instead of focusing on her symptoms, she will recollect the traumatic events that had occasioned them. The treatment is a smashing success and gives birth to psychotherapy.

She calls it a "talking cure" and refers to it as "chimney sweeping." If we translate chimney into memory and sweeping into remembering, hers is a theory that might read: there exist in the mind memories that are pathogenic; remembering them (specifically, reexperiencing with feelings) is pathocurative. Breuer conceptualizes the phenomenon as catharsis and abreaction, and this ushers in our modern theory of therapy. It becomes the kernel of Freud's theory: hysterics suffer from unconscious reminiscences, therapy is a way of reminiscing and making memories conscious. Breuer's theory centers on the phenomenon of states of consciousness, Freud's on the concept of repression, but Breuer bequeaths both the theory and the therapy to Freud—and the rest, as they say, is history.

Freud retains the format of hypnotism but stops hypnotizing, then substitutes free association for guided recall. These changes are based less on theoretical considerations than on clinical ones; he emphasizes the priority of clinical events over theoretical ideas and insists that the latter emerge from the former. But Freud is not content with a theory of therapy, he wants a theory of neurosis. More than that, he wants a theory of psychology which he calls metapsychology ("our psychology"). In his theoretical excursions he leaves psychotherapy behind. He loves psychotherapy less than metapsychology; he is less interested in explaining how psychotherapy works than how people do.

His theory conflates a theory of neurosis with a theory of therapy. Neurosis is a result of forgetting, therapy is a process of remembering; forgetting is a result of repression, therapy is a way to undo it because repression is manifested in resistance and can be breached by interpretations. This required of patients a new activity: in addition to remembering their traumas, they had to learn about (become "acquainted" and "conversant with") their resistances. This required of therapists a new activity: their interpretations had to be didactic and explanatory.

Complications grow when resistance takes the form of transference. Therapy is iatrogenic, it inflicts a transference neurosis; treating it becomes a major task. This requires a new activity on the part of patients: in addition to remembering and gaining insight into their resistances, they had to understand their thoughts and feelings toward the therapist, and analyze them by tracing them to childhood traumas. This activity gets treated the same way as the repression; the model remains hypnosis-with-a-difference; transference calls for no change in method, though it does require the analyst's remarks to become more didactic.

Finally, Freud introduces a concept that he calls *working-through*. Analyses of the memory and transference resistances were, by themselves, ineffective for a permanent lifting of the repression, a working-through had to be done. It isn't enough to uncover the childhood trauma, it's necessary to trace and uncover its subsequent course of development and each of its manifold effects. These have to be treated seriatim and the theory had only an associationist concept to account for this requirement. The concept of secondary gain is invoked, to combine with the laws of association, but the therapy grows increasingly didactic in its efforts to undo these sequelae. (Where Socrates could stick to education, Freud had to resort to teaching by instruction. But if Meno had suffered from an ignorance of Greek history, Socrates, too, would have had to shift from educating to teaching.)

On Working-through

Why a piecemeal working-through was necessary is a question Freud answered in two ways. Each of the pathogenic memory's associations had to be cathected and thereby severed, was his first formulation. Later he postulated id resistances in conjunction with a repetition compulsion. But he wrote very little on the subject, and the same is generally true for subsequent Freudians. I stress this because working-through, however it might be construed, may be relevant to my "core event."

The last of Freud's basic concepts on therapy,[5] working-through is a theoretical, as well as clinical, stepchild and also something of an embarrassment to the family. It has the earmarks of being ad hoc. Ernest Jones and Peter Gay, in their comprehensive biographies of Freud combined with detailed presentations of his work, each devotes a paltry paragraph to it. Jones writes: "It concerns the constant struggle in analysis between the analyst's endeavor to get the patient to recollect the buried memories and the patient's tendency to substitute for this repetition in action. Freud then drew the important distinction between simply [sic!] discovering the nature of a given resistance and conveying of it to the patient, allowing him to 'work through' the knowledge and assimilate

---

[5]It appeared in 1914 under the title, "Remembering, repeating, and working-through" (*Standard Edition*, 12:145–156. London: Hogarth Press, 1958). Inasmuch as repeating is remembering, working-through is repeatedly remembering.

it."[6] Gay has this to say: "But at long last the time may come when the patient, steadily relapsing, steadily forgetting insights painfully won, will begin to absorb, to 'work through,' his hard-won knowledge."[7]

But knowledge of what? Freud consistently insisted that it was knowledge of resistance. He wrote: "This working-through *of the resistances* may in practice turn out to be an arduous task for the subject of the analysis and a trial of patience for the analyst. Nevertheless *it is a part of the work which effects the greatest changes in the patient* and which distinguishes psychoanalytic treatment from any kind of treatment by suggestion."[8] Consequently, you would think, it was destined to be a major part of psychoanalytic theory and that analysts would carefully examine its clinical and technical ramifications. Instead, it is given short shrift and treated as simply more of the same.

Erwin Singer, in his *Key Concepts of Psychotherapy*, mentions it grudgingly ("No discussion of interpretation can avoid [alas!] at least brief mention of the concept of 'working through'") and then grounds it in learning theory. "The patient needed time to assimilate the knowledge he had gained and this assimilation demanded what contemporary psychologists call 'reinforcement'."[9] This alludes to Freud's remark, "One must allow the patient time to become more conversant with this resistance with which he has now become acquainted, to *work through* it, to overcome it, by continuing, in defiance of it, the analytic work according to the fundamental rule of analysis."[8]

Fenichel, in his lucid and instructive *Principles of Psychoanalysis*, puts it clearly: "Consistent interpretive work, both within and without the framework of transference, can be described as *educating* the patient to produce continually less distorted derivatives until his fundamental conflicts are recognizable. Of course, this is not a simple operation resulting in a single act of abreaction; it

---

[6]Jones, E. *Life and Work of Sigmund Freud* (Vol. 2. New York: Basic Books, 1955), p. 236.

[7]Gay, P. *Freud: A Life for Our Time* (New York: W. W. Norton, 1988), p. 304.

[8]*Op. Cit.,* p. 155, emphasis added.

[9]Singer, E. *Key Concepts of Psychotherapy* (New York: Basic Books, 1982), p. 217.

is a chronic process of working through, which *shows* the patient again and again the same conflicts and his usual way of reacting to them, but from new angles and in new connections."[10] Thus is there a shift from interpreting the resistance to interpreting what is resisted, and the line Freud drew, between interpreting the resistance and allowing the underlying stuff to emerge thereby, has been blurred.

If we want to become mathematicians we will have to work at it. Why shouldn't the same be true of becoming a nonneurotic? If it is, then we wouldn't opt for an insight-abreaction experience as the core experience, for we'd have to add on the work and find a way to explain it. Learning mathematics doesn't begin with discrete episodes of understanding followed by work, but the reverse: episodes of understanding occur as a consequence of arduous work. Analogously, episodes of Disclosure might lead to insight, it's the therapeutic work that will generate the insight, and working-through, qua therapeutic work, generates understanding rather than the other way round.

Working-through could have been a basis upon which to reformulate therapy (after all, it's the part of therapy which "effects the greatest changes in the patient"). While it isn't synonymous with Disclosure, I would venture that the bulk of our patients' work consists of something akin to it. The question is whether working-through is simply more of the same. Even if it is, rather than appeal to anything didactic (involving teaching and training), or anything that relies on the dynamics of change, per se, or anything that defines our work as therapists as the active and principal work of the therapy, I believe that we can construe working-through as an ongoing process of Disclosure.

The Case of Successful Treatment

A prominent analyst once presented publicly a case of successful treatment. By every index of cure, of substantial and significant change, the case was a smashing success. And yet: (1) the patient never engaged in free association, even though she was on the

---

[10] Fenichel C. *Principles of Psychoanalysis* (New York: W. W. Norton, 1935), p. 31, emphasis added.

couch and was given the free association instruction; (2) the patient disagreed with, or ignored, all interpretations and showed no evidence of making use of them; (3) the patient developed no transference (or it was never uncovered because of 2); (4) resistance was never dealt with (or was never uncovered because of 2); (5) there was no evidence of flight into health, the treatment lasted two years, and the patient credited it for her recovery.

This, as I recall, was it, and if the presenter had more to say, he never got the chance because of the uproar that ensued. I don't recall the remarks, I only recall how heated they were. Their overriding tenor was "Not possible!" For one thing, it was not a psychoanalysis, for the patient, after all, wasn't analyzed. The presenter agreed, and was willing to call it psychotherapy. All right, but how come it was effective?

My point is that no one considered that psychoanalysis might be therapeutic all by itself, that the sheer format is therapeutic. Free association is not necessarily and in all cases necessary; resistance and transference are not, in all cases, necessary; neither is insight. What then does it? What I am calling Disclosure, of course! I am willing to assume that the patient in this case did it, and to a significant extent. I'm willing to go out on a limb and claim that she must have done a significant and substantial amount of it, and that's why her therapy was such a success.

Then What's the Core Event?

When he shifted to free association, Freud shifted the focus from remembering, construed narrowly, to disclosing construed broadly. Patients are unable to associate freely: he attributed this to resistance (it follows that when they can free associate they are effectively finished with therapy). Moreover, if they do it at all they do it sporadically. The bulk of their talk can better be described as narrative. And while I'm not ready to claim that narrative is synonymous with Disclosure (in my special sense), and I want to argue that it isn't, there isn't a long step separating one from the other.

Patients talk about many things; not all of it is Disclosure and neither is all Disclosure talk. They can have silent thoughts and feelings, and there can be Disclosure in that. Having a dream isn't

Disclosure, not necessarily; telling it may be no different—it may not yet, and not necessarily, be Disclosure. Disclosure implicates our sense of self. It is things about me, personally, that I disclose: my memories, my beliefs, my thoughts, my wants, my conflicts, my feelings. (Disclosure has to have the "warmth and intimacy" that William James took as criteria for our personal memories as well as for our personal self.)

By speaking my mind I can find out what's on my mind. I can be surprised that I knew what I know and held the views that I do. Such experiences can be construed as constructing (I'm not uncovering, I'm creating) but this fails to capture my experience of it. I don't feel I'm "making it up." The ideas were "there" and I'm revealing them to myself. It can feel as if I'm discovering them there.

What about the experience of having understood? It seems cogent to therapy but may be too limiting. Do I want to contend that the case of successful treatment was engaged in understanding? How about Anna O? *Understanding* is too specific a term. Disclosure may be more effective when it comprises understanding, but this doesn't mean that you can't have therapeutically beneficial Disclosure absent understanding. What I want is a term that means *un*covering and *dis*covering what is inside oneself.

The word *catharsis* is overloaded in the emotional dimension. It suggests a passive release of affect (a "letting it all hang out") that lacks self-reflection, active self-inquiry, as well as the act of discovery. I need a word that implies work and is self-directed in two senses—directed by as well as at the self. The process I wish to capture is one in which we explore ourselves with a degree of activeness and purpose and no motive other than to understand and experience authentically. Moreover, we have to be listening also. It has to be spoken (or written), heard (or read), and felt. We have to witness it in one or another sensory mode; it isn't enough to just experience it without having the experience of experiencing it.

In one sense, I am talking about remembering, in another revealing. I need a word that encompasses both and captures a degree of surprise and wonderment. For the experience has emotional concomitants, and one of the most reliable is a feeling of astonishment, ranging from minimal surprise to maximum awe.

Then can I not rely on *Disclosure* to have these layered meanings and connotations? Do I have another option? If not, then my task is to make it relevant to therapy, inasmuch as therapy is an ongoing and extended process, and it may therefore be necessary to distinguish between episodes of Disclosure and a process of therapeutic Disclosure, the one being embedded in the other.

Learning the piano takes a process of lessons that are connected and interrelated. There are subevents and episodes; we have to develop habits (such as playing scales) that lay the groundwork for learning to play musically. Therapy, too, has to lay groundwork, and a theory of therapy has to specify the groundwork conditions. Not unlike a theory of piano pedagogy, it can only be based upon empirical evidence, upon observation and experience.

Learning the piano is an apt analogy in that it doesn't imply a prior defense or require us to theorize about how come we didn't know how to play it to begin with. Yet it entails experiences of discovery. A significant aspect of such discovery is the emotion that accompanies the acquisition of a skill, an emotion commonly called exhilaration. I propose that this emotion accompanies (or is embedded in) Disclosure. It is the ahah experience the Gestalters used to make so much of. The feeling is one of "click." When things fall into place, we feel exhilarated; there's a sense of surprise and satisfaction, perhaps of wonderment and even awe.

We feel surprise when our expectations are, and also aren't, fulfilled. "I was right, I knew it!" and "I was wrong, I didn't know it!" are accompanied by surprise. When viewing scrambled figures or solving cryptic clues, we experience tension; the solution resolves it and does it so suddenly that we feel surprised. How do we know the solution is right? We simply know! The unscrambled figure brooks no doubt; it's the only thing it can be, is our experience. The mode is passive, the solution is passively received; we stare until the figure clicks into place. There's no question here of being wrong; we see what we see because it is there to be seen. The solution to the cryptic clue, by contrast, is right because all of its parts are accounted for and they fit together. But here we can be fooled into thinking we were right when we actually weren't. This can happen when the solution didn't account for every element and yet we thought it did. We can settle for the imperfect fit because of ignorance, laziness, or some combination thereof. We can have a false sense of fit in the verbal sphere, which we don't have in the visual one.

Psychotherapy as Literature

Our patients tell us stories; they tell us and retell us the story of their lives, both past and present. We interpret these stories according to our theories, which can be considered stories of our own. Given the appeal of modern literary criticism (deconstructionism and new historicism), it is tempting to borrow those ideas and press them into service for our theory of therapy.[11] In my opinion it's a temptation worth resisting.

For one thing, the narrativist stance endorses our changing (or "glossing") our patients' story, and this can be hazardous. Not only does it require that we regard narratives as a species of fiction, it fosters our active participation, not merely in facilitating and perhaps also supervising the telling and examining of the story, but in the story itself. The meanings we seek to extract tend to be ours, not the patient's; our effort becomes less to evince the story than to interpret it. To be sure, there's no gainsaying that we must perforce shape the story with our interpretations, because the meanings we find will inevitably be influenced by our own theory. This doesn't mean, however, that we cannot discipline ourselves to constrain and limit such influence. The fact that theory is unavoidable doesn't justify giving it full and unrestrained license.

How does our theory of the patient inform our theory of the therapy? We are dealing with two theories here and they are really quite separate. Our theory of therapy can stand or fall on its own, and we are better off guarding against the intrusion of our theory of patients, who, after all, have a theory, too. We can let their story emerge according to their theory. To be sure, we might help modify their theory, but this isn't the same as imposing our own. These considerations might require eschewing any literary

---

[11] I am referring to the work of Donald Spence (*Historical and Narrative Truth: Meaning and Interpretation in Psychoanalysis.* New York: W. W. Norton, 1982) and Roy Schafer (*Retelling a Life: Narrative and Dialogue in Psychoanalysis.* New York: Basic Books, 1992), among others.

pretentions. It might help not to regard patients as authors and story-tellers; it might be better not to regard their narratives as texts; let them be autobiographies of a certain kind. It simply might not be helpful, to them or their therapy, for us to take a literary approach to their "material."

Moreover, disclosing isn't merely narrating and story-telling. It is making history, yes (this is probably unavoidable), but the emphasis needn't be on the making: this obscures the vital element of discovering that is the hallmark of the core experience. That this vital element necessarily involves construction doesn't mean that construction is the vital element. There is some therapeutic value in regarding our patient's story as the way it actually was, as a fact; it may often be better to approach it as historical truth than as narrative truth, for this puts the emphasis on evincing and discovering it rather than on fabricating and creating it. When we amend and modify the story, we aren't coauthoring it or even critiquing it, we are editing it. We aren't making it a better story, we're making it a more complete, coherent, and truer history.

Deconstructionalism and the new historicism are, after all, just theories. They are interesting ones, but whether they improve the quality of our therapy is an empirical question. For some patients they probably do, but for many they probably don't. There are patients who resist all efforts on our part to tamper with their story; it is set in stone. They nonetheless benefit from therapy.

Saying and Thinking

To bolster the distinction between thought and action, we have invented the metaphor of an "inner world." But the rationale for monastic silence has less to do with inner worlds than with issues of spirituality. As I understand it, the reason for the silence is less to move inward than to commune with matters of spirit. So the distinction is between psyche and soma; mind and matter; thought and observation; and we have conflated thought with spirit.

We also conflate vocalization with speech. Infants vocalize, toddlers babble, children speak; adults do all three when they verbalize, vocalize and sing, babble and chatter, and speak. Is it only because we feel less alone thereby? Does silence always bespeak aloneness? Does it not also suggest unreality? Silent thought—pure mentation—is divorced from reality.

In any event, little attention has been paid on our part to the subject of speaking. Some clinical observations have been made on the role of particular words, but nothing on the psychological implications of speaking aloud. Yet, it isn't uncommon for patients to say, "It's one thing when I think it but another when I say it," and further, "It's yet another thing altogether when you say it." To say it aloud gives a thought a kind of reality it didn't have when it was a thought. Hearing oneself say it is significantly different from hearing it said by another, especially when the other is a significant other. These are vital aspects of Disclosure.

"I am Special"—A Fourth Case

When I first met her, my analyst (who had received a phone call from my referrer as well as from me) headed for the seat at the head of the couch and said, "You know the standard instructions." I assumed the couch and was off and running. She must have made remarks during the session but I had no recall of them.

What I did, however, recall—and it reverberated in my mind—as the statement, "You know the standard instructions." It said "you know psychoanalysis" and "you are special." I already knew the latter but I didn't yet know much psychoanalysis. As far as I knew, I was going to be exposed as a covetous narcissist with a huge Oedipus; I was going to resist heroically, and fall into a state of terminal transference, and (if I was good) I'd work through everything—and emerge as Homo Analysand. I was in for surprises.

The biggest surprise turned out to be that the therapy grew to matter in ways that were astonishing to me. As it happened, my Oedipus was no big deal, my preoedipal complexes were more interesting. But what counted above all was the experience of revelation, and it was exhilarating (as well as painful). Moreover, I was astonished by how, and also by how much, my analyst's remarks contributed to the experience.

There were, to begin with, the reverberations of "you know the instructions." It became the basis of my first revelation. From the meaning I took from the remark I discovered things about myself. This process of discovery made the ensuing therapy exhilarating, as well as painful. But it was exhilarating and painful only to me and not to my analyst. She bore my process of discovery with admirable equanimity, though she occasionally expressed surprise and seemed to share my exhilaration.

I want to dwell on her "you know the instructions." Strictly speaking, it's an interpretation and not an instruction; I did know them and she was merely articulating that knowledge. Since it was no mystery how come she knew I knew them, the question was why she made the interpretation when she did. At one level she was saying, "I am not giving the standard instruction because you know it." In this way, she gave the instruction while at the same time acknowledging that I knew it (and perhaps was also saying that she chose not to define herself as the silent analyst).

The timing of the interpretation conveyed the message "you are special," and this is what I call a diagnostic interpretation. I regard it as having been a technical error. Not that it was incorrect (I certainly was special), but why set it as the agenda? Why not let my agenda take precedence and let me begin by dazzling her with my sophistication? Why take the wind out of my sails? In any case, what this is meant to illustrate is the power a therapist's speech can have.

Meno had invested power in Socrates' authority. He had observed the awe and respect his master had for the philosopher, and this had evoked the feelings that lay dormant in him for his original masters, his parents. His submission to the treatment was, in several senses, regressive. This of course is the transference which sets the stage for mental events that are so awe inspiring. Each of us has had the experience of submitting to the authority of primary caretakers.

But notice what I'm disclosing. Specifically, I am remembering-reminiscing. To be sure, I'm doing something else as well: formulating and conceptualizing my experience. But isn't this part and parcel of it? So if we widen the meaning of remembering to include the near past, and we narrow the distance between the near past and the present, we see the merit of construing the "core event" of therapy as remembering-reminiscing—which takes us back to Freud's insight into the role of memory in psychotherapy: neurotics suffer from reminiscences, and reminiscing alleviates the suffering.

Postscript

Another personal vignette, this time from the nearest past, the present. If this were a talk I was giving and I had the courage to give it extemporaneously and without much preparation, I'd have had the opportunity to discover some things about the subject— specifically, things that I believe and feel, which I didn't fully realize that I believed and felt. So why would I not do it? For one thing, because your experience might not be therapeutic, and that would be unfair. More importantly, however, I'd be afraid of making a fool of myself, and worried about feeling embarrassed and ashamed, and these feelings would be distracting; they could interfere with my work by making me, among other things, cautious and guarded. And this, I believe, has important implications for the format of our therapy and our behavior as therapists. When we believe in the therapeutic value of Disclosure, we therapists make it our business to do everything we can to protect our patients from being afraid of making fools of themselves. We do our best to facilitate and promote this core event, in every sense of it and in all of its forms.

SIXTEEN

THE "ANALYTIC EXPERIENCE" AND THE "CORE EVENT"

Our treatment of the theory letter gets mixed reviews: we could have made you out to sound less pretentious and dogmatic; we should have summarized your thesis to make sure we got it right; you miss our comments and questions (we might at least have made some suggestions on naming the "core event"). Before we make amends, we want to comment on the "analytic experience" which you describe in your current letter, and which you had decided not to include in the theory lesson. Susan and I disagree with that decision. Not only are we moved by your depiction of the "analytic experience" but we feel that it's bound to be a significant event with substantial therapeutic impact. We appreciate that it's difficult to write about this kind of event without sounding maudlin, and also that you wouldn't want to make too much of it; it's an experience that patients may never have and their treatment won't suffer for it. Still, it's clearly related to the core event, and merits more than a mention.

The "Analytic Experience"

During the course of some Psychotherapy sessions a special event occasionally occurs that is difficult to capture in words (it's one of those experiences each of us has to have had in order to really comprehend). Nevertheless . . . .

We will imagine ourselves in P's position, speaking periodically and regularly for an hour at a time to a person who helps us speak openly, freely, and reflectively, and whose remarks bespeak an intensity of listening and a degree of dispassion that is rare and

147

remarkable. As we gradually assimilate how distinctive, and also how safe, these conditions are, we talk about ourselves, our past and present, our dreams and dreads, our most intimate thoughts and deepest feelings. We also come to have ideas and feelings about the person who is helping us do all this, and we recognize them to be largely our own products, for that person is so impartial and impersonal. With this recognition comes a heightened sense of our inner reality, the range and richness of our me-ness. Fine, but so far we are engaged only with the therapeutic process.

During the course of this therapeutic process, however, something special might happen. Perhaps accompanied by a change in our state of consciousness, a reverielike or deeply contemplative state of mind, we are now talking "from the gut" and with feelings that are rare. They may be new feelings or long unexperienced old ones but they feel profound. We might be having a new insight into ourselves, or into what we were talking about; it's the sense of revelation that counts, the sense of being in touch with something deeply valid and authentic about us. It doesn't have to be so new and so startling, yet it does feel awesome. We are now having an "analytic experience."

From our vantage point as therapist, the experience can be difficult to discern because patients might slip seamlessly into it and not recognize it for what it is. But if we sense that they are having an analytic experience, we may choose to articulate it, for they can be shaken, if not frightened, by it. It is usually accompanied by a sense of defenselessness; it's an experience that feels free from one's usual inhibitions; patients feel wholly open to their inner reality, and for this reason it is likely to be accompanied by anxiety. So we might want to empathize with those feelings and offer some support. All that's usually required is to say that we know what they've experienced. We might also say that such experiences can be beneficial for therapy. Subsequently, we may have occasion to offer the interpretation that they were defending themselves against their recurrence.

Some teachers refer to such events as "peak experiences"; you prefer "analytic" because it emphasizes their being heightened experiences in knowing. In your view, they are acts of acute understanding and therefore likely to have a profound effect ("They are probably the stuff out of which basic change is wrought and against which major defenses are deployed"). But their relationship to the core event is tangential, and you didn't want to distract our attention from that central and ubiquitous aspect of Psychotherapy. That's why you decided against including the "analytic experience" in the theory letter.

The "Core Event"

A theory of therapy must describe what our patients do, for this will describe what we have to do. The core of what they do—the smallest common denominator and sine qua non—is a mental act that has the earmarks of (1) remembering but without necessarily a sense of pastness or datedness; (2) uncovering but without necessarily a sense of its ever having been covered; and (3) discovering but without necessarily a sense of its being new. It's an experience we all have, and the only mystery is why we have no name for it.

There's an emotion that goes with it, for which we have names. At one extreme it can be exhilarating and include a sense of awe; at the other extreme it ranges from interesting to fascinating. To some degree it's arousing and exciting. In any event, the emotion is a vital ingredient—and you mentioned in this regard that our interpretations should articulate it ("You are feeling surprised that . . . ," "It's fascinating to you that . . . ," and when we say, "You're wondering if . . . ," we might bear in mind the emotional denotation of "wonder").

Here's a point that Susan thinks you missed: the experience also includes a sense of identity, as expressed in, "I'm in therapy, I am a patient," in contrast to, "I am sick, I need help." Just as, "I am studying psychology, I'm a psychologist," and, "I am taking piano lessons, I'm a pianist," it's something that is part of my life as a vital activity and isn't confined to the sessions.

Back to your thesis. Acts, or call them *episodes* (neither of us is happy with *experiences*), of what we are provisionally calling

Disclosure are therapeutic. We take this to be an empirical proposition, which means that we need an empirical theory to explain it,
which means that our theory has to do nothing more than describe
the episode and specify the conditions for its occurrence. The theory
may need to consider stages of Disclosure, and developmental
stages too; it may need to draw distinctions among varieties of
Disclosure; it may need to say something about defenses that regulate Disclosure; perhaps it will need to describe false or ersatz Disclosure. But, as you write, "Beyond doing all of this work, there
isn't much point to theorizing. The chief value in theorizing is to
compensate for our inability to fully describe the phenomenon and
specify its conditions. Theories are promissary notes."

On Metapsychology

And they "get in the way." My understanding of your thesis is this:
you want us to be as open, sensitive, and attentive to our patients
as we can possibly be, and theorizing, especially if it isn't empirical, can hamper us. You want us not to impose our theory on our
patients—who, after all, have their own which gets in their way,
too. And a good way for us to help them get around their theory,
and disclose their mind as fully as they possibly can, is to get out
of their way. This requires us to take their Disclosure at face value
and keep from looking for deeper meanings and truths that lie beneath and behind.

Susan has studied some Wittgenstein and hears some echoes of
his views in what you've written. Susan says we can think of theory
as a framed filter, or lens, which we cannot possibly look around;
the best we can do is keep it clean and transparent, and also keep it
in mind. She agrees that, inasmuch as our goal is for patients to listen to themselves and thereby observe their own Disclosure, and inasmuch as they are also wearing a filtered frame, we need to minimize
the extent to which our theory adds a layer of distortion to the
filtering process. But just as they cannot look around their frame,
neither can we. Anyway, our theory is we hope better than theirs.

She is troubled by your characterization of Freudian metapsychology as nonempirical and your criticism of the distinction that is traditionally drawn between it and clinical theory. Defense, for instance, is taken as a metapsychological concept and resistance as a clinical one; we've been taught that they are congruent concepts that merely occupy adjacent levels of discourse. You dispute this view. Freud didn't subscribe to this kind of epistemology; he viewed resistance as a "manifestation" of defense, and that's an idealistic way of thinking, in that it posits a domain of reality that lies behind and beneath the one that we can observe directly.

My personal view is that when patients forget a session, this can be the result of a defense, namely repression, but it isn't necessarily the expression of a resistance. Resistance is when they want out of the therapy. For instance, when they experience a flight into health, then it's a resistance (and my favorite one); it isn't, strictly speaking, a defense, though it makes use of defenses. I find it more congenial to think of forms of defense—such as projection, isolation of affect, reaction formation, counterphobia, and the rest—which are transformations and distortions and disguises. To call them resistances begs the question of resistance to what.

Susan says we have to include a resistance to the therapeutic process itself, and that's fine with me. It's a short step from the idea of flight from therapy, and it calls into play patients' defenses in a variety of mixes and forms. But true resistance, I would think, has to count as an impasse and probably needs to be approached as such.

Cryptics and Other Puzzles

I am especially interested in your comparison of scrambled figures with cryptic puzzles, in that it points up a difference between the perceptual and verbal modes that may have implications for therapy. The problem of judging correctness and truth remains deeply problematic outside of perception, where we express understanding in the perceptual mode ("I see!" we say, for seeing brooks no doubt and is reassuring, and we like to translate things into perceptions because seeing is believing). But when it comes to our ideas and thoughts, and especially our memories and feelings, we face a distinctive problem in respect to ascertaining what's factual.

The good cryptic has to make verbal sense (e.g., "The slumber that envelopes the inventor of psychotherapy"). We solve it by finding the interpretation that's cryptically concealed ("Bertha"). In order to do it, it's necessary for us to already know the solution (the interpretation), in the sense that it has to be recognizable and familiar. We know that our solution is right when it takes account of every component of the clue. The conditions of false insight are misreading and ignorance, a blithe slovenliness, a lack of patience, a deficiency of frustration-tolerance. Maybe that is why "verbal puzzles" require therapy: insight in the realm of thought is problematic in a way that it isn't in the perceptual realm.

This may be a good rationale for the requirement of extended therapy, of working through, for not only do we have to become familiar with the solution, we also have to learn how to solve cryptics. This takes learning to work with patterns and tolerating ambiguity and frustration. Moreover, we can have the sense of click and of rightness for cryptic clues of one or two sentences, but our mind's cryptics are longer than that; putting the pieces together can only rarely achieve a perfect fit; typically, we have to be content with a good-enough degree of fit.

In any case, I find this intriguing and illuminating—and surprisingly, so does Susan. She thinks it's relevant to the concept of reconstruction, for which the only criterion we usually have is a subjective sense of rightness and confidence.

Disclosing and Suffering

We think your dissertation might have a gap that bears on this question: Isn't it desirable, and maybe even necessary, to specify which kinds of suffering are amenable to the benefits of Disclosure? Shouldn't we be able to say what sorts of problems Psychotherapy is appropriate for? Surely, not all psychological suffering can be ameliorated by uncovering and discovering, and not all the time.

Moreover, Meno figured out a theorem, Anna O recalled specific traumas, and the patient who had such a successful treatment obviously talked about particular things. Selection is unavoidable. Is it not also therapeutically germane? If patients are depressed, say, what should they talk about? What topics can we expect them to choose that will be relevant to their suffering? It may well be the case that they are likely to benefit most from disclosing particular mental (call them "ideational") contents. Do you not think so? You mentioned convalescence as a metaphor for therapy; but we don't recommend a month's vacation at a spa to cure an ingrown toenail, we would advise somehow convalescing the toe in order to promote its healing.

Anyway, Susan believes we need a theoretical guideline for the kinds of disclosing that are specific to psychological suffering, as well as a technical guideline for our role in fostering selective disclosure. I'm not sure. For while Breuer selected the symptom for Anna O to work on, and Freud chose to address his patients' resistances, Anna O did much of the choosing and Freud's patients were not freely associating so much as deciding what to talk about. So I think we might settle for saying that our patients can be trusted to choose the right topics; we can be neutral with respect to content because they will not be. They can of course be mistaken in their choices. We could even make a case for presuming that they will be, else they wouldn't need therapy. Nevertheless, Susan and I agree that even when we do instruct patients with respect to choosing content, what we're instructing them to do is "disclose on it!"

The Problem of Nomenclature

Let's see if we can help find a name for the "core event." Disclosure has unfortunate connotations. We looked it up and found "the act or instance of disclosing; *exposure*; something disclosed;

revelation." It suggests a telling of secrets, making public what is properly private; it calls to mind confession and purging, if not betrayal. Then what about Revelation? For "reveal" my dictionary gives "to divulge or disclose; make known; bring into view; expose; show," and for "revelation," "something revealed; an act of revealing, especially a dramatic disclosure or something not previously known or realized." So revelation (except for its divine connotations) is apt. Perhaps we can create a new predicate for it, and say *to revelate*, instead of the bland *to reveal.* Esthetically, this leaves something to be desired, but "Is P revelating?—no, he's just recounting something" sounds good to me. And revelating does imply an emotion of some surprise, it suggests something of a "Wow!"—a feeling that is clearly felt.

But there's a significant difference between being engaged in disclosing something and being engaged in having a revelation about it: sometimes it's more accurate to say, "P is disclosing," other times it's more accurate to say, "He's having a revelation." My inclination would therefore be to use both words interchangeably and acknowledge that they overlap to a significant and substantial extent.

From the patient's perspective disclosure/revelation is an act rather than an experience in the phenomenal sense (it isn't like "I am seeing a patch of red" but more like "a patch of red is being seen"). Gaining clarity, on the other hand, is an experience, as are understanding and discovering (clarity, understanding, and discovery form a nice acronym, by the way: CUD). They can be construed as mental acts, too, but they strike Susan and me as more specifically experiential than Disclosure is. Susan, however, really prefers to stick to *therapeutic process.*

We'll stop now. We hope you agree that it's time we got back to learning how to conduct Psychotherapy.

SEVENTEEN

THE CONTENT
OF INTERPRETATIONS

Interpretations, our stock-in-trade, will take us at least three lessons to cover because an interpretation has three dimensions, content, form, and timing. Even though they aren't orthogonal, we will have to study them separately, despite the fact that an interpretation's form can be predicated on its content, its content is influenced by its form, and both are contingent on its timing.

Timing, in that it pertains to the key question of why we make interpretations in the first place, is fundamental. Clinical considerations, in conjunction with the way we construe the therapeutic process, provide the basis for our timing criteria. Therefore, our basic answer to the timing question is: we interpret when (and also because) the therapeutic process requires an interpretation in the interests of facilitating and optimalizing it.

In other words, our chief way of supervising the therapeutic process is making interpretations. By supervising we mean restoring the process when we judge that it has faltered, maintaining it when we judge that it may falter, and improving it when we judge that it needs improving. Inasmuch as these are clinical calls, timing has to be learned by practicing; there are few guidelines to help us evaluate the condition of the therapeutic process, and the judgment can only be made intuitively and on a case-to-case basis. Nevertheless, you will teach us as much as you can about it—after we've learned what to interpret and how to.

You start off with a simple question: What is an interpretation? Your answer is also simple: "I count as an interpretation any attempt to reflect or translate a patient's narrative." Thus, if the patient had said, "I think it's raining," the remark, "You think it's pouring," is no less an interpretation than, and formally may be no different from, "You think God—or more precisely, your father—is pissing on you in contempt for the puny size of your penis."

In other words, any remark that can be prefaced with "in other words" counts as an interpretation, no matter how little the other words deviated from the narrative and how slight and superficial a translation it was. Moreover, that assessment can never be ours, it has to be our patient's. You assure us that you have not infrequently made remarks that you judged were not profound and your patient judged otherwise. Likewise, we can look forward to being surprised, if not also chagrined, to learn that an interpretation that we thought was not, our patient labels gratuitous. It usually isn't easy to know it in advance; the best we can do is try and steer a course between those we deem too superficial and those we deem too profound, and then be ready to revise our deeming.

We want to avoid the extremes because we have promised our patients to say useful things, and superficial remarks, as well as profound ones, are often not very useful. They are likely to baffle them, on the one hand, and shock them on the other.

- What you said seems pretty much exactly the same as what I said—so why did you say it? It cannot be "useful" simply to repeat what I say, so maybe I'm missing something. Surely you aren't someone who makes redundant remarks!
- Where did you get that idea from! It is farfetched, outrageous, and deeply upsetting to me. I wish you would take it back.

But you avoid the terms *shallow* and *deep*, and sidestep the popular dictum, *"Neither too deep nor too shallow."* You apparently don't want to commit us to a particular conception of depth.

Susan is a believer in the dynamic unconscious, I am not. She believes we have thoughts and memories, as well as feelings, that are unconscious by virtue of repression, and one of therapy's chief tasks is to "lift" those repressions. I believe our thoughts can exist outside of awareness, and our memories may well be irretrievable but not necessarily because of repression. I think that feelings, insofar as they can be separated from thoughts and memories, can at best be suppressed and then expressed in transformed ways, and that it's therapy's task to untransform them. Would you care to arbitrate our dispute? My hunch is, you would rather contend that it makes no difference in practice—no matter how we construe depth, it's our patient's construal that counts.

Fair enough. But it is still a useful guideline to keep from making interpretations that are too shallow (redundant and gratuitous), on the one hand, and too deep on the other. In any event, you prefer to conceptualize the issue as clinical tact. As you write:

> Anyone in the position of patient is bound to feel vulnerable, and psychotherapy patients are likely to feel acutely so. They need assurances that they will not be hurt more than necessary, won't suffer undue shame and humiliation. Our neutrality and impersonality may heighten the sense of vulnerability, and therefore we must be especially tactful. This means being so in tune and in touch (hence "tactile") that our behavior naturally takes into account our patients' feelings and avoids upsetting them unduly, hurting them unnecessarily, trespassing on their self-regard inappropriately.

To the degree that tact is synonymous with such sensitivity, it goes without saying that we should be tactful. So when we say "tact" in these letters, we also have in mind other considerations.

It's one thing for our patients to experience the shock of revelation when the revelation was theirs, it's another when the revelation was provided by us. Their being apprehensive about what we might say to them is bound to interfere with their work. Patients might have entered therapy with the belief that they were in for rude shocks and therefore will be in a state of readiness for them (if not in a state of guardedness). This expectation has to be explored, for it can hamper the therapeutic process. In fact, we are well advised to treat the matter as business, when the opportunity presents itself, and tell our patients flat out that we don't plan to say anything that will be too upsetting to them.

At the same time, however, avoiding things that might be upsetting runs the danger of timidity and pussyfooting. So, as in all matters technical, the crucial variable is balance. Still, if we had to choose between the Scylla of tactless shock and the Charybdis of pussy-footing timidity, we should choose the perils of Charybdis. "Be tact-ful" sounds like "Be gentle" ("Have mercy on poor P!"), but even if it does it's not such bad advice. Only when it inhibits us from mak-ing an otherwise sound and timely interpretation is it not good, and then we may say that the concept of tact was misused.

Put another way: a sound and timely interpretation, almost by definition, is not tactless. It can embarrass, shame, and even anger a patient, but if it did it unduly or excessively then it was untimely—ergo tactless. The key judgment is "undue" and "excessive," and it's where experience is likely to count for a great deal. The crucial consideration is that patients not be thrown into such an upheaval that they can't use the interpretation productively.

Back to the question of what an interpretation is. We can define interpretation broadly as any remark that says something about the patient. This definition, in your opinion, is both accurate and use-ful. But interpretations come in a variety of types which are far from equal. Certain of them are proscribed by Psychotherapy, or, if not altogether proscribed, then to be used only in special and circumscribed conditions. There is only one type that can be used freely, and even then considerations of timing are a key constraint. This prescribed type of interpretation is one that you name "em-pathic" (with apologies to me in anticipation of my objections), although you occasionally slip and just name it "good."

Yes, *empathic* isn't good for the kind of interpretation you de-scribe; empathy pertains to emotions and feelings. I appreciate your reluctance to call it good, so I'll find you a name for it after we've examined what it is, and more importantly what it isn't. In the mean-time, where you've written "empathic" I'll write "good." This cap-tures the tenor of your remarks and I'm sure it's what you have in mind (so it counts, you see, as a *good* interpretation).

A good interpretation is one that addresses itself to what is in (or on) our patients' mind. A good interpretation doesn't say anything about our patients excepting what is actually (or potentially) in (or on) their mind. A good interpretation says nothing about patients other than their mental content. It doesn't say, for instance, what kind of mind they have or, God forbid, what kind of person they are. The good interpretation restricts itself to the actual and potential contents of a patient's mind.

But you know that neither Susan nor I is fond of "mental content," she prefers "consciousness and awareness" and I like "phenomenal experience," so you suggest that we reread the preceding paragraph substituting those terms for mind and mental content. You ask us only to bear in mind that consciousness comes in states (like pre- and un-), that there are levels of awareness, and that not all phenomenal experience is fully phenomenological.

Perceptions, cognitions, wishes, memories, or combinations of them as well as conflicts among and between them, can be in and on a patient's mind. Perceptions can be intense and vivid, clear and accurate, distorted and illusory; cognitions encompass thoughts, expectations, knowledge, beliefs, and opinions. Wishes include desires and needs, and combinations of and conflicts among them, as well as dread of them and attitudes toward them (like "dangerous" and "forbidden"). Memories come in shades and colors, and in personal meanings and symbolic significances; and when we add daydreams and night dreams, images and imaginings, and when we realize that the categories mix and amalgamate, then we can see that we have more than enough to work with. This then is the stuff out of which our interpretations should be made; good interpretations restrict themselves to these "mental contents."

Which means, for one thing, we have no need to traffic in explanations. We can prudently dispense with the why question, as in, "Why do you have this particular mental content?" We have our hands full enough finding out what is on the patient's mind, without distracting ourselves with the child's why question. (Susan bristles at this; she assumes our interpretations will have to provide dynamic and genetic formulations, and in this sense explain things to patients. I, on the other hand, am glad that I'm not going to have to figure out their "dynamics.")

But *why* isn't just a distraction, of course, it's an intellectu-alization. That's a defense mechanism—and a good one (these letters stand in tribute and testimony to it). So if we wanted to strengthen our patient's defenses, then explanations can be useful. Except there's a fundamental difference (and for Psychotherapy it's also an important one) between intellectualization and insight. The latter consists of uncovering and discovering what is in our mind, while intellectualization involves figuring out the reasons it is there. The reasons can only be conjectural and theoretical, they can never be true or factual; an insight (seeing into what's there) can be valid.

Disclosing the contents of our mind is an empirical matter, ex-plaining how our mind works is a theoretical one. There is noth-ing wrong with theorizing, we do it all the time and so do our patients; even if we count it as a defense, we don't denigrate it; like most defenses it's perfectly indispensable. But we can (and you believe we should) do without it when we make our interpretations, which should be made from the stance of an empiricist, one who observes and describes. This is already a huge task and more than enough to keep us usefully occupied.

When we offer him a piece of theory, we are providing P with a short-term palliative. Explanations in psychotherapy serve the same functions as first-aid in medicine; they are short-term, ameliora-tive treatments. As such they can be useful, and under certain cir-cumstances altogether necessary. If P is suffering from debilitating anxiety, and our goal is to help him reduce it, then an explanation of why he might be feeling anxious can go a long way toward achieving the goal. Even such a blatantly nongood interpretation as, "You are feeling anxious because you are an anxious person," can serve a useful function when the goal is to reduce the anxiety that P is currently feeling. It's a Band-Aid.

The same applies to what we're calling diagnostic interpreta-tions. "You are an anxious person" is a prototype. It clearly does not address P's mental content, so it doesn't fall into the category of good interpretations. Not that it's necessarily bad, it simply isn't good. Now, an explanatory interpretation is easy to spot because it includes, at least implicitly, a "because." A diagnostic interpretation is harder to spot because it can depend on how P takes it. More-over, he will usually understand that we are offering an explana-tion; the same isn't the case for a diagnosis (in either case, however, our explanations and diagnoses, both, will usually be warmly wel-comed and often also expected).

So the matter of diagnostic interpretations is more complicated and subtle. Briefly: diagnosis comes in two forms, classification and troubleshooting. Why is my car malfunctioning? (1) Because it's a nineteen-eighty-four Ford (classification), and nineteen-eighty-four Fords malfunction; (2) because its carburetor is broken (troubleshoot-ing), and cars malfunction when their carburetor is broken. It is type 1 that we must avoid; type 2 should be kept to a minimum.

But our quarrel with diagnostic interpretations is based on the fact that they do not address mental content. Still, the question remains, What's wrong with them? Here we fall back to the em-pirical position: they aren't bad, and neither are they dispensable, they just aren't efficacious for Psychotherapy. We will discover for ourselves that an interpretation of mental content, no matter how invalid it is, has an effect that is fundamentally different from one that is diagnostic and explanatory, no matter how valid it is. For one thing, it orients patients to search for such interpretations them-selves; it facilitates their uncovering and discovering of their ideas, thoughts, illusions, fantasies, conflicts, and memories.

Now, it was clear at this point in our lesson that you were as-siduously excluding a key ingredient in your lists of mental con-tents, namely emotions and feelings. So you turn to them here and it becomes clear why you'd been leaving them out, for here is where your views are startling enough to merit being considered idiosyn-cratic if not eccentric. Emotions and feelings and moods—affects, in other words—belong to a category of mental events that is both very special and especially problematic, and not only do you ad-vise us to be extremely careful and circumspect when we work with affects, you go so far as to suggest that we might even want to leave them alone altogether.

Affects are states of mind (if not also of body) that are distinc-tive (if not also unique). They are not mental contents, nor are they ideational phenomena, they are concomitants or aspects of mentation, and ubiquitous ones. Each and every cognition and conation has an affective component (in fact, every cognition has a conative component, too, and vice versa); we take this for granted. We also take it for granted that the affective component cannot be expressed and communicated and translated into words in the way that cognitions and conations can (the same is true, of course, for perceptions). To be sure, feelings and emotions can be described and expressed in language, but not the way that an ideational mental content can; their indigenous mode of expression is nonverbal and their principal mode of observation is by way of empathy.

But they play a big role in psychotherapy, and therapists pay lots of attention to them. "Yes, but how do (did, will, would) you feel?" is a common and popular question (we call it a probe), and naming a feeling for patients (we call it an articulation) is a common and popular interpretation. Anger is probably the most favorite emotion of all, and the all-time favorite interpretation is undoubtedly "you are (were, would have been, will be) angry" (it is also, you parenthetically mention, undoubtedly the worst).

When it comes to our percepts, we can be very sure of ourselves: "No, it's a truck I saw, I'm sure it wasn't a bus"; "Yes, I heard a man's voice, and it wasn't a woman's"; "I felt cold but no pain." When it comes to our cognitions, we can be quite sure of ourselves: "No, I don't think I'm worthless"; "But I am satisfied to be a man, I don't wish to be a woman"; "No, I'm not really conflicted about whether to continue therapy." But when it comes to our feelings and emotions, we are prone to be least certain and most suggestible: "I don't feel happy but I guess you're right, I must be happy"; "I didn't feel remorseful, but now that you mention it, I probably did"; "Yes, I suppose I'm feeling hurt because of the canceled session." Compliance is one thing, suggestibility is another, and in the realm of affects, since their referents are states of mind that can be quite amorphous, we have to be alert to both.

At the very least, we need to be wary of interpretations that are restricted to affects or that pivot on them. Ordinarily we will make sure to include a reference to the mental content of which the affect was an aspect or concomitant, but we must try hard to make the content primary—and we might also consider going so far as to dispense with the affect altogether.

At this point you remind us that our basic instruction says that we will "listen" to P. This implies that we'll listen to what he says and not watch him say it. It seems to Susan and me that this is arguable. True, we didn't say "observe," we said "listen," but we haven't promised to restrict ourselves to "what," so we can still listen to "how." We can "hear" the resentment in his account of a failure, the victory in his account of success, listen to the music as well as the lyrics. In fact, we can hardly help it. Still, your advice is to stick, as much as possible, to the lyrics and let the music play by itself.

This is reminiscent of our hands-off position vis-à-vis action that you mentioned in your third letter—*"Let Nature Take Its Course"*—and also of your attitude toward latecoming qua narrative. But you amplify the principle and take it to an extreme that Susan finds intriguing but strikes me (and I'd guess it would most of your colleagues) as bordering on the irresponsible. "Don't interpret nonverbal behavior!" you say. "Don't automatically regard it as narrative, especially when patients clearly didn't intend it as such." This means that we shouldn't interpret the way they said what they said, because those interpretations are bound to be confrontational and diagnostic, and will make them self-conscious and guarded, and that is significantly different from being self-reflective.

Moreover, interpretations of nonverbal behavior tend to render patients passive in a way that interpretations of their verbal behavior won't. ("You're sneering," we say, but can P say, "No, I'm not"? Strictly speaking, we would have to say, "I see you sneering," not, "I think you're sneering," and certainly not, "I have the idea, or a hunch, that you're sneering." It has to be a statement of fact that is based on our perceptual experience, and P can hardly say, "What makes you think so?") Moreover, it has been your experience that Psychotherapy can proceed effectively with never any reference on your part to patients' nonverbal behavior during the sessions, providing, of course, that they had made no reference to it.

But affects are significantly different from all other nonverbal behaviors, and while affects aren't, strictly speaking, mental contents, they are conscious experiences and aspects of phenomenal awareness. Accordingly, "You are feeling sad," and "You are feeling angry," aren't confrontational and diagnostic interpretations (which is why we are calling them articulations). P can disagree with them—"No, I don't think it's what I'm feeling" (though with less assurance than he can say, "I don't believe that things are gloomy and hopeless," or, "No, I'm not thinking that I want to hurt someone")—but he can't be so sure. He can say, "What makes you think it's so?" but he can't easily disavow it, because it's a feeling and not a thought. Still, you don't find it hard to contemplate a course of Psychotherapy in which affects are never articulated; we interpret mental content exclusively and leave the feelings (like we've left the actions) to human nature. Instead of saying, "You are sad because you believe that things are hopeless," or, "Your sadness expresses a sense of gloom and foreboding," and instead of saying, "You are angry at me because you want to attack me," or, "Your anger expresses a desire to hurt me," we can simply interpret the belief and the wish, and leave the affect alone (it's what we do with nonverbal behavior).

Among your reasons for advocating such a radical stance is that you've seen therapies sink into a bath (a bathos?) of feelings, where therapist and patient wash themselves (if not also each other) in the warm waters of emotions. "Yes, but where's the feeling?" is the constant question. And it's a facile one because patients commonly believe that therapy deals chiefly with their feelings, and most patients expect that we will devote our full attention to their feelings and interpret, if not simply expose, them as bad stuff, and help them expel them—for it's a purging they need, a ventilation of bad feelings so that good ones can take their place. Too many therapists not only support this view, they foster it.

In any event, you never probe for feelings and emotions, you are conservative when it comes to articulating them, and you make sure always to include their cognitive or conative concomitants; you formulate every affect interpretation so that it pivots on the mental content and the affect plays a subsidiary role. There are, however, two big exceptions: the "clinical affects," namely those that fall in the category of anxiety and of guilt. (Whether guilt is a state of mind is debatable; we usually refer to a "sense" of guilt, and the affect is best described as remorse or regret. So your rule-proving exception is restricted mainly to anxiety.)

Anxiety takes various forms and finds expression in language that ranges from being upset to feeling worried to being filled with dread to feeling panicky. Whatever their forms, we should rarely contemplate not articulating them, for they may play a special role in signaling underlying conflict and perhaps the threatened emergence of dangerous thoughts and wishes. In other words, we might subscribe to the "signal theory of anxiety," and take the position that anxiety can be articulated—for its own sake, so to speak—because it can signify the activity of powerful ideas (i.e., mental contents) that are straining at the threshold of consciousness.

Interpretations like, "You believe you are depressed and this worries you (or fills you with dread)," and, "You see yourself as a bitter person and that upsets you," and, "You're afraid of being angry," are therefore always good. "Afraid of," in the context of "afraid of being angry," isn't the emotion fear; we aren't afraid of being late, or afraid of feeling victorious, in the same sense that we are afraid of the bear.

And what's wrong with "being afraid of the bear"? Nothing, so long as it's clear that a variety of mental contents are implied: "believing that the bear is dangerous"; "expecting that the bear will attack"; "wanting to avoid attack," and so on. The same isn't true of feeling happy and sad, elated and gloomy, and even "rageful." These are likely to be states of affect that are not specific to mental contents, they are mood states. Would we ever want to articulate a patient's mood? It has all the drawbacks of a confrontation; it constitutes the music without any lyrics; it simply isn't efficacious in the work of uncovering-discovering. It is also, in certain respects, a facile thing to do, for it's easy to "work with" feelings and moods; it deals with experiences that are amorphous and tends to degenerate into vagueness and finding words that allude to experiences without clarifying them.

Moreover, inasmuch as they are nonverbal experiences, they can only be approached confrontationally. "You say you're sad but you sound happy"; "when you speak of your brother you speak bitterly"; "there is a ragefulness in your voice and your face which does not jibe with what you're saying." These are confrontational interpretations and as such leave patients with very little room to disagree. Even when proffered with empathy and tact, they crowd P.

We return in conclusion to the issue of depth, in order to distinguish between interpretations that may be characterized as weak and those that may be strong. Weak ones are our bread and butter; we will make them freely and frequently. They may be regarded as redundant and unhelpful by patients, but we will have no way of being sure in advance. Often what we thought was going to be weak (superficial or gratuitous) turns out to be otherwise, and vice versa. Equally often, moreover, what we thought was going to be a valid, if not strong, interpretation will turn out to be invalid. But rarely will this detract from the therapeutic process; it can even enhance it because a patient can readily provide the valid one. (The same, as we've already mentioned more than once, is not true for explanatory and diagnostic interpretations; they cannot so readily be disconfirmed.)

But occasionally we will need to make a strong interpretation, one that comes as news to P. It can surprise him, even shock him, but we do it not for those reasons; we do it to provide P with an incentive to continue the ordeal of therapy. A better way to put it is: a strong interpretation makes the therapy interesting and vital, and it defines us as "the one who has interesting and vital things to say." An even better rationale speaks of us as occasionally "participating" in the therapeutic process (as a kind of partner) rather than always just "supervising" it.

Suffice it to say, Psychotherapy requires that occasionally we proffer a strong interpretation, and we can often prepare it in advance. So from time to time we have to think up a strong interpretation that we can give P. If we come up with a good strong one, and it has to be a strong good one, which means that it cannot be explanatory or diagnostic (and it needn't be all that valid either), we will appreciate the value it has. In any event, we must think hard about it; we must not be timid about it; and to repeat, we needn't worry about being wrong. "Better to be strong and wrong than nongood and right," you write.

This covers the first of our three lessons on interpretations. Now let's find a name for our good ones. *Empathy* won't do (my thesaurus sends us to *sympathy*, and that word is clearly inapt). *Disclosing* and *revelation* might be pressed into service, though "a disclosing interpretation" would obviously be better than a "revelatory" one. But we cannot speak of "a disclosure" in the same way we can of "a confrontation," because it's something a patient does, not us.

I was tempted by words like *perspicuous, lucid, insightful, concordant,* and *putative,* but they don't sit right. A "perspicuous interpretation" is tempting but a bit fancy. How about a "lucid" one? I like this the best, it's simple and elegant. Susan sees nothing wrong with "a mental content interpretation," and I'm willing to settle for "a content interpretation." (The implication that it's one that we can be contented with is a nice touch.)

Enough!

EIGHTEEN

THE FORM OF INTERPRETATIONS

For our lesson on how to interpret, we are making use of the opening paragraph in *Portnoy's Complaint*.[12]

> She was so deeply imbedded in my consciousness that for the first year of school I seem to have believed that each of my teachers was my mother in disguise. As soon as the last bell had sounded, I would rush off for home, wondering as I ran if I could possibly make it to our apartment before she had succeeded in transforming herself. Invariably she was already in the kitchen by the time I arrived, and setting out my milk and cookies. Instead of causing me to give up my delusions, however, the feat merely intensified my respect for her powers. And then it was always a relief not to have caught her between incarnations anyway—even if I never stopped trying.

This narrative has four parts. If we've decided to offer an interpretation, we might have to select one of them. The bases on which we make such a selection aren't examined in this lesson, and we have arbitrarily selected one in order to carry out a comparative study of the following forms:

1. You wanted to see her in the act of transforming herself.

This interpretation isn't completely redundant, for Portnoy didn't explicitly say that he had this wish (he wanted to catch his mother "between incarnations," whatever that means). Anyway, redundancy

---

[12]Roth, P. *Portnoy's Complaint* (New York: Knopf, 1962). Portnoy is presumed to be in psychoanalysis with a Dr. Spielvogel, and the book is presumed to be a transcript of the sessions.

(or call it shallowness) doesn't count as a formal feature, and we've chosen a weak interpretation in order to systematically vary its form and keep our attention fixed on the variations.

Then what are its formal features? To begin with, it is succinct; it makes one point and makes it with a single sentence. This is good form. "A good interpretation," you say, "is succinct without being curt." The distinction is a subtle one, but if we wanted to avoid being curt, we might do it by prefacing the remark with "I take it," or ending it with "I gather." Susan isn't sure that this ameliorates the curtness, but I think it can, and my guess is that you will side with me—you've already shown us that you favor such locutions.

A second formal feature of the interpretation is its explicitness. There is nothing allusive or vague about it, as would be the case for, "You wanted to see a certain part of the transformation," or, "There was something about the transformation that you wanted to see." The criterion is whether Portnoy can ask what we had in mind ("What 'certain part' did I want to see?" or, "What do you have in mind by 'something about the transformation'?"). The good interpretation is explicit; there is nothing vague about it; it doesn't allude or imply, and neither does it provoke a patient into asking us to be more specific and say more. At the same time, neither does it direct a patient to be more specific and say more.

Finally, inflected in a direct way, the remark is assertive. It implies that "I know (or believe) this to be a fact." Susan thinks this defines us as down-to-earth; I think it may also define us as dogmatic. We agree, however, that, even though you specify that all of the variations in this study—in fact, all of the interpretations that are ever given in your letters—are to be given with a degree of warmth and enthusiasm, a great deal depends on our tone of voice and the way the remark is made. Our first variation of the interpretation makes this point.

2. You wanted to see her in the act of transforming herself?

Inasmuch as the wording is identical to form 1, it is equally explicit and succinct but its punctuation attenuates the certainty of voice as well as the dogmatic element. However, and again depending on tone of voice, it adds a possibly incredulous element, if not also a challenging one. We could be saying, "This is a fact?" thereby defining ourselves as the skeptic, and this isn't a definition we want. A simple rewording can prevent this.

   3. Did you want to see her in the act of transforming herself?

It gets rid of the skeptical-challenging element and substitutes an interrogatory one. But the interpretation is now more clearly a directive, at least to the extent that it directs Portnoy to answer with a yes or no, or with a don't know or not sure.

   There's no gainsaying that forms 1 and 2 are also directives, at least to the extent that they direct Portnoy to pay attention to the interpretation. All interpretations do this. Susan argues that the three forms are equivalent in respect to their directiveness, while I think they can make a significant difference nonetheless.

   When we append "I gather" or "I take it" to form 1, we are implying the question, "Am I understanding you correctly?" (But we aren't digressing into this matter, because directiveness isn't a formal feature of interpretations, and the role of direct questions is a topic we're postponing.) Suffice it to say that all forms of interpretations ask a question and a direct question asks it more directly.

   4. I believe it is possible (or likely) that you wanted to see her
      in the act of transforming herself.

This is equally explicit and succinct, and its form is conjectural. "This is a speculation," is what it says. "I have a hunch that . . . ," might be the way we'd put it. It defines us as the one who speculates, and it's an altogether appropriate definition for us, for the uncovering–discovering process benefits from a degree of speculation. We will want to keep it within bounds, naturally, because we don't want to be far-fetched and reckless (if we did, we must skip ahead to form 10 which is a deep speculation for which we'd also use form 4). But speculation and conjecture can be useful for the therapeutic process. We can also invite Portnoy to participate in it by using form 5.

5. What do you think of the possibility that you wanted to see her in the act of transforming herself?

This is a direct question. Inasmuch as it retains the speculative element, however, it doesn't ask directly for confirmation–disconfirmation; rather it asks Portnoy to consider the conjecture and see whether it fits. It is somewhat open-ended and also implies an interest on our part in how he regards such "possibilities." The directive is, "Listen to this conjecture and see what you think of it."

Susan and I like this form, and so do you. It is succinct without being curt, it's explicit, it has no hint of skepticism or challenge, and it avoids coming across as assertive and dogmatic. Furthermore, though it's a question, it doesn't feel interrogative; it doesn't probe, nor does it impose a fresh topic. In short, it feels right.

When we are not certain we should say so, when we are speculating we should say as much, for this allows us to say speculative things about which we are not certain and invites our patient to do the same. Psychotherapy thrives on active exploration (rather than on passive ventilation) and the freer it is, the better. So we can say, "Look, I have an idea about this . . . ," and cast it into question form by adding, "What do you think of the idea (or possibility) that . . . ?" thereby inviting the patient to join in. And we do it with intensity and objectivity; with tentativeness but authority; with a measure of warmth and caring.

The spirit in which we should make an interpretation is captured by the word *proffer.* The interpretation is given to our patients for their vouchsafing. We have no ego involvement in it. Once we've proffered it, it belongs to them. If they dispute it, fine; if they ignore it, fine. Our most prudent conclusion, as a working hypothesis, is that it was incorrect (either in respect to its content or in respect to its timing, or both). Moreover, it isn't uncommon for patients to dismiss an interpretation only to voice it later on as if it were theirs. This might ignite a small spark of satisfaction in us, but nothing more.

Now, if we use form 5, or any other, each and every time we
offer them an interpretation, our patients are going to be distracted
by it. So there's bound to be value in varying our form. However,
there are some additional ones which we may not ever want to em-
ploy, even though they are commonly used by therapists. What follows is a sampling, and your critique, of them.

6. It sounds like you wanted to see her in the act of transforming
   herself.

This is probably the most common and most popular way to frame
an interpretation. Your guess is, that at this very moment, thou-
sands of therapists all across the country, of all stripes and persua-
sions, are saying it to their patients. Nevertheless, you advise us
not to use it. For one thing, it has a passive-receptive voice, and
defines us accordingly. Our stance is that of the passive rather than
the active listener, the one who listens for the sound of things rather
than for their sense. And it is allusive, too, in that we allude to what
a patient's narrative "sounds like" instead of elucidating what it
might mean.

You advise that we discipline ourselves in the use of the active
voice. You advise us to avoid the passive-impersonal voice, as in,
"It seems to me that. . . ." Instead we should say, "I think . . . ," "I
believe . . . ," "I gather . . . ," and "I'm wondering. . . ." This not
only defines us as one who plays an active role—who actively
thinks, actively believes, actively gathers, and actively wonders—
but it invites our patient to do the same.

Other passive forms are: "I get the feeling that . . . ," which is both
passive-receptive and intuitive (we listen passively-receptively and
with our fingertips); "I can't help wondering if . . . ," which could
also be apologetic and implies a passive helplessness; "It strikes me
that . . . ," which speaks for itself. There is little value in these locutions; they run the risk of teaching patients a lesson they don't need.

7. It's interesting that you wanted to see her in the act of
   transforming herself.

This, of course, implies that some things that Portnoy is going to say will be more interesting than others, and defines us as someone who makes that judgment. It raises questions of "interesting in what respect" and "interesting to whom." At best, it implies that the reason we selected this piece of material is because we found it to be interesting, or at least more interesting than the other pieces. This is quite a different rationale from, "I selected it because I had an idea about it and I thought my idea might be useful."

8. What's important is that you wanted to see her in the act of transforming herself.

This might imply that some of the things Portnoy wants are more important than others, and defines us as the one who judges the fact. It raises the same questions and problems as form 7. Words like *interesting* and *important* are worth avoiding inasmuch as they imply valuation and consequently a breach of neutrality. The same is true for the next variation, which adds another ingredient.

9. What you really wanted to see was your mother in the act of transforming herself.

Even if we cast this interpretation in one of the forms listed above, it conveys this message in addition: "What you say you wanted, or thought you wanted, isn't true, or is only a superficial kind of truth; I will tell you the real truth." It defines us as one who deals with underlying, if not hidden, meanings that are more meaningful, if not also more true. It also defines us as an authority of sorts, an authority not on psychotherapy so much as on psychology.

Next we add two variations to the list, even though their formal characteristics are of a different order.

10. What you wanted to see was your mother naked.

This is a new idea. Portnoy said nothing about his mother being undressed. We have made a bold inference and given a strong interpretation. To be sure, this isn't, strictly speaking, a formal feature but it touches on the matter of depth and defines us as the one who delves therein (it's the other side of shallowness and redundancy). We can argue that it's merely a piece of speculation—and what's the difference between a deep interpretation and a speculative one? But since you hesitate to criticize a strong interpretation, you digress briefly to point out that, in proffering one, it can be helpful to couch it in form 5 and define it clearly for the patient as a piece of speculation. It is also important to keep our strong interpretations simple and succinct.

Since most of us are obsessive-compulsive, we tend to rely on such tendencies as circumstantiality and uncertainty. For this reason, it is difficult for us to keep our interpretations simple. Often what we do is offer an interpretation that contains several ideas for our patients to choose from. While this keeps them in the active position, it can attenuate their defense against the unacceptable idea. Better to break the larger interpretation into parts and present them one at a time. This gradual, or stepwise, approach is generally appropriate for formulations that contain a genetic idea, and is especially well suited to transference interpretations.

In any event, among the most effective strong interpretations are those that are succinct. When they are well-timed, interpretations such as the following can have a significant effect:

- You were yearning for your father's approval.
- You love your father deeply.
- You wanted to kill your father.
- You believe that beneath the surface you are really insane.
- You believe that beneath the surface you are homosexual.
- You have felt, all your life, that things just aren't fair.
- You have felt, all your life, that you are a mistake (accident).

Timing is the crucial consideration. We must be convinced that our patient already knows what we are putting into words, that he or she is now ready for it in this sense. The function of this kind of interpretation in particular is to articulate clearly what is preconscious or to release an emotion that is straining at the threshold.

So the thing to notice about the strong interpretation that we offered Portnoy is that we had no reason to believe that the idea was at the threshold of his consciousness and we have changed the subject. We are no longer addressing the idea of his teachers being his mother in disguise, and neither are we talking about her ability to transform herself into them. Instead we're introducing a new idea and raising a voyeuristic issue that has sexual implications. The problem with doing this is, that while it may actually have been what underlay his experience at the time, it may not have been—and if this happens to be the case then the interpretation would amount to a deflection, if not also an imposition on our part. Even if it happens to be valid, there remains a sense in which we've deflected him from the narrative and diverted his attention.

This problem also applies to our next example, which grinds us into a new gear.

11. This is a screen memory of a primal scene.

Here we have, among other things, a purely diagnostic interpretation. It isn't addressed to what Portnoy said, or to what he thought, wanted, intended, expected, was afraid of, or was conflicted about—none of these things. In other words, it does not address mental content. Instead it diagnoses; it provides a formulation (of an intellectual nature, necessarily), a way for Portnoy to conceptualize the experience and thereby understand it (formally it isn't different from "you were an inquisitive child").

Another property of this interpretation worth noting is that it applies to the entire narrative rather than to a particular part of it. It explains to Portnoy what sort of narrative it is and raises the question of what he's to do with the explanation. Can we picture any response other than a grinding halt? He may choose to contest the interpretation, but this would be tantamount to changing the subject. Or else he might accept it and then, if he didn't ask us what the memory was screening, begin a search for the screened memory. In either case the memory at issue would fall by the wayside. Another way of putting it is: an explanation has a tendency to draw attention to itself and away from the experience that it explains; the explanation may become more interesting and important than the experience.

Before we study the perils and pitfalls of explanations, we examine a close relative: a formulation that can be called a connection in that it simply connects parts of the narrative to each other.

12. Your relief at not catching her in the act of transforming herself is connected with your wish to see her in the act of transforming herself.

This is a favorite form of interpretation of many therapists (and patients like it, too). It isn't a causal explanation; it's an associationistic conception, if an A is associated with a B type, and we can now fall back on associationist theory and use the handful of categories (like contiguity in time and place, similarity and contrast), and explain the connection in that way. Ordinarily, however, matters rest with our pointing up the connection.

Portnoy will probably become interested in exploring it, but clinical experience suggests that it is apt to be intellectualized; he will probably now engage in a process of reasoning, and out the window goes disclosing-discovering. The enterprise may nevertheless result in some significant insights, so we don't decry the connection, we just use it sparingly. We might restrict it to those occasions on which we have a strong interpretation in mind but deem it likely to be tactless. At such times we can consider offering parts of the interpretation and proceeding gradually, in the stepwise fashion. But each part must be able to stand on its own; it should not be an incomplete or truncated interpretation, and it must not be allusive. For these reasons the connection can be a good first step.

Let's say we use form 12 with form 10 as the strong interpretation in mind. The dialogue might go as follows:

Us   I have a hunch that your relief at not catching her in the act of transforming herself was connected to a wish to see her in the act.

P   That's interesting. I think it must have been, because why else would I have felt so relieved when I didn't get to see it. I wanted to see it, but at the same time I must've not wanted to.

Us   Perhaps then your relief was associated with an idea that she would punish you for seeing it.

P   No, I don't remember being afraid of what she'd do to me. It had more to do with being afraid of something I'd actually see. There was something terribly exciting about, but at the same time terribly—oh, forbidden, I think.

Us   Could it be that you thought you might see her naked?

P   I didn't think of that! And it's so obvious it embarrasses me. I was a horny little bastard, and she was beautiful. I don't remember ever seeing her naked until I was twelve or thirteen, when she was past her prime. But when I was little she always wore a slip or paraded around in her underwear.

Us   So isn't it quite possible, then, that among the things you wanted to see was your mother naked?

Finally, we have the explanation, the interpretation that says why. It raises some basic issues that we'll study in our next lesson, where it will be argued that explanations of virtually every kind rarely make good interpretations. In the meantime we'll settle for these points: (1) explanatory interpretations are causal formulations, in the sense that they pivot on a *because*; (2) they can restrict themselves to mental contents, linking them together ("You wish to tell me this story because you believe I'm interested in early memories"); (3) they can be hybrid with diagnosis ("You were an inquisitive child because it satisfied your voyeuristic needs").

Back to the narrative, and let's notice that its parts are already connected in a causal way. The reason Portnoy's teachers were his

mother in disguise is *because* she was imbedded in his consciousness, the reason he ran home is *because* he wanted to see the transformation, the reason he was relieved at not catching her in the act
—is left hanging. So here's a weak interpretation qua explanation:

> 13. You were relieved that you didn't catch her in the act
>   because you wanted to maintain the delusion that all of
>   your teachers were your mother in disguise.

It makes sense, but how is Portnoy going to respond? "I guess so,"
might come first ("It makes sense"). Next might come, "Then why
did I want to maintain the delusion?" Will we respond by com-
pleting the circle and saying, "Because she was so imbedded in
your consciousness"? Unless we're prepared to draw from the experience of our other patients, or (God forbid!) from our theory,
our only other reply is likely to be, "I don't know."

Many therapists would judge it appropriate to direct Portnoy to
search for the answer, and they might do it with a directive like
"What comes to mind about it?" This amounts to suggesting that
he free associate on the topic, and it's also tantamount to simply
saying, "I don't know—what do you think the answer might be?"

But the key question is whether explanations simply beget further explanations, each of which will lead Portnoy further away
from the narrative, or whether they can enrich and deepen the narrative and will lead to his uncovering more mental content. In our
next lesson we will learn the answer to this question.

NINETEEN

EXPLANATIONS, DIAGNOSES, AND PSYCHOANALYTIC INTERPRETATIONS

I have persuaded Susan to let me give your lesson on explanatory interpretations (which begins on a polemical note and then grows lecturely) the same treatment as the theory letter: edit it, reorganize it, and add subheadings. "The Perils and Pitfalls of Explanations" is the title that she preferred; I leaned toward "Ours Is Not to Question Why"; we compromised with:

Don't Ask Why!

Why Not?

Explanations are a menace. Our need for reasons is the source of tragedy and has led to acts of cruelty and destruction. Explanations, according to one reading of history, are sources of strife as well as sheer stupidity. We use them to exonerate ourselves and justify our worst behavior. They bolster bias, vanity, and venality, blind us to our most beautiful feelings, deflect us from our best impulses, filter and distance us from the world—instead of making things lucid, as they purportedly should, they too often blur and obscure them.

Surely, though, I am referring only to bad explanations, those that are false. Good ones are intellectually satisfying and esthetically gratifying, aren't they? They subserve, after all, our need to understand. This, in my view, is at least arguable. Be that as it may, however, a key problem for us is their relationship to understanding. For even if we claimed that the goal of therapy was to achieve

179

understanding, we would have to acknowledge that achieving it isn't synonymous with arriving at explanations.

We therapists can avoid why explanations and strive instead to understand how. Our interpretations can steer clear of causes and reasons, and focus instead on perspicuous articulations and descriptions. Insofar as causes and reasons help achieve clarity, they may be useful. Not only, however, are they instrumental, at best, but they can be diverting and misleading.

P speaks of a distressing experience: it may be natural to wonder why it happened. It is practically irresistible. We can nevertheless discipline ourselves to keep from asking why—and if P asks, we can regard it as a defense. For instead of wondering why, we (and he) are better off wondering what—not what caused the distressing experience but what occasioned it. And by its "occasion" we mean its context, we never mean to suggest that a context is a cause. A context is part and parcel of the experience. In our quest to understand what happened, it is therefore germane to ask what else happened or how the parts and aspects of the distressing experience fit and work together.

To repeat: nothing is more natural than asking why, and we are naturally inclined to explain events in causal terms. All our lives, we've been looking for reasons. Our first questions were why questions. Why? Because children need to know how things work, and they conflate why with how. Or maybe it's because cause and effect is built into the fabric of phenomenal experience. (Do you see what's wrong with explanations?) But bear in mind that most of the reasons that we find satisfying are conventional in nature, they have traditionally been reduced to either God or nature (and in our psychoanalytic era drives have replaced God and nature). Be that as it may, the most effective question to work with in Psychotherapy is not why but what, and the most effective *what* is mental content. To be sure, emotions and feelings come a close second, but mental content is where the paydirt is.

The Trouble with Generalizing: Diagnosing

Explanations generally pivot on a generalization from particular events and individuals to collections of them. In addition to asking why a particular event occurs, we ask why these particular sorts of events ever occur, and not only for this individual but for all like individuals. Normative explanations, we know from clinical experience, usually provide little more than reassurance. Moreover, in seeking sameness, we have to attenuate distinctions—and preserving them often makes matters clearer. That's why we can favor similes (metaphors, models) over theories that generalize: a simile offers a like thing and it never aspires to be true, only fitting. A simile (or model) provides insight in a fundamentally different way than a normative explanation does. It rarely offers a reason why, it usually is content to suggest a way how.

Consider the question, "Why do I behave this way?" and the answer, "Because I am a person who behaves that way." It isn't altogether empty, in that it asserts that in all like circumstances I behave that way, and this can lead to an examination of the "like circumstances." The question becomes, "Why do I behave this way in all of these circumstances?" and the answer might be, "Because all persons like me do." The task now becomes one of elucidating "like persons"—another generalization that's going to beg the question—which eventually becomes, "What about me, and persons like me, explains my behavior in this circumstance (and in all like circumstances)?" We can now no longer resort to generalization. Or is it more accurate to say that we can never, not in principle, avoid it; even when we are being as specific as we can be, is there not a necessary ingredient of generality?

In any case, we can minimize generality by restricting it to P and also to the circumstance. For even if we'll eventually end up saying, "Because it's the way you are, in this circumstance—haven't you noticed?" it's better than, "Because that's the way people are—haven't you noticed?" (And why is it better? Because that's the way therapy works best—haven't you noticed?)

The chief pitfall is diagnosis. Saying "I did it because I'm a lazy person" isn't saying much—it is tantamount to still being a lazy person. Saying that laziness is a learned habit is a counsel of despair, unless I'm willing to unlearn it (and there are ways to do it). However, saying "I did it because I have ideas that aren't fully conscious and therefore are poorly understood by me," is saying a great deal, so far as psychotherapy is concerned, for it's a fact, though a different kind of fact than my laziness is. Laziness is an inference from a plethora of facts; it is a concept about me, not in me (that's what we mean by diagnosis). Note the insignificant difference between, "I did it because I'm lazy," and, "I did it because I believe I'm lazy." The former is tantamount to, "I walk funny because I'm a cripple." If we say, "I walk funny because I believe I'm a cripple," it has a quite different meaning.

Consider this example: Child has broken a dish; Parent says, "You have broken a dish"—this is a confrontation. Child says, "I know it" (i.e., the confrontation was gratuitous), "but of course you had no way of knowing; you made the confrontation because you want me to know it"—this is an interpretation.

So Parent says, "The reason I want you to know it is that I want you never to break dishes."

"You believe, then, that knowing what I've done—understanding what it is I did—will help prevent me from doing it again," says Child. "But you could have given me to understand that you didn't want me to break dishes; it wasn't necessary to point out to me that I broke a dish." Notice that Child is asking for no interpretation whatever; Child neither wants nor welcomes an interpretation.

Or say Parent said, "You broke the dish because you're bad," or, "You broke the dish because you want to hurt me." Both are diagnosing explanations. A content interpretation would simply be, "You know that the dish you broke is my favorite dish"—it's an assertion of psychological fact. Similarly, "Look, you broke what you know to be my favorite dish!" is an assertion of fact together with the directive, "Be aware of what you did so that you won't ever do it again." The interpretation is combined with a confrontation, and its purpose is to modify Child's behavior.

More on Mental Content

"What can I learn about my patient today?" is first cousin to, "What am I supposed to hear today?"—which can be translated to, "What is in and on my patient's mind?" What sorts of things can be in and on a patient's mind? I have already enumerated them, and called them mental contents. For the purposes of this discussion, I will refer to them as they have traditionally been referred to in the literature, as ideas.

A patient's motives and drives aren't ideational except insofar as the patient has theories about them. At the level of our theory

the difference between an expectation and a motive, as well as
the difference between a wish and a drive, is attenuated by defining them operationally. But at the level of the patient's theory the
difference can count. To be sure, "I have such-and-such a drive"
might be synonymous with "I have such-and-such a wish," but it
can connote something quite different.

Compare "I have a need for food" to "I wish to eat." The former
connotes a sense of being driven by, not of driving oneself; it feels
more involuntary and less under control. We may choose to relinquish wishes in a way that we can't so readily with drives. For
one thing, we own them in a subtly different way. These are among
the considerations that support my contention that P's ideas, not
his motives, are the appropriate subject for our interpretations.
Ours is not to question why, let's stick to what.

An Interpretation Is What?

To begin with, *interpretation* is an unfortunate term. We adopted
it from the interpretation of dreams, wherein we extract meaning
from a dream; wherein we replace its manifest content with a la-
tent content which is deeper and truer; wherein we explain the
dream. The mode is didactic and detective; we are good scholars
and mentors, good diagnosticians and troubleshooters—but are we
good therapists?

The mode is congenial. We were once, after all, children, and
things were mysterious to us. We had an urgent need to know the
facts of life; we hungered for facts and our appetite was insatiable.
Our parents were eager to explain, eager to teach, for nurturing
and explaining go hand in hand and being the good teacher is
being a good parent.

All service providers, be they dentists or car mechanics, take
pains to explain our problems, even when it serves no practical
purpose. Do we need to know what's wrong with our teeth or our
car? Yes, we apparently do, but not because it will serve any practical purpose in the work that's going to repair the problem.

Yes, Simon, analogies (unlike similes) are hazardous and psychotherapy is distinctive, so I'll quit analogizing. The relevance is
this: the role of therapist implicates the socially familiar roles of
parenting, doctoring, mentoring, teaching, repairing. The problem

is to identify and isolate our distinctive role and the ways it differs from all other socially familiar ones. It can lie in our abjuring of explanations.

But we spend so much of our professional life sequestered with patients—and playing the role of parent and teacher is so congenial, it breaks the tedium and satisfies our need to do something. What better way than by providing explanations? And isn't it easy to persuade ourselves that they are good for what ails the patient? In my opinion, they have the value of maintaining P's interest in therapy and also making him feel safe. Explanations provide intellectual security and little more.

Our work is maximally useful when it pivots on P's experience of gaining clarity, understanding, and discovering—the core of the therapeutic process. Each of our guidelines can have the fundamental and overriding purpose of promoting and facilitating the process, and our basic question is: "What can I do, here and now, to improve it? What does this particular P, at this particular juncture in therapy, require of me in order to optimalize his therapeutic process?" This has the value of overriding these kinds of questions: "What can I do to elicit P's memories?" and "How can I help him gain insight into his defenses and dynamics?" and "What can I do to show him that our relationship contains the seeds of transference, or mirrors the relationships he has with significant others?" much less "What can I do to help him change?" Those questions are potentially subsidiary and subserving, but otherwise they are potentially diverting and distracting.

On the Uses and Misuses of Psychoanalytic Theory

How, then, do we square Psychotherapy with an adherence to Freudian theory? In other words: How does a psychoanalyst do Psychotherapy? By giving psychoanalytic interpretations, is the short answer. The long answer is: psychoanalytic theory, specifically what is referred to as its clinical theory, provides a lode of good interpretations, and so rich and abundant is the lode that one can mine it without having to resort to psychoanalysis's metapsychology. The clinical theory is well-stocked with ideas for good interpretations, while the metapsychology, insofar as it deals with mental mechanisms and processes, can only provide explanatory ones.

You will hear it said that we analysts teach our patients our theory; we use our theory as a source of interpretations that explain, and we provide explanations that are drawn not only from our clinical theory but also from our metapsychology. In practice, however, most of us rely on the former alone—and as a source not of explanations but of interpretations of mental content. Our clinical theory provides us with an abundance of ideas for discerning what's in and on our patient's mind. Not all of them will prove valid, of course, so we make sure to be discriminating and judicious. Given this caveat, let me spell out some concrete ways that our theory helps us formulate our interpretations.

Let's start with the infamous castration anxiety and its first cousin, penis envy. The theory posits that we are likely to have a primitive regard, perhaps fascination, for the penis and its magical powers; we have unconscious ideas in respect to penises, both present and absent, evident and hidden; we have a propensity to view a wide range of things, like our body appendages as well as other "appendages" (like our babies and pets, as well as cars and tennis racquets), as penises, with all of their attendant ideas and fantasies.

There is, in this theory, a wealth of interpretable mental content, interpretations which in their baldest form translate to such propositions as: "Holding a tennis racquet sometimes feels like you are holding a penis," and, "When you broke your tennis racquet it felt somehow as if you had broken your penis," and, "Having a baby is uncannily like having a new penis," and, "Holding your baby can evoke some of the same sensations in you as when you hold your penis." Our technical guidelines insure that a patient will feel free to ignore, if not reject, such interpretations; they will have been made with such tact, and in such a timely fashion, that the element of imposition will be minimal (if P believes that these interpretations don't fit for him, he will at worst find them "interesting"). Moreover, it is often possible to convey them without using the word *penis,* by saying "a part of your own body."

Issues of potency can pivot on penis ideas ("I cannot be potent so long as my penis is so feeble"), as can issues of shame ("It is forbidden to show my penis"). Narcissistic issues are readily translated into penis terms ("See, I have a penis!"). And penis envy ("Mine is smaller than his," and, "I have nothing because I have none") can provide the template for a host of feelings that pivot on depreciated self-image ("I'm not a man/woman; my penis is too small and fragile; my penis is hidden inside; my penis isn't real, it's a toy").

Now, if penis envy and castration anxiety can provide such a wide range of interpretable content, then think of what we can get from the psychosexual stages—with their grand themes of orality, anality, and phallicity—and culminating in the classical Oedipus complex, with its multifaceted references to the "family romance" that bears on a host of basic and ubiquitous human issues.

The Problem of Defense

A basic concept in psychoanalysis, defense plays a major role in most forms of dynamic psychotherapy. But inasmuch as defenses cannot be counted as mental content, how can a therapist who is conducting Psychotherapy deal with patients' defenses? To answer this question, I have to start with Freud, for he initially construed ego as a collection of mental contents, and therefore eminently interpretable as such.

Freud's topographic theory posited that ideas could have the status of consciousness, preconsciousness, and unconsciousness. In principle, there was nothing in our mind that couldn't be expressed as a memory, a thought, a wish, and therefore in the form of "this is what is in (if not at the moment on) my mind." There was one major exception: the processes and forces that determined and secured our idea's status in respect to consciousness, preconsciousness, and unconsciousness.

Ego denoted those ideas that pertain to our self-image (attitudes, values, and ideals, having to do with who and what we are), and that enter into conflict with those ideas that do not pertain to our self-image. These, let's call them ego ideas, were not different in kind from other ideas, but they had the privileged power to fuel conflict (with nonego ideas), and thereby generate symptoms. The unconscious was made up of repudiated nonego ideas (that were repressed as a consequence of their conflict with ego ideas), and they were dynamic in two senses: they are kept unconscious by force, and they strive to gain consciousness. These dynamic forces, inasmuch as they aren't ideas, required didactic and diagnostic explanations. But the ego ideas and the nonego ideas could readily be interpreted, as could the conflicts between them.

Freud was first and foremost an interpreter of dreams, and psychoanalysis was always based on the act of interpreting. As we interpret a dream, we interpret a mind; as we elucidate the meaning of a dream element, we elucidate the meaning of an idea. Nevertheless, we cannot, in the same way, interpret the dream work (the processes and mechanisms by which, according to the theory, the dream was formed). The dream work can only be explained, and the explanation must perforce remain part of our theory. The theory's explanation can provide a template for our interpretation but it cannot be part of the interpretation itself.

When he observed that ego ideas could become dynamically unconscious, Freud felt it was necessary to redefine ego and reformulate his theory. No longer was ego a category of ideas, it became a status of them (like conscious, preconscious, unconscious had been, and now were "demoted" to the status of mere descriptive categories). Moreover, ego—inasmuch as it was driven by a powerful id and buffeted by an overbearing superego—no longer enjoyed a privileged position. In an important sense, ego became synonymous with defense; it was now a process of mind; it denoted the way the mind regulates and protects itself. As such it could no longer be interpreted, it had to be explained.

"The Ego Plays a Trick"

Let's join the psychoanalytic community, gathered to celebrate, with presentations honoring his career, Heinz Hartmann's 70th birthday. When it comes time for him to address us, Hartmann speaks of how good and glad he feels. This, he points out (as a good psychoanalyst should), is enigmatic—"But the ego plays a trick." We all rise to applaud this apt and beautiful formulation.

"The ego plays a trick!"—a succinct phrase freighted with significance—and to my ears, it sounded natural and self-evident. In fact, it was the first time I heard the term *ego* without experiencing a twinge of uneasiness (my intellectual upbringing, in the embrace of English empiricism and American pragmatism, had made me leery of metaphysical and animistic concepts).

Notice, first of all, who is feeling glad: it isn't an ego, it's Hartmann. He is speaking and feeling; his ego is the tricking agency, the defense. Defending against what? We didn't need him to spell it out for us. He was telling us that he had thought about the event, had anticipated it with joy, and done all the things necessary to prepare for it. All of these actions, thoughts, and feelings are subsumed under the rubric of the subject of the discourse, the "I." Taken as a whole, it is that subject we want to explain psychoanalytically—and it is "his," not his ego's. It needs explaining because he had a set of competing thoughts, feelings, and wishes: depressive thoughts, sad feelings, and grim anticipations; wishes that it weren't so, that he was not at the end but at the beginning. What wanted explanation is how come these were absent—and here is where we get "the ego." That's what pulled it off, said Hartmann (and he should know, for he was the expert on the subject).

He didn't say, "I played a trick on myself," because he wanted to say that all of us do it, not just him. Inasmuch as we "have" egos (which might mean that we aren't infants, say, or cats), we have a propensity to play tricks on ourselves. It's the ego in us that does the deed, and the deed is a defense.

If he were P, "You are tricking yourself," would be a diagnostic as well as confrontational interpretation. On the other hand, "You believe that you are tricking yourself," in that it addressed his idea, would count as an empathic interpretation. Accordingly, we could take the view that a defense interpretation can avoid being explanatory when P already has it in mind, as a theory about himself. Unfortunately, this won't solve the problem.

Take projection: we say, "You believe (or realize) that you are projecting," and this "sounds like" a good interpretation. Is it not the same as, "You believe that people hate you"? In both instances, we are articulating P's theory about himself, and that theory constitutes a piece of mental content. There is, however, a potentially significant difference: being an object of hate is an idea that belongs with his self-image, while projecting may not.

Our problem may lie in the fact that *defense* is an unfortunate term. It connotes a warding off of noxious stimuli and protecting ourselves against attack (the paradigm is shutting our eyes). But we don't always do it to fend off the world. Consciousness, as William James insisted it had to be, is selective. Defense can serve the interests of selection, enabling us to focus and concentrate by screening out irrelevant stimuli. Moreover, all defenses, even projection, can be construed as fundamentally adaptive. Accordingly, our goal may perhaps be to strengthen them, perhaps repair and redeploy them, but not to "breach" or weaken them.

Still, so long as we are committed to making good interpretations, however we choose to construe defense, the practical implications are the same. Whether we take it as the goal of therapy to repair them, or redeploy them, or whatever, we can rely only on the therapeutic process to achieve that goal, not on interpretations that would have to be diagnostic and confrontational.

Where does this leave us in regard to the widely accepted dictum *"Defense before impulse"*? We cannot honor it. The dictum provides a guideline for exactly not interpreting certain mental contents (impulses); it enjoins us to wait until the defense is analyzed. But who does this analyzing? When we do it, we are being didactic and confronting; when our patients do it, they are being autodidactic and intellectual.

We can take the position that it should be a goal of therapy, as distinct from its being a process of therapy, to modify patients' defenses. But this is equivalent to saying that the goal of therapy is change. We don't pursue change directly; it's the therapeutic process that brings it about. Does this mean that the theory of defense is of no practical use to us, it plays no role in our interpretive work? If we see our patients projecting, are we helpless to help them in it? To be sure, we cannot point it out to them, but is there nothing we can otherwise do?

If we rely on the topographic theory and the proposition that ideas have intrinsic force, in the sense that they strive and compete for consciousness, then we can construe repression as the activity of the ideas that contravene those that are unacceptable. The repudiation of repugnant ideas is achieved by other ideas that contravene them, and these ideas are likely to be ego ideas, for they are stronger. This can most easily be observed in projection, where the unacceptable idea is externalized rather than repressed; it is stripped of any reference to self-image, while its counterpart idea is strongly maintained.

Say P is talking about a conviction that his brother hates him and a conviction that he loves his brother, and we form the opinion that projection is at work; we might formulate an interpretation composed of four parts. (1) "The two convictions are connected"; (2) "You do not love him, you hate him"; (3) "This idea is repugnant to you"; (4) "Because it is repugnant to your self-image, and because you want to protect the integrity of your self-image, you . . . ," and we are now deep into the defense interpretation which is clearly an explanation. But why not simply leave (4) out? It has already served a valuable function by providing us with a template for our first three interpretations. Why not settle for that, and rely on the therapeutic process to do the rest? In other words, let's accept the working hypothesis that Psychotherapy will prevail against the defense (just as it's going to prevail against the neurosis) in some mysterious, inscrutable, and wonderful way ("Convalesce that defense!").

I will be examining resistance and transference, which are, after all, forms of defense, in a separate letter. In the meantime, we'll follow Simon's advice and settle for saying that resistance is best reserved for episodes of flight from therapy. Such flights (flight into health, into illness, into despair, into distrust, and the like) make use of a patient's defenses, but they are appropriately regarded as impasses. They must therefore be treated as business and not narrative, but with this difference: we can now resort to explanations. For when therapy is in a state of impasse, we may use our Band-Aid treatment (our short-term ameliorative measures), and explanations can play a useful role. This is when we can be didactic, when we may play the role of teacher and mentor. But we do it only when the integrity of the therapy is at issue, when matters are at a point of impasse.

When P says, "My brother hates me," there is no impasse. And there may also be none when he says, "You hate me." Inasmuch as this is transference, we'll be examining it later. But I want to mention a key feature of it that pertains to how we might work with defenses when they have a transferential focus. When P says, "My brother hates me," we have no basis for adding a part four to our three-part interpretation, and saying, "No, he doesn't, so that idea is false." That would be an invaluable step in exposing the defense. But when P says, "You hate me," we *can* do it; we're in a position to say, "I do not hate you, so that idea is false." P now faces a dissonance that requires him to reflect on the way his mind works, his defenses, and it was done without recourse to explanations.

TWENTY

INTERROGATING, PROBING, AND CLARIFYING

We were surprised that you didn't realize, prior to actually writing about it, that interpreting defenses was so problematic. You had thought that defenses could be interpreted when a patient caught a glimpse of them, and when they could be formulated as an interpretation of ideational content; now, it turns out, you have serious questions about it (another proof of the power of Disclosure and how teaching isn't so different from being in therapy).

But you needn't have apologized for taking us on yet another excursion into theory, for even I got caught up in the issues that you raised—and Susan was fascinated by what you wrote about psychoanalysis. You'll be glad to know that I am shifting away from my atheoretical stance, and Susan's commitment to psychoanalytic theory is getting stronger.

Reading our letters has made you aware of how repetitious you are (we've noticed it, too, but tact prevented us from drawing attention to it). You take the opportunity to point out that our patients repeat themselves, often a great deal, and it isn't always in the interests of defense. To be sure, it's often predicated on a conviction—and sometimes it's a wish—that we won't remember the things they tell us. But obsessionality within bounds is simply a personality trait, and needn't be taken as a disorder; we have to accept it as a natural expression of the therapeutic process. Therefore, provided we haven't got a timely transference interpretation in mind, when our patient says, "I was talking to Mary, she's my wife," we needn't say, "Did you think that I had forgotten that Mary is your wife?"

Today's lesson interrupts our study of interpretations in order to deal with the question of questions. Let me say in advance that unlike your lesson on explaining, this one is dismaying to me. Not that your position comes as a surprise, but I expected to be asking my prospective P lots of questions, and I find it hard to imagine doing without them. Don't therapists ask questions? They do it a lot, you assure us. So despite the fact that your arguments are by now familiar, I still have misgivings. They are founded on the fact that I, too, want to be free to ask P questions and you are hobbling me.

A direct question is of course directive. But you advised us to cast our interpretations in question form, and you pointed out that even when we don't, they amount to indirect questions. Any remark we make asks the patient something—to pay attention to what we've said, at the very least. So why is the difference between a direct question and an indirect one so significant? And granting the difference, surely we don't want to place a value on indirection. Is it that when we conduct business we are direct and forthright but when we conduct narrative we are indirect and disingenuous?

All right, I'm getting this off my chest. It's daunting to imagine never asking a direct question, and that's what you're asking me to do. Well, not exactly "never"—"Keep them to a minimum," you write. "Try to keep from wanting to ask them."

Once again, you start by drawing a sharp distinction between a clinical interview, which is diagnostic in nature and purpose, and a therapy session which isn't. Then you draw a distinction between questions that ask for information and questions that ask for feelings. You call the former interrogations and the latter probes.

I hope you realize you're loading the dice when you use these terms. They're loaded with pejorativeness, calling to mind police interrogation and all manner of third-degree procedures. So naturally I don't want to interrogate P, and neither do I like the idea of probing in a nosy and intrusive way. On the other hand, "direct question" seems so benign; it even sounds desirable, at least insofar as being indirect is not.

We're talking about the distinction between a question that asks for information that wasn't provided and a question that asks about information that was provided. You don't mind casting aspersions on the former, for which purpose you're glad to use the terms *interrogation* and *probing*. An interrogating question (and I think we might settle for an interviewing question) is one that asks for information, a probing question is one that asks for feelings. You give us the assignment of studying the implications and ramifications of asking Portnoy how old he was when the event he recounted took place. By way of fulfilling the assignment, here's a rendition of the dialogue Susan and I had on the question:

"How Old Were You?"

S   Why did you ask?

Me   Because he didn't say, and the age might be relevant.

S   That he didn't say goes without saying, but there may have been a reason he didn't. In fact, there has to be. Why not ask him why he didn't mention it?

Me   I can inquire into that afterwards.

S   "Inquire into"—such a nice sounding phrase! What you mean is you'll say, "So why didn't you mention your age?"

Me   I'm not going to be asking two direct questions in succession. But I might not have to; he might give the reason, after answering the question, by explaining why he omitted mentioning his age.

S   He also might not. He might answer the question and then ask you why you asked it. What will your answer be? Surely it won't be, "Because the age is important"?

Me   I wouldn't mind putting it that way but I couldn't. So I'd say something to the effect of it's helping us understand the event.

S   Us? I didn't hear Portnoy trying to understand it.

Me   True. But look here, I didn't interrupt his narrative with my question. I'm assuming that he had finished his account and was now engaged in trying to understand it.

S   That's a big assumption. I'll be generous, though, and grant it. But I take it that we agree with each other: there's no justification for interrupting his narrative with the question.

Me Not with a question for information. A question for clarification, however, is permissible. It's even desirable because it subserves my promise to "try to understand."

S   That's true but beside the point. You couldn't well say "It isn't clear to me how old you were." So let's get back to it. Please stop stalling and tell me how knowing his age will help either of you understand the event he's recounting.

Me Before I do that, let me ask you: Are you denying that knowing the facts of an event can help in understanding the event?

S   That would be silly, Simon. How many facts are necessary is the question. We can never know all of them, after all.

Me So we're arguing about the relevance and role of a particular piece of information, not of factual information in general.

S   Yes. Like, for instance, how come Portnoy's mother didn't pick him up from school? And how come he came home by himself? I think this is a bit odd; it was his first year in school.

Me I didn't notice that. But now that I do, can I not ask him those questions? I think they may be more pertinent than his age.

S   They may actually be related to his age, because it sounds like (oops!) Portnoy was too old to be starting school. But look here, Uncle's assignment is to ask Portnoy how old he was. We can't change it to, "How come you went home by yourself?"

Me If we were his patients we could. And he wouldn't even hit us with the interpretation, "You're changing the question because it's an easier one to deal with," because that's an explanation and a diagnosis and a confrontation all rolled into one.

S   All right, I'll go along, so long as you promise to come back to the age question afterwards.

Me   It's a promise. I am now asking Portnoy to tell me how come he came home by himself when he was in his first year of school. That's a direct question.

S   If I were Portnoy I'd ask you a direct counterquestion, and say, "Why do you want to know?" Or better yet, I'd put it this way: "The school was around the corner on the same block as my apartment, and there were no streets for me to cross, so it was perfectly safe for me to do it. Why did you ask?"

Me   "Because it struck me as odd, and that distracted me."

S   "Oh, I see. You did it for your sake, not for mine."

Me   "Exactly. I had no ulterior motive other than to clear my mind of a distraction that was interfering with my ability to listen."

S   "But why did it strike you as odd, in the first place? And were you not suggesting that I might find it odd, too? Say my response had been, 'I never thought of it, but now that I do, I don't find it odd. You, however, do, I gather.'"

Me   I'd rather Portnoy found it odd, too. This way I'm going to have to inject my personal opinion on the matter.

S   The same is true the other way, too. Once you say, or even imply, that you've heard something odd (or peculiar or dissonant) then your personal view is necessarily impli- cated. The fact that you were distracted by it is unfortunate, and there's no reason Portnoy should have to undistract you.

Me   Yes, but it isn't asking him for so much. While I'm at it, let me mention another piece of the narrative that dis- tracted me. The final line is, "And then it was always a relief not to have caught her between incarnations anyway, even if I never stopped trying." He was trying to catch her "between incarnations," not in the act of transforming herself. Did you notice that?

S   No, I didn't. What's your point?

Me   It suggests that he wanted to see her when she was neither his mother nor his teacher. That's intriguing, isn't it?

S   Yes, but what has it got to do with asking him any questions?

Me   This: My inclination would be to get at it by saying, "What do you mean 'between incarnations'?" This is a sort of clarification question, in that it asks what he means. Strictly speaking, it isn't a question for the purposes of information.

S   Strictly speaking, however, neither is it a clarification question. It doesn't ask Portnoy to explain what he meant to say.

Me   Oh, come off it! You're quibbling because you're embarrassed that you didn't spot the "between incarnations."

S   But I still think your question is a directive. It's tantamount to saying, "Tell me more about it." A clarification question, for it not to be a directive-to-explore, has to be addressed to the meaning of what P said. Unless it was incomprehensible, his utterance has to have been ambiguous—it can mean different things, and we're only trying to find out which one he intended. "Did you mean X or did you mean Y?" is the form of our question, and we can spell out the X and the Y, so that when P puts the counter-question—"What do you mean 'What do you mean?' Isn't it clear?"—we can say, "No, I'm not sure whether it means X or Y."

Me   It's paradigmatic form is, "I don't understand (1) the meaning of the word you said, (2) the sense in which you intended it." The directive is only to clarify, not explore.

S   And there's a potential duplicity in misusing the question. We must truly not have understood what P meant to say.

We mustn't use the question when what we haven't understood is the meaning of the experience or act that is being spoken of.

Me You're sounding a lot like Uncle. If I were permitted to interpret that, I would suggest that it's because you're feeling guilty that we're not doing his assignment.

S I think you're right, even though it's a confrontation. The interpretation took some of the sting out of it, and that's why I personally still think it can be okay to be confronting so long as we follow it with a good interpretation.

Me You're still sounding like him. Maybe he'll let us make an occasional confrontation, just like he's letting us ask an occasional direct question.

S I hope so, because it's the only way we're going to be able to interpret P's defenses.

Me But I agree that my question isn't a legitimate clarification question. It was based less on a piece of unclarity than on a piece of potential significance. Still, why don't we work briefly with the between incarnations idea and see if we can come up with some good strong interpretations?

S I think we should use the technique of gradualness for it.

Me Then I'll begin with, "It's possible, isn't it, that you wanted to see her when she was neither your mother nor your teacher?"

S "I'm not sure I understand what you're suggesting."

Me "Well, you said 'between incarnations.' This suggests that she was somebody other than your mother or your teacher."

S "Oh, I never thought of that. But it's an intriguing idea. Do you have any thoughts who she might be, or do you want me to think about it?"

Me "Well, I can suggest that she's—oh, just a woman, perhaps, and . . . uh . . . maybe she's unrelated to you."

S "Unrelated to me? What on earth do you mean?"

Me   "Okay, then what about her being related to your little sister? Maybe she isn't your mother, she's hers."

S   "That's interesting. But I think it's more likely to be that she's related to my father, she's his wife. I would have wanted to see her as his sexual object. Maybe I wanted to see her naked."

Me   "I see. You believe in the Oedipus complex, I gather."

S   "And I take it that you don't."

Me   "That's a personal question, so I don't need to answer it. And anyway, it's your theory that counts because you're the P."

S   And you don't sound like much of a T. Look here, Simon, I believe we've bungled enough and it's time to get back to the issue at hand. You were defending the question, "How old were you?" You were claiming that knowing Portnoy's age could help understand the event he recounted. My question was how.

Me   I can think of several hows. Let's use this one: it's bound to make a difference if he was four, as compared to his being six. A four-year-old will be more prone to magical thinking, and will be more attached to his mother, than a six-year-old. So if it turns out that he was six, I would expect him to regard the event as an aberrant one, and if he didn't, I'd want to explore the matter.

S   That will be a breach of neutrality. You'll be shifting from the role of therapist to the role of diagnostician.

Me   Not if I took the position that I wanted him to explore it. In fact, want isn't quite correct here, expect is more apt. And I'd expect him to do it for the sake of his coming to understand the event. I don't believe that my neutrality has to extend to issues like this.

S   Yes, I know. We've been over this ground already, and you are nothing if not stubborn. All right, I'll concede this, for the sake of this argument, because I think the question wasn't useful nonetheless. You could have initiated an exploration by making a simple, if speculative, remark, "I'm wondering if you regard the event as a normal piece of magical thinking." I'll bet he'll give his age in response to that interpretation.

Me   I won't take the bet. But if I made this interpretation, I'd be broaching the subject of normal, and I'm loathe to do that. It would be tactless at this point. So my direct question serves the interests of tact, you see.

S   We can't be sure of that. There's a sense in which any direct question can be tactless. For one thing, it can imply that the information should have been provided in the first place. Portnoy might take the question as an admonition that he was remiss in not giving his age. "I should have mentioned it," he might say (or think it to himself), "I'm not very good at recounting, and you are going to help me improve it." Or else he might say/think, "The age is important, else why would you have asked for it, and now I know that it is important." "I should have known it in the first place," he might also add.

Me   There's no need to rub it in. I'll concede that these messages may be communicated by interrogations and probes. It's quite unavoidable. But all communications carry unintended messages. Interpretations do it, too.

S   Not nearly to the same degree. When we say "I have this idea about your account," we aren't implying that P should have had that idea. The idea, after all, was ours. But when we ask for information, we are drawing attention to the fact that it was missing in the account. There's a big difference here. A direct question can be a criticism, if not a scolding; not an interpretation—if it's a good one, that is. Moreover, a question imposes a topic, an interpretation needn't—and a good one doesn't, inasmuch as it meshes with P's topic.

Me   Whoa, not so fast! When we say "I understand what you have in mind," aren't we criticizing P for not understanding it? Aren't we saying "You don't understand what you have in mind, and maybe you should, that's why I'm telling you"?

S   You have a point but it's not a strong one. When we say "I understand," we don't imply "and you don't." We might even be implying "and you do, too." That's what I meant by meshes. Moreover, saying, "How old were you?" doesn't imply that Portnoy didn't know how old he was, it only implies that he should have mentioned it. So we're talking about whether the remark blends with what P was thinking about. Portnoy wasn't thinking about his age at the time, and your asking for it therefore counts as an act of not blending in.

Me   But what if he thought that he had in fact mentioned his age, and he is now engaged in trying to understand the event. For me to blend in and be on the same wave length, I have to know it also. Now can I ask him how old he was?

S   No, but you can ask is he assuming that he had mentioned it. Strictly speaking, this isn't a direct question, it's an interpretation.

Me   But it doesn't strike me as any better than the direct question. "Didn't I mention my age?" Portnoy might say.

S   "I don't recall that you did."

Me   "Oh, shame on me! Here I've been assuming I did—which is just like me, to make unfounded assumptions. I feel awful."

S   "You feel I have criticized you, I take it."

Me   "And I defy you to convince me otherwise!" Anyway, by your own criteria it wasn't a good interpretation. Portnoy wasn't thinking about his assumption; it wasn't nearly on his mind.

S   Okay, then I take it back. I guess it was too confrontational. This leaves us with no way to inquire into his age.

Me   Then let me begin again, this time with my favorite rationale. Let's say I was distracted by the thought, "But how old was he?" The reason I had this thought is beside the point. I had it; it was plain distracting; I wanted to set the thought aside so that I could listen fully. That's why I asked.

S   In other words, you were not intending to promote any self-inquiry on Portnoy's part.

Me   My hands are clean. I am treating the matter purely as business.

S   Then the question is whether you should have been distracted—and since I think you shouldn't, I would go a step further and ask you to consider whether you were not being disingenuous. I let you off the hook before on this issue, but now I'm going to challenge you on it. Were your hands really clean?

Me   Why wouldn't they be?

S   Because you, too, have an unconscious (I happen to know it for a fact). You had the idea that Portnoy was engaged in magical thinking, an idea that for reasons—some professional and some personal—was forbidden, so you repressed it. But like all good unconscious ideas, it strove for expression and struggled with the defense. This struggle distracted you by making you anxious.

Me   Neat! So my distractedness was a neurotic symptom.

S   And you should have regarded it as such, by asking yourself why you were feeling it. That's bound to be more useful for Portnoy in the long run than asking him questions.

Me   Okay, then let me ask you a direct question: Why are you so darned strict with me?

S   That's not a direct question at all, it's an interpretation, so I am quite free to not answer it.

Me   Touché! Let's go get a bite to eat.

TWENTY-ONE
INTERPRETING, INTERVIEWING, AND LISTENING

You agree with me: Susan's "you're assuming that you mentioned your age" is no better than my "how old were you?" It might even be worse in that it uses an interpretation for ulterior purposes, and not to promote the therapeutic process. If we want to know his age, no matter for what reason, we can either ask for it or live with the frustration. Our choice may depend on where therapy is at. If this was indeed Portnoy's first narrative, we are better off avoiding anything that would smack of an interview. Your point that interpretations should be "proffered" in the spirit of, "Consider this, it might be helpful," is very useful here.

Our basic instruction has two sentences: (1) "I will listen and try to understand," and (2) "When I have something useful to say, I will say it." In our minds they should be connected. We are listening in order to understand, our criterion of "useful" is to share our understanding with the patient, and that's pretty much all. So even though we could recast our "are you assuming that you mentioned your age?" into a formally good interpretation—"If I understand you correctly, you have the belief that you have mentioned your age"—it hardly satisfies the criterion. There is little chance that Portnoy will take the remark as contributing to his work. At this stage of his therapy he is more likely to take it as the directive, if not also as the criticism, that was well-exemplified in our dialogue.

That compliment, and your comment that we needn't have been so harsh on ourselves, was welcome, as was your lesson on how we should have proceeded. Having made the error, not only do we have a way of fixing things, the repair can serve a valuable function in the therapy (yet another value that accrues to our emphasis on technique, which not only helps us avoid mistakes but helps us get out of them). When Portnoy reacted with embarrassment and self-reproach, we could have taken the opportunity to discuss the matter in a businesslike way. "I do understand your feelings," we might have said, and then gone on to say something about the unintended meanings that our interpretations would unavoidably have.

For it isn't uncommon, especially when therapy is young, for patients to feel that we have a hidden agenda. After all, they don't yet know what we mean by "useful," and they are likely to have some ideas of their own. What those ideas are—and it is vital that we get to know them—will often be revealed in responses to our interpretations. We should therefore listen for these responses and address them. Patients have to learn that we intend them to feel as free after an interpretation as they did before it (they should in fact feel freer). This is an ideal that can only be approached, and it's bound to take time. It won't always suffice to tell them that we never intend our interpretations as directives ("Whenever I make a remark or an observation you needn't feel called upon, as far as I am concerned, to make any response"). Moreover, we can also say the same for direct questions and probes, although it would border on the absurd ("Of course I don't have to respond," says P. "But why on earth would I not want to? After all, you must have a good reason for asking").

It's easy to lose sight of the fact that every communication carries multiple messages, many of which are unintended, and that in the emotionally charged arena of psychotherapy, these messages are likely to be emotionally charged. An interpretation that explains why P behaved cruelly toward his brother (e.g., "You have long believed that he usurped your position as your mother's favorite child") can serve to exonerate him, and, "You still feel envious of his position as her favorite child," can fault him. All interpretations, even those that aren't diagnostic, are liable to carry an additional burden of meaning that ranges from sanction to prohibition; they can imply advice, criticism, evaluation, blaming, and exonerating—and they do. Is there nothing we can do about it?

A behaviorist's answer would be: (1) reinforcements are indigenous to interventions; (2) not only is it futile to try and cancel them out, it flies in the face of therapeutic effectiveness. We can agree with (1), though only in principle, and we must respectfully disagree with (2). Without dismissing or minimizing them, we can be sensitive, if not vigilant, to the reinforcement ramifications, and articulate them to our patients at every opportunity. By so articulating we might make it clear to them that while these ramifications may be unavoidable in principle we don't intend them in fact. Accordingly, we must be prepared to follow up an interpretation by drawing attention to the unintended meanings it had. You offer these examples of how this can be done:

Example 1

P has been scolding us (for speaking in a pedantic way, say), and we've offered this interpretation: "What do you think of the possibility that a reason you are scolding me is that you want me to scold you in return for not having paid your bill?" "You're right," responds P, "I'm feeling guilty about that." Then, after a pause, he says, "Oh, I feel like such an ass!"

We now have two choices. We can interpret the feeling in respect to the bill paying, or we can interpret this as his reaction to our interpretation. The latter has all the priority.

Therefore we say, "You're feeling foolish, I take it, as if I actually did scold you." So P says, "I sure do!" pauses again and adds, "But I also still feel sore at you."

We again have two choices: we can treat this as narrative and say, "I think you feel hurt by my having raised the issue of the unpaid bill," or we can make the businesslike observation, "It's paradoxical; you scolded me because you wanted me to scold you, and then, when I pointed it out to you, it felt like I was actually doing it." Again, the latter has all the priority.

Example 2

We've made an interpretation—"What do you think of the possibility that you wanted your mother to cuddle you?"— and P has said, "That makes a lot of sense. Yes, the reason I was so nasty to her yesterday is I wanted her to cuddle me like she used to when I was little. So instead I let her have it. That explains it." Then, after a pause, he says, "I feel better now that I know that. She really deserved it, didn't she? Treats me like a stranger. You know something, I feel relaxed. My stomach is quiet for a change. You're a great therapist!"

Instead of basking in the praise, we make an interpretation that has two functions. One is to articulate and the other is to edify: "You feel warmly toward me right now for two reasons, I think. One is, I helped you understand why you were nasty to your mother yesterday. The other is, the explanation lets you off the hook; it means I'm taking your side against her—maybe also that I am excusing your behavior." (We might even go ahead and add, "In a sense I did what she didn't do—cuddle you.")

Example 3

"Women are so self-indulgent, and my wife is one of the worst. The minute I get home from work she wants to be treated like a queen; I should make her a cocktail, I should entertain her with stories from work, I should help her prepare supper. But haven't I been working all day? So of course I exploded when she got angry because I refused to set the table." "But I don't know why I exploded as terribly as I did," he adds, "I didn't mean to. It was just too much of a tantrum."

"You may have had some doubts over whether her anger might not have been justified," we say.

"Oh, very clever! You think I was feeling guilty, eh?"

Let's imagine that P now bursts into tears and says, "I'm crying because it's true what you said; I did feel guilty." Here's what we should now say: "I think you're crying for another reason, too, and it's that you're upset with me. For in pointing out that you may have felt she was justified, I seem perhaps to be taking her side against you."

What's noteworthy about these examples is that each of our initial interpretations can be faulted on the grounds that it actually carried the unintended message, or carried it too strongly. It's also worth noting that they are explanations, which raises the question of why they were given. There's no reason to infer that P wanted an interpretation. The issue, then, is one of timing. A poorly timed interpretation is likely to be fraught with unintended messages. Nevertheless, even well-timed ones can carry them, so the examples are useful.

Next you direct a little lecture at me, in respect to my complaints about being hobbled by your injunction against asking direct questions. You are not unsympathetic. You tactfully acknowledge that your position vis-à-vis interviewing is idiosyncratic. Most therapists do lots of it. The probe for feelings is practically their stock-in-trade and they frequently ask questions for information, it's such a natural way of fostering and furthering therapy. Questions not only help patients deepen their self-inquiry but they serve as tangible evidence that we are actively involved. Moreover, therapists might agree that an excessive reliance on them can transform a session into a clinical interview, but would contend that a judicious mix of questions and interpretations can prevent that from happening.

Your first response to this argument is to stress the passive position that questions and probes cast patients into, something that needn't be the case for interpretations. Then you point out that they cast us into the role of mentor and troubleshooter in a way that interpretations need not. Moreover, they also exert a subtle but significant influence on the nature of the interpretations that we give, for in the context of interviewing, our interpretations tend to become diagnostic explanations that treat patients more as an object than as a subject of inquiry. Finally, rarely asking direct questions, and virtually never probing, serves the valuable function of ensuring more active listening on our part, and this can help our patients discover for themselves the benefits of active and autonomous self-inquiry.

For the spirit of inquiry that accompanies extensive reliance on interviewing differs fundamentally from the spirit of inquiry that occurs when there is little, if any, reliance on it. It simply makes a profound difference to the way a typical session proceeds, when we rely entirely on what our patients choose to tell us. The special kind of passivity on our part that is embodied in working only with presented information engenders a special quality of participation on their part.

This is not to say that our passivity necessarily causes them to be more active, because it doesn't. Patients, too, often take a passive position. Not a more passive one than ours, of course, for they are speaking and feeling, while we listen and occasionally offer comments. However, the "special quality of participation on their part" refers to the fact that when patients are working in the interviewing format, they are likely to be less passive than when they aren't, but their activeness will never lead them into a relatively free kind of mentation, a kind of stream of consciousness that approximates the spirit of the free association mode. This, however, is not the case when the interviewing format is not being used; they will often slip naturally into that kind of mentation, without having been instructed to, and without the disadvantages of taking it as an externally imposed task. This will secure for them the vital benefits of free association, which include such therapeutically valuable features as a lowered level of self-consciousness and defensiveness, as well as an altered state of consciousness, that facilitates an openness to spontaneous and fleeting thoughts and feelings.

Moreover, it also allows and encourages a kind of listening to themselves, and of a kind that corresponds to the way we listen to them. For patients to listen to themselves, to observe their thoughts and feelings, is quite necessary; discoveries derive from such listening. Interviewing tends to prevent it. Interviewing can obviate the necessity for it. What can happen, paradoxically, is that because we are doing that work for them, patients don't have to listen to themselves. Interviewing can make them more passive than is optimal.

Since discussions of activity-passivity have a way of becoming theoretical and abstruse, we'll rest with the claim that the best place for our patients isn't at any of the extremes of activity-passivity's various dimensions, but fluctuating in between. When we ask questions and probe, when we use the interviewing mode for anything other than business matters, we are likely to push them toward one or the other extreme. Two guidelines are available to safeguard us against an undue use of direct questions: (1) *Question only toward an interpretation*; (2) *Be prepared to answer the counterquestion, "Why do you ask?"* In most instances, our answer to the counterquestion will contain an allusion to the interpretation, so the guidelines do overlap.

We must allow also for the answer, "Because I don't comprehend what you are saying or meaning to say." All other kinds of answers (e.g., "Because I believe the answer might be important"; "Because you are leaving out many of the details"; "Because I'm interested") are to be avoided as justifications for asking a direct question. This is a particularly important technical point, for the conduct of Psychotherapy at least.

What about questioning toward an interpretation? Here's where you take exception to Susan's argument. If I wanted to offer Portnoy the interpretation about magical thinking, and I figured it would be valid only if he were 4 at the time, then I had a justification for my question. Were he to ask me why I asked, I could say it was that I had an idea, and wanted to be sure that it stood a good chance of being correct, and then I'd go ahead and tell him what the idea was. In fact, I might have included the interpretation along with the question ("How old were you? I'm asking because . . ."). This is something that you often do, especially early in therapy. It's a way of saying, "I might be wrong, but . . ." Later on in therapy you might simply ask the question, but if a patient puts the counterquestion you always give the interpretation.

Next you examine how interviewing might work in Portnoy's case. Say we chose to inquire into the relief he experienced at not catching his mother between incarnations. "Why was it a relief?" we ask ("I wonder why it was a relief," is equivalent in directing him to examine the matter). This might be productive. It might also, however, not be. There's the possibility that he will simply shrug and say, "I haven't the faintest idea," and if he then says, "Why did you ask? What's your thought about it?" we are the one who's put in the position of actively exploring and uncovering.

Or say he had left the feeling out. We might be tempted to infer it with, "What do you think of the possibility that you felt relieved at that?" Where might this affect interpretation lead? "Yes, I did feel relief; I guess I didn't altogether want to catch her; I wonder why," and that's fine. But he might also say, "Can you tell me why I'd feel relieved," and we're back in the driver's seat.

What about the clarification question? You agree with Susan that "what do you mean 'between incarnations'?" isn't one. We couldn't claim it was ambiguous if he were to respond, "What's unclear about it?" The best we could claim is that it isn't the same as "in the process of incarnating herself." To be sure, he could correct himself and say, "Well, that's what I meant to say; I misspoke," and we could pursue it by saying, "I do understand that you meant to say 'in the process of incarnating herself,' but I have a hunch that you said it accurately, because. . . ." But what then was the point of the question?

Anyway, it wasn't a clarification question, it was a probing (of a fishing for significance kind) into something that rang dissonantly in our ears. We heard a "glitch," something "interesting," and we inquired into it. The best way to do this is with the speculative interpretation that I had suggested, and the gradual way that Susan and I carried it through was fine. You don't think we bungled it. We were pursuing a line of interpretation in a stepwise way.

You raise the intriguing possibility that I "heard" the glitch because I was listening right. You did not spot it, just as Susan didn't, perhaps because you were reading rather than listening. Good listening enables us to observe such glitches in a patient's narrative, which in turn enables us to do useful interpretive work.

Let's suppose the weak interpretation we had given him was incorrect and Portnoy corrected it: "No, I didn't want to see her in the act of transforming herself; that's not what I said; I wanted to see her between incarnations." We could acknowledge: "That's what I took it to mean; I gather it doesn't." But we shouldn't add, "What then does it mean?" There's no good reason to. He may go on to say what it means, or he may say, "I have no idea what it might mean," or he may drop the subject—it's up to him. We've been as active as we prudently should be, especially if the therapy is young.

Early in therapy, we should try to avoid questions of any sort, even when we need the answer for an interpretation that we have in mind. We should rather let the opportunity slip away than slip into the interviewing mode. After all, the interpreting mode, too, has its hazards when therapy is young and our patient's beliefs and attitudes toward our interpretations are unknown. Moreover, if this was the very beginning of Portnoy's therapy, then we wouldn't know why he's recounting that event. Was it his earliest memory and he believes that therapy is a process of systematic reminiscing? If that were the case, our best response would be to listen.

In any case, however, early in therapy we have to establish the role definition of the one who listens. We must bear in mind that we've told our patient that we would listen and try to understand, and inasmuch as we didn't say, "I will try to listen," we did promise to be good listeners (if not also good understanders). But no matter how good at it we were to begin with, we will have to learn it anew because, as you write, "The kind of listening that we do in our work is an acquired skill, if not an art." So here's your lesson on:

The Art of Listening

When we sit down with a patient, it should be with a wish to do little more than listen. We have no wish to talk (though we have no wish to be silent, either), we don't want to make interpretations (though we are glad to make them whenever necessary). In short, we have no urge to "do something," we are content to listen. In order to approximate this state of "desirelessness," it may be helpful to bear in mind that "How can I help my patient today?" isn't a helpful question to ask ourselves, unless our answer isn't, "I can be of help by listening to what he or she wants me to hear today." Without intellectual scruple or emotional qualm, our basic orientation toward each session is to hear what our patient wants us to hear.

What stands out for me from the Talmud lessons of my childhood is the recurring question, *"Mai komashmalon?"* I recall my teacher translating it as, "What does it mean?" and explaining that it directs us to unravel the multilayered meanings of the text. But *mai komashmalon?* literally translates to "What is here to be heard (or to be listened to)?" or "What is one supposed to hear?" In other words, we are enjoined to listen to the words rather than simply read them, the point being that knowledge and understanding flow from the listening mode, and this, I believe, is even more quintessential for therapy.

Learning to be a good listener takes knowing what makes a good story. A good beginning is one that grabs our attention, and the body of the story holds and builds it by creating anticipations so that we engage in a process of confirming and disconfirming them, and in this way participate actively. Story-tellers create surprises and suspenses, listeners relish them. Finally, the overall form of the story comes to a good closure; the ending connects with the beginning; the story's structure is simplified and unified because the false leads, the disconfirmed anticipations, split away. Listeners now understand the story, in the sense of apprehending its structure and seeing how the parts fit together; they can remember and review it for themselves.

Good listeners are active and resourceful in their anticipations but they also avoid short-circuiting. They modulate their need for confirmation-disconfirmation; the suspense is allowed full play and the anticipations remain alive. Quick confirmations could spoil the story. Tolerance for suspense—first cousin to tolerance for ambiguity—is essential, and too many anticipations and hypotheses can spoil things. There's a requisite balance between actively figuring things out and passively taking them in. Good listening requires hearing everything, and this requires a measure of passive receptivity.

When he wrote about free-floating attention, Freud advocated a kind of listening that is closer to the passive than the active. His advice is usually taken to mean a kind of reverielike state in which we drift along with the patient without much concentration. In this way we allow our associations free rein, and this allows ideas and hypotheses to come freely to mind. At times this mode can be fruitful, but only at times.

A useful aspect of this advice is the freedom from pressure that free-floating attention entails. For no matter where along the dimension of active-passive we are, we must listen with ease and equanimity. A sense of effortless attention and calm interest should be our goal, even while we're listening to narrative that is strained and uncalm, and we are emotionally empathizing with it.

The way we listen to music might be useful, and not just as analogy. Naive listeners hear only the melody. Even they, however, are being affected by the bass line, as well as the harmonies and rhythms. Trained listeners hear them and can discern their significance. Similarly, experienced therapists hear not just the verbal account but also the tone of voice, choice of words, use of metaphors and idioms, changes in rhythm and tempo. Not that they listen *for* them (though they occasionally do that in order to confirm a hunch) but they listen *to* them. While it is humanly impossible to be constantly on the alert for all cues, it isn't impossible to be open to them. The passive modes of listening are usually best suited to this task.

So we must listen actively and passively, to the music as well as the message. We try to maintain a balance between the different modes, judging when the balance should be shifted in one direction or the other. Notwithstanding the fact that all of this is far from easy to do, we have to do it with ease.

There are two criteria for good listening: remembering and understanding. There is nothing that convinces patients that we were listening more than our having remembered what they told us. Not everything is open to understanding, but, in principle at least, it is subject to recall—and the experienced therapist remembers. I would go so far as to propose the hypothesis that when a narrative has been well listened to, it is fully recalled.

It can be impressive how well an experienced therapist remembers the contents of a session, and every aspiring one has had the awful experience of having totally forgotten a session that took place an hour before. But there occur, even in the accounts of seasoned therapists, significant distortions and elisions, so a sense of conviction that we have accurately remembered cannot be fully relied upon. There are wide individual differences in ability to remember. Experience is a factor, and our mode of listening mediates it. If our listening was active, if appropriate schemas were at work, then what we heard will be better remembered. However, if there was too much confirmation-disconfirmation, and our listening was without a balance of passive taking in, then much will be forgotten and only that which was relevant to our hypotheses will be remembered.

Patients have feelings about our ability to remember. At best they take it as evidence that we care, but it's often not so simple. It's not uncommon for them to react with uneasiness, if not dread, for our heightened recall may mean that we're paying too close attention, which in turn means we're getting too close.

They also assume that we won't remember what they tell us, particularly details such as names of people they mention infrequently. While this is a fair assumption, it can be carried to extreme. Some take pains to remind us who the person is ("I was with John, he's my brother-in-law," or "John, the guy who works in my office"). This can reflect the assumption, if not also the wish, that we won't remember. (Sometimes it also serves to avoid the feelings that would be evoked if we had to ask, "Who is John?") Still, it's worth bearing in mind that our ability to recall what they tell us is likely to be extraordinary. Patients cannot be expected to realize that our way of listening enhances our ability beyond its everyday levels, so a degree of astonishment and doubt is quite appropriate (and I don't hesitate to tell them that it isn't as difficult for a therapist to remember details as they might suppose).

There can a temptation on our part to show off our memory. This is no different from a desire to impress patients with our powers of understanding (both are apt to be based on a need to demonstrate our potency). Related to this is an unwillingness to ask about something that we've forgotten, for it may betray the fact. Awkward situations can arise ("Oh, you're mixed up, I'm talking about my brother-in-law Peter, not John who works in my office"). They can be avoided if we don't hesitate to ask when we feel uncertain. (If I find that I repeatedly forget who a certain person in my patient's life is, or about a certain event, then I suspect there's a reason for it. No matter where it resides, and it's not always with the patient, the reason is worth uncovering.)

Then there's the feedback: how we respond while we listen. Ordinarily, listeners use a variety of interjections to indicate that they are listening, and to encourage the speaker to continue. We say "yes" and "I see," we grunt and "uh-huh," and there are the nods, smiles, shrugs, and the rest. For Psychotherapy, I advocate eschewing them. Yes, all of them! I am convinced that they are unnecessary. In my experience, the two criteria of having listened, remembering and understanding, are sufficient; the signals and gestures, in subtle but substantial ways, steer and guide; they selectively reinforce; they are actually quite directive.

Impassive listening isn't easy to cultivate, it takes practice as well as conviction. The same holds for patients: even if they know that we're listening closely, it may be difficult for them to accept and tolerate our impassivity. For these reasons, many therapists feel that it just isn't worth it. Furthermore, not only does it raise the specter of the machine-therapist but it seems to deny the fact that communication—that most basic of human needs—needs a range of gratifications. All of us need the signals which confirm that we are communicating and being listened to. Nevertheless, my conviction here is strong: all of this may be true for ordinary communication and for ordinary conversation, but Psychotherapy isn't ordinary.

When I first began listening impassively I did so with misgivings. It felt artificial to me. I wasn't sure that I could do it well and that my patients would tolerate it. So it came as something of a revelation that I could do it well enough, that most of my patients accepted it, and that it seemed to make a significant and substantial difference. They still spoke to me but they spoke also to themselves. At times, it was as if part of them was listening in the same way that I was listening. At such times I sometimes had the uncanny sense that there were three of us in the room.

Now, it's easy to suppose that patients, when they are faced with an impassive, nondirecting therapist, will fall into a detached kind of monologuing. But that needn't happen at all, and most of the time it just doesn't. Our presence remains integral and our participation remains vital. The fact that we are listening guarantees that they, too, are listening—and the fact that they are listening can vitalize their therapeutic process.

TWENTY-TWO
TIMING

Having learned how to break our silence, we now have to learn when to. This won't be easy, for timing is tough to teach, in anything but the most general terms, and we're forewarned not to expect much help from you. We will have to rely on our intuition and clinical experience (in conjunction with our supervision). But you needn't be so despairing; your lesson gives us a number of concrete suggestions, and the timing exercise is instructive.

Our chief timing criterion can easily enough be framed in the context of our conception of the therapeutic process: we speak when we judge that the process might benefit from something we could say. In practice, though, rarely is this judgment easy to make. We also have to decide what intervention might best serve the purpose, and while in the majority of instances, it will be a good interpretation, it's easy to lose sight of the fact that interpretations may be construed as bearers (and barers) of insight, but attaining insight isn't synonymous with the therapeutic process. Insightful discovery can be a result or outcome of the process, but the process itself denotes our patient's principal way of working. Thus, our fundamental timing question, "How does interpreting relate to the therapeutic process?" boils down to: "How does our principal way of working relate to our patient's?"

A fair summary of today's lesson might be the following. Timing would be much easier if:

- There was no real difference between patients needing an intervention for their sake and their therapeutic work needing one for its sake.
- We could readily distinguish between supervising the therapeutic process and participating in it.

- We never had to worry about interpreting prematurely.
- We never sensed that an interpretation was required when we had no inkling of what was in and on our patient's mind.
- Our chief criterion for speaking up was that we understood something a bit better than our patient was understanding it at the moment.
- We never had to worry about missing an opportunity to say something useful.
- We didn't have to decide what aspect of our patient's narrative to address, and therefore what should be the content of our interpretation.
- We were never in the position of knowing that a particular interpretation was needed, but we knew that its form was going to be bad.
- Patients never said anything that strained our credulity.
- We didn't have to worry about reinforcing a patient's poor performance.
- We never had a good interpretation in mind when it wasn't timely to proffer it.

After dutifully summarizing your remarks about these issues, we'll do the timing exercise.

You ask us to imagine P speaking about his long-standing hostility toward his brother, and doing it well; he is speaking openly, freely, and feelingfully, reminiscing and reconstructing, and sticking to the subject. Now we imagine ourselves having an insight into P's hostility or spotting something relevant to it that he was overlooking. We are to imagine even further that we have reason to believe that were we to share our insight with him, or draw his attention to what he was overlooking, P's hostility might diminish and his relationship with his brother improve. The question is: Are we going to do it? The answer: apparently not. How come? We don't have the requisite reason. The therapeutic process was proceeding optimally and *it* had no need for an intervention.

The distinction we have to make is between P needing our intervention and his therapeutic process needing it, and I, for one, doubt if I would ever feel comfortable making it. Susan, on the other hand, has no problem here. She thinks the distinction is a vital one. She only doubts whether she could make it in practice.

You point out that not only is the distinction a difficult one to make in practice but it flies in the face of the principal criterion that many of your colleagues use—which happens to be the criterion that I find so congenial. It pivots on the patients and on their readiness to comprehend and apprehend. The critical consideration is their state of mind as reflected in the condition of their resistance and transference; when these conditions are right, the time is right. Accordingly, I (and most of my teachers) would draw no distinction between whether P could use the intervention and whether he needed it. The latter I would take for granted; if he can use it, he needs it.

That, of course, isn't the criterion you want us to give priority to. Whether P can use the interpretation is, at best, a secondary consideration, and when we say that P needed it, in this respect, we must actually mean that his therapeutic process needed it. The efficacy of this criterion, you concede, is open to question, and it's one of those guidelines that might look good on paper but won't work well in practice. Your clinical experience has convinced you, however, that it can have a great efficacy and contribute substantially to P's well-being.

So what we're going to do with our insight is let P arrive at it himself. After all, if he is working so well, we can reasonably expect him to achieve this insight (or arrive at others of equal value, perhaps insights that haven't occurred to us), and if our expectation is realized, then his achievement would be all the more effective. His relationship with his brother may benefit more from an insight arrived at by himself rather than one received from us.

The ground on which we base this hypothesis is the familiar one of changes in our patients' behavior and experience being a natural consequence of the naturally functioning therapeutic process. The process is therefore what has to command our attention; when it falters or breaks down, it's then that our insights and observations and formulations (i.e., our good interpretations) can be useful.

So if P experiences an impasse, he blocks, say, or grows guarded, feels a twinge of fear or pang of anxiety, it is then that we can "do something" with our insight and observation, and usefully intervene with an interpretation of this form:

> I have an idea why you blocked (why your thoughts
> drifted away from what you were talking about, why you
> feel guarded or anxious). It's because you came face to
> face with a painful thought about your hostility toward
> your brother, or you might have caught a glimpse of
> something about it that you've been overlooking.

As it stands, this interpretation is allusive and vague. We should be in a position to suggest what the painful thought was and what P was overlooking. But you mention parenthetically that you might say the above and then pause to see whether he knew what the painful thought was, or whether he sees what he'd been overlooking. You might even commit the error of asking him whether he knew what you had in mind. And why would you?

> As with most pieces of poor technique, I never intend to avoid them
> entirely. Calling them "bad" in these letters usually implies only
> that we should use such techniques rarely. "Do you know what I'm
> thinking (or referring to)?" needn't be too different from, "Do you
> understand what I'm saying?" In any case, however, if P said that
> he didn't, I'd go on to tell him. An interpretation of that form is likely
> to be more effective than one that says, "I think I know why you
> are hostile," or, "I see something you're overlooking," because P
> can learn something about himself that will not only benefit his re-
> lationship with his brother but also enhance his work in therapy.

Back to our chief criterion: there are difficulties with it. One has to do with the fact that improving the therapeutic process is always possible, in principle, and therefore so is justifying an interpretation on these grounds. Whenever we feel the impulse to offer one, we can too easily persuade ourselves that the interpretation might improve our patient's work, and that judgment is difficult to prevail against.

A second problem is the potential reinforcement effect of applying the criterion too routinely. There's a good probability that patients will notice how we offer them help whenever they aren't speaking freely. It doesn't take much acumen to learn that one has only to falter and grope, or even slip into a guarded posture, and "useful" things will be heard. So if we speak only when patients aren't working well, they have an additional incentive to avoid it. This might constitute another timing consideration, and could be formulated in the terms of our main criterion in the following way: "I offered the interpretation because the therapeutic process needed it because withholding it would have been negatively reinforcing." But we're sure you'd agree that this makes matters so elastic as to be quite useless. The reason we think you'd agree is you several times make the point that our central timing criterion can only be regarded as the principal one, it can by no stretch be the exclusive one.

The stage of therapy is another one. Interventions, and not just interpretations, change their function as therapy develops. During the beginning phases they can serve purposes that become quite unnecessary, and even gratuitous, during the later ones. For instance, at the beginning, patients have to learn the way we participate, the way we listen empathically but objectively, and formulate understanding without judgment and criticism, and we need to make interventions and offer interpretations in order to help them learn that.

Another lesson they might have to learn is that there will be little real conversation or dialogue between us. So we'll have to time our interventions in such a way that they do learn it (and this will also actualize our own freedom of choice). We do it in practice by calling attention to their efforts to solicit remarks from us, and by discussing their reactions to our nonresponsiveness. (That would have to be done in the business mode, of course, which suits me fine, though Susan would rather always do it with interpretations.)

There are further ways that the stage of therapy can make a difference. Early in therapy, especially during the trial period, we must

I. H. Paul

participate more frequently. But after that we have to establish our role as "supervisor" of the therapeutic process, and therefore we need to draw back from participation. If this wasn't hard enough, once that role has been established, we can occasionally lapse from it and participate as a kind of partner. We do this in the interests of variety, if not also in the interests of vitalizing the therapeutic process, and we do it by occasionally allowing ourselves to offer an insight or discovery for its own sake (and we thereby define ourselves as the one who also makes discoveries). But we do it not so much to show patients how it's done, nor to lead them to discoveries, but more in the spirit of active participation.

So, "Look here, I've noticed something about your hostility toward your brother," we might say to P, and say it in the spirit of its being intriguing and helping us understand things about him. But we are cautioned to do this only on occasion, for this kind of participation can have undesirable consequences (fostering, for instance, a "symbiotic transference"), and therefore has to be kept in balance. As therapy progresses, however, our participation can increase; more of our interpretations can be made for their own sake, but the ubiquitous transference and role definition implications have to be borne in mind throughout.

Our chief timing criterion throughout the course of the therapy remains supervision of the therapeutic process, and it is hobbled by the lack of reliable guidelines for assessing the condition of the process. Certain of them—like those that pertain to disruptions of speech flow, and deflections, diversions, and changes of subject— can be spelled out objectively enough, but they have limited reliability as well as utility. If we relied on them mechanically, we might shortchange the value and quality of the stream of consciousness. We have little choice, then, but to be subjective, and fall back on intuition in order to judge when a patient is "working well."

Moreover, and more often, we'll judge that the process requires us to say something, except we have no idea what on earth to say (an intervention is called for, there's no ambiguity about it, but we have none to offer). For this reason it's a good idea to have an interpretation or two in hand, either derived from earlier in the session or from previous ones (and also from what we've rehearsed between them). This, incidentally, resolves a paradoxical proposition in respect to listening well: we can listen better when we have an interpretation in mind inasmuch as we aren't worried about being caught short—so we're calm, poised, secure in the knowledge that if we had to say something, we have something to say.

We are going to be more prone to intervene prematurely than fail to intervene when it's necessary: that's your guess. Your recommendation in respect to guarding against such prematurity is for us to take a flexible and permissive position toward what a well-functioning therapeutic process ought to look like. A broad and liberal conception, you believe, is likely to be more prudent than a narrow and stringent one. We'll have to learn to be both lenient and conservative in judging how well our patients are working; we'll have to try and give them enough "space." But we will also take comfort in your claim that good interpretations, even when they are poorly timed, aren't likely to spoil the therapeutic process (it isn't such a fragile thing). In general, then, we should worry less about poor timing than about poor interpretations.

Moreover, our patients will teach us what the right timing is going to be for them. Each therapeutic process, after all, is distinctive, if not idiosyncratic, so our timing criteria cannot be uniform across patients. Some will require more frequent interventions, others less; some will require interventions to help break their silences, others won't.

Furthermore, an interpretation can be invalid and still be timely. It's wrong to hold to its validity and lay all the onus on timing. If patients disavow an interpretation, they may be correct. For us to assume that it was merely badly timed runs the risk of smugness. This is not to say that an invalid interpretation cannot be efficacious. But we must never become ego involved in our interpretations, always bearing in mind that we proffer them to patients for their use.

Now, whenever we sense that the therapeutic process requires us to say something, we have two options: one is an interpretation, the other is a redundant remark. With no good interpretation in mind, we are limited to redundancy (merely paraphrasing what the patient has said). This might be better than nothing, and chances are often good that we'll add something significant to our remark, something that turns out to be useful. It could be little more than a choice of words and still would make a difference.

Another timing issue is when patients recount things that strain our credulity. It's important to keep from defining ourselves as the skeptic. Taking at face value what our patients are taking at face value is prudent, and good timing requires a sensitivity to those moments when they are ready to experience some doubt, when they are prepared to reconsider the condition of their memory.

In addition to asking ourselves whether the therapeutic process now needs an interpretation, we ask whether the interpretation we could now give is a good enough one. Is it going to be sufficiently succinct, too diagnostic, too deep? These questions touch on formal requirements of different types of interpretation. For example, self-image interpretations are best if succinct and unencumbered with explanation (e.g., "You see yourself as a person who mustn't be hostile to those who are close to him"), interpersonal interpretations have to be expressed in an impartial way (e.g., "What do you think of the possibility that you have old and unresolved feelings of rivalry with your brother?"), and transference interpretations work best when they are fully articulated but divided into graded parts. Our timing decision will sometimes be made on the basis of how readily we are able to formulate the appropriate interpretation.

The timing question can therefore be further refined as: Does the content lend itself to an interpretation that I could now give in its optimal way? Of course, what's the point in thinking about such formulations, we might wonder, if it was not something that we were prepared to say aloud? Why have it in mind in the first place? But that's an unrealistic position to take. The formal features of the particular interpretation we have in mind will often determine whether we keep a particular formulation there.

This seems like a good time to stop discussing timing and start the timing exercise. It consists of a narrative, and our task is to intervene in a timely way. Since P won't "hear" our interventions, we have to proceed as if we hadn't made any, and therefore they have to be independent of each other. It would also be unfair to read ahead and base our interventions on what he's going to say. All we know to begin with is that P is a 20-year-old student, Henry is his 17-year-old brother, and therapy is fifteen sessions old.

The Timing Exercise

> I have to tell you about another scene I had with Henry yesterday. [pause]

We've evidently heard about these scenes, and P is going to describe yesterday's. During this pause we might have the impulse to encourage P to get on with the account with a gesture that lets him know we're interested in hearing it. We will naturally resist this impulse. We might also want to address his "have to," by saying, "I take it you feel under some compulsion to tell me about it." This isn't the time to do it. Better to store the "have to" in our memory and return to it if and when we can make an interpretation that began with, "I think I understand now what you meant when you said 'I have to tell you about the scene'."

> It beats me why. God only knows what I was after!
> [silence]

Why this silence? Is he thinking about what he was after? Is he waiting for us to inquire into it? "You felt that you were after something, I take it," is possible here, but Susan thinks it's gratuitous in this context, and that P will take it as the direct question "What were you after?" I agree. I myself would find it hard not to comment on his "God only knows." It suggests that not only is he helpless to know what he was after but so am I.

Your intervention at this point is a combination of ours: "If I understand you correctly, you feel that you were after something, but what it was is a complete mystery." You're not sure this is the right time to say it, though, so you would probably hold off.

I just couldn't stop myself, I guess.

Here is where a defense interpretation could already be made ("You're disavowing responsibility!"), but it shouldn't be made; it would be too flagrant a confrontation. Surprisingly, you do not agree. P has given us an opening: it's his "I guess." It suggests that he has some doubts, and you would want to articulate them by saying, "I take it you aren't altogether sure you couldn't stop yourself." At one level, you are merely saying, "Do I understand you correctly that by saying 'I guess' you are expressing some doubts?" But at another level you're suggesting that P may have an inkling that he is disavowing responsibility. This way of dealing with defense is neither confrontational nor diagnostic, and it bears importantly on the question of timing.

There's something weird about the thing, I get so caught up in it, so . . . so out of control. [silence]

It isn't good technique to interrupt a narrative, but this one has not gotten off the ground—and if anything, it's P who is interrupting it. In any case, the therapeutic process isn't going well, so an intervention might be useful. Susan thinks he is again disowning responsibility, and the only interpretation she'd be willing to give is one that said as much. Inasmuch as it would have to be diagnostic, she is willing to keep it to herself.

I personally think there might be value in drawing a connection between his feeling "weird" and "out of control." So, in a half-clarifying half-interpreting way, I'd say, "Are you saying it felt weird because you were so out of control?" This, it seems to me, is an intervention that satisfies our main timing criterion, and P might find it useful, too.

I was writing my English paper and Henry put on a record, one of his beloved Brandenburg Concertos, and it

disturbed me, so I wanted him to turn it off. But instead
of just asking him, I yelled. And then I went into my
regular act, calling him an inconsiderate bastard, and
selfish, only thinking of himself, and everything. As if he
were living by himself, off in his little ivory tower.
[pause]

"Instead of with you," completes the thought, and my inclination
would be to do it. Susan's isn't, and she faults me for participating too actively in the therapeutic process. But isn't it worth helping him explore why instead of just asking Henry he yelled? Isn't
the context of his going into his "regular act" worth elaborating?
I would take it for granted that P wanted to figure out why he re-
acts to Henry with such hostility, and that the reason he paused
here is that this issue is relevant to it.

You, too, would speak up here, but instead of saying, "instead
of with you," which is, after all, a bit redundant, you would comment on his "off in his little ivory tower." For one thing, you'd
want to make sure you understood it in the same way that P intended it. If this was the first time he had used this metaphor,
you'd ask the clarifying question, "Do you mean that sarcasti-
cally, or is it something you wish you did, too?" I like your intervention better than mine because it takes P's words seriously,
if not literally, and I think it's always a good idea for us to do
that.

The whole scene was predictable, no different than it's
been for years now. Actually, it's more than a scene, it's a
one-act play with three scenes. Scene One: he argues,
"The door was shut; I didn't know you were working; I
didn't realize the music was so loud." When I don't let up
and scream at him for being thoughtless and everything,
he goes into Act Two: he apologizes, says he's sorry,
looks contrite, ashamed. Then, when that doesn't do me
any good and I keep on letting him have it, he sulks.
That's Act Three. He tells me I should stop picking on
him so much; starts feeling sorry for himself. [pause] He
cowers. [pause] Of course, that only makes me more
furious. God only knows why! [silence]

"Of course" implies that there's no mystery here—except only for God, of course. There might be value in articulating this, it's the second time he's used the expression. Susan worries that we'd be setting ourselves up as something of a God if we spoke at all at this juncture. She thinks his "God only knows" is a warning to us, and it would put us in a paradoxical position even to say so. I see her point.

Your comments at this juncture center around the content of the narrative, and you're using the time to formulate strong interpretations—not to be given now but possibly later (the only intervention you would consider for this silence is the standard silence-breaking one, "What are you thinking?"). The "act" that P described has all of the earmarks of ritualized enactment perhaps of mortal combat, or of sex, perhaps a combination of the two. "When that doesn't do me any good" is suggestive of sexual frustration, and his reaction to Henry's "cowering" suggests that he sees it as an accusation.

> So I go into my humiliation routine—he's a weakling, a nebbish, a baby. I don't have to describe that act to you again, do I? [silence]

This is probably a rhetorical question (it's session 15, after all). "I take it you don't want to," is nevertheless timely enough.

> I can be such a bastard to Henry. He gets me so fucking mad. [pause] You know, he was right in a way, because he didn't know that I was working; and he did shut the door; and the music wasn't all that loud. But I couldn't accept any kind of apology from him. [pause]

We note the "couldn't" and the sense of helplessness (perhaps it's impotency) that he reports. We could interpret this now only if P were thinking about it during the pause, for otherwise it would not have been done with an empathic interpretation. This touches on the timing criterion that asks: "Does the interpretation that I could now give have an appropriate form?" In this instance it would probably take on diagnostic features.

And he doesn't fight for his rights, anyway. Right away
he starts in apologizing and sulking. God, I can't stand
that! Because . . . [pause]

"You wish he was more manly; maybe you wanted to see whether
this time he would be different." That's Susan's interpretation, and
I think it's good. It alludes to the issue of potency without at the
same time being allusive. But you have no comments at this juncture, so you'd probably think that this interpretation was premature.

Because I can't do that—apologize, or anything like that.
I . . . I wish I. . . .

"Could?" completes the thought but we are cautioned against mind
reading. There's the significant difference between supervising and
participating, and the latter should be reserved for strong interpretations.

You know, I think I actually wanted to. I wanted to make
up and leave him alone. But I couldn't control myself.
[pause]

"You felt powerless to stop hurting him," is a timely interpretation in our opinion (Susan would say "impotent" but I think it's a
bit presumptuous of her).

Your preference would be to address his "leave him alone," because you have a hunch that he's struggling with a wish to draw
Henry close to him, which conflicts with a wish to destroy him.
In fact, you composed the transcript with that wish and conflict
in mind (and therefore in P's mind, so your calling it a hunch is
somewhat suspect). But since you included other conflictful wishes
as well—namely, that Henry was stronger than he, or was his older
brother, or his sister—and you might want to offer one of them in
the form of a strong interpretation, you'd be inclined to wait and
see which of them could usefully be proffered.

You know something, I think I did want to make up, but I
didn't want to leave him alone. That makes no sense,

does it? I mean, I could see apologizing for bugging him,
but I couldn't stand the idea of not bugging him. Something makes me have to beat up on him. It's almost as if I
have to prove something. [silence]

Consequently, if we'd been listening well and formulating hypotheses as we listened, we'd now be prepared to offer a good strong
interpretation. The time feels right for it, for the account seems finished; P has repeated the idea of his having to prove something,
and he's fallen silent. Under these conditions even an invalid interpretation can be useful. In fact, it might even be more useful than a
valid one, in that P could actively invalidate it by providing one
that is valid. (Moreover, it defines us not as the one who understands
but as one who tries to understand, and that's even better.)

Susan therefore opts for raising the theme of homosexuality
here (and we did not read ahead!) because she thinks that "bugging" is close enough to "buggering," and Henry has been depicted
as having homosexual traits. "I wonder what you think of the possibility that one of the things you want to prove is that Henry isn't
homosexual," is how she'd put it.

My preference would be to settle for, "I have a hunch that the
'something' that makes you have to beat up on him is a wish that
he would be stronger than you and beat up on you." And you would
venture, "What do you think of the possibility that what you feel
you have to prove is that you are really his older brother."

He's only three years younger than me but it feels more
like ten, he's so. . . . He's so weak. Such a baby. I've got
strong feelings about that.

Now can come: "I have a hunch that at some level you wish he
was your older brother and you were his age."

He has no friends, except for Albert, who is just like him
in many ways. They're not into sports, just music. They
don't go out with girls. They're probably screwing each
other, for all I know.

"It isn't clear to me whether you believe they are or not."

No, I didn't mean to say that. I don't really believe it. But they sure behave like homosexuals, and that bothers me. [silence]

Okay, where do we stand now? Is it time to suggest that he has some concerns and conflicts over his homosexuality? You don't think so. It feels tactless, you say. On the other hand and by your own convictions, P's anxiety might be signaling a conflict that is threatening to become conscious, and we might want to help resolve that conflict and reduce his anxiety (it might be doable if we could formulate an interpretation in the form of, "It bothers you because it brings to your mind your own worries and doubts about your homosexual leanings," for which we'd have to have some basis derived from previous sessions).

But you don't judge that P is all that anxious. This silence might well be a contemplative one, during which he is trying to figure out why the idea of Henry being homosexual bothers him. If so, allowing him to do it himself could be useful for the therapeutic process.

What bothers me most of all is how weak he is, how vulnerable, and also how closed in he gets. I mean, he comes home and goes straight into his room, like he just wants to be by himself. With his damned records. If he was at least into books, into studying for school, if he was a brainy kid, or something like that. But he isn't. I mean, what's going to become of him? He's probably not going to get into college. [pause] When my folks aren't around any more, who is going to take care of him? [long silence]

Not only the long silence, but the fact that it's the end of the transcript makes this the obvious occasion for an intervention. We have plenty of choices—perhaps too many. Still, P's main concern is quite evident: the task of taking care of Henry will fall on his shoulders and, "Instead of taking good care of him, you're afraid you'll destroy him." That interpretation would almost count as a weak one. Stronger ones might suggest that he felt responsible for Henry's weakness, that he destroyed him when they were little, perhaps. That would be my choice.

Susan thinks P might have a long-standing fantasy that Henry wasn't his real brother; this might tie in with the wish that Henry was his sister, so she would try for a line of interpretation that led in that direction.

You, however, would seriously consider the option of allowing P to contemplate the question in the meditative mode—and if you wanted him to meditate aloud, you'd quietly say, "What are you thinking?"

TWENTY-THREE

DIAGNOSING AND "HOW DOES THIS THERAPY WORK?"

That psychotherapy in general, and Psychotherapy in particular, isn't the treatment of choice for all prospective patients, goes without saying. How we assess P's suitability for Psychotherapy is a question we are now ready to tackle because the answer is now simple: if he is willing to accept the conditions of our therapy, if he can tolerate its strictures, its constraints, and also work productively within its format, then P is probably qualified for Psychotherapy. This criterion is wonderfully circular but also eminently pragmatic. If P can stand doing without advice and feedback, if he can sustain a self-directed monologue, then. . . .

We arrive at this determination by giving him a trial run. Even when they aren't defined as such, the first sessions of Psychotherapy are a trial period. Not only are we assessing his qualifications but P is assessing ours. Therefore (and despite your having written this several times already), we must give him a good sample of how we work: the way we listen, the way we understand, the way we interpret; and some of our interpretations (some of them should be strong ones) are given for this purpose.

At the same time we are assessing P's qualifications, so we listen not only in the standard way but in a diagnostic one. We listen for signs of thought disorder, of borderline features, and of suicidal ideation. Still, the question of whether therapy will do him more harm than good may remain, and it isn't easy to answer. To be sure, we can answer it on psychodiagnostic grounds, but this may be little more than the other side of the same coin. The two ways of approaching the question are conflated insofar as we necessarily make the diagnosis on the basis of P's capabilities for self-directedness, for psychological mindedness, for impulse control and frustration tolerance, and the like.

Nevertheless, we can approach the question diagnostically in two ways: (1) by diagnosing P's personality and pathology, looking out for psychotic features, clinical depression, debilitating anxiety, as well as for symptom type and severity, and (2) by diagnosing P's life situation and reality problems, how urgent they are and how debilitating. These two sets of considerations will converge on the assessment of whether he is suitable either for psychotherapy in general or for Psychotherapy in particular.

You prefer to approach the question in terms of P's qualifications. You listed some of them in your second letter, in today's letter you extend the list and give us their diagnostic implications.

- P must talk; if he is severely depressed, or organically impaired, he won't be able to.
- P must talk openly and freely; if he is too paranoid or too fearful, or inhibited and constricted, it will mitigate against openness; if he is manic then his talk will be driven instead of open, and if he is schizophrenic it may be too chaotic.
- P must attend regular sessions; if his character is such that this isn't possible (he is too immature, too poorly integrated, too impulse ridden, too prone to acting out), he won't be able to.
- P may be too anxious, or his symptoms too urgent; the anxiety and symptoms may be too debilitating and exhaust too much of his resources for normal functioning (there are therapies that deal with anxiety and with symptoms in a direct and focused way).
- P's life situation must not be so dire that it has great priority. Psychotherapy takes time; P must have the time (there are therapies designed to help him resolve reality issues).

These determinations properly belong to supervision, so there's no point in examining their specifics in clinical detail. Instead, we can take a broad approach to the diagnostic question, and it's a conservative one. So long as P accepts the treatment, we should be loath to declare him unfit for it. We should proceed on the conviction that Psychotherapy—with modifications of one sort or another—is appropriate for a wide range of prospective patients, and give it and P the benefit of the doubt. For one thing, there is no reason to believe that Psychotherapy will harm him. For another, we will be able to tell whether it is harming or being of no avail, and we can readily relinquish some aspects of the method and introduce measures that are supportive and mentorly. Our form of therapy, like others, can be modified in ways that are appropriate and responsible.

In good free association style, we go from the question of diagnosing suitability to the question of diagnosing in general, and we get a lesson on its perils and pitfalls, which leads us somehow into the question of how Psychotherapy works in the first place.

The Perils and Pitfalls of Diagnosis

We are better at diagnosing than at treating. If our patients could be cured by figuring out what's wrong with them, our work would be easier: we listen to understand, and when we've understood, we share our understanding with them; we "disclose them to themselves," and they get better. But the unfortunate fact is, diagnosis, even when it's by the patients themselves, is not the cure.

This dismal observation was the basis of the dismal slogan, *"Insight is Not Enough,"* which led to radical modifications in psychoanalysis, if not the abandonment of its methods. Many of us who refused to accept that view fell back on the position that if insight was not enough then it wasn't enough of an insight.

But isn't psychotherapy an extended diagnosis? It's what many teachers teach. Erwin Singer, for example, asserts that diagnosis is a protracted process and therapy becomes "paradoxically" a diagnostic investigation "in which the inner situation of the patient unfolds in ever-sharpened forms," and, "equally paradoxically," the diagnostic process is in itself the therapeutic process. "If the aim of therapy is the patient's gaining insight and knowledge concerning the nature of his existence," writes Singer, "his

I. H. Paul

profound grasp of his 'diagnosis' is synonymous with a good deal of cure."[13]

This is a claim that isn't easy to dispute. Isn't every piece of repair work predicated on a piece of troubleshooting diagnosis? "We will work together on diagnosing your problems," we say to P, "and this will be therapeutic; it will in effect constitute the therapy," and there's nothing wrong with that so long as (1) the work is done by P, because we are dealing with healing rather than with doctoring, and healing requires no healers, though they can be helpful in providing the optimal conditions for healing to occur, and removing the roadbocks and anti-healing factors; (2) we say "Disclose thyself!" rather than "Diagnose thyself!" It might boil down to that.

Let's switch over to the dialogue mode and examine this issue together. Let's have P, in an early session, put the question, "How does therapy work?" What's your reply?

Us   "I don't actually know."

U   "But do you not have some ideas about it, some theory?"

Us   "I don't believe it would be useful for you to know my theory."

U   "How can you be sure? What makes you say that?"

Us   "It's no different from your doctor saying, 'It will not help you with your headaches for me to tell you my theory of how aspirin works.'"

U   "But your theory of therapy might be of some use to me; it could influence my work and also enhance my motivation. So you may choose to share it with me." How would you frame your answer?

Me On the acts of gaining clarity, understanding, and discovering (CUD). "I believe therapy can work by means of getting a clearer understanding of yourself and your problems, and discovering things about yourself."

---

[13]Singer, E. *Key Concepts of Psychotherapy* (New York: Basic Books, 1982) p. 133.

S   What about transference and resistance, regression and catharsis? These are elements in my theory of therapy that I believe are instrumental in its efficacy. Do I include them in my answer?

U   Generally, no; sometimes, only if necessary, yes. We may believe in the power of transference, we may have faith in the value of resistance, regression, abreaction, and there may be more elements in your theory of therapy. They needn't, however, be explained to P—not necessarily.

S   But I don't want to appear to be minimizing the role of such phenomena because without them my formulation can sound too intellectual. P might construe things in purely cognitive terms, as if he and I will be "figuring out" his personality and problems, and that's all that's going to happen in therapy.

Me If we wanted to avoid that impression, we might add a few words about emotions and feelings, amplifying our answer to include not only the understanding of them but also the possibility of his coming to experience some old, long forgotten feelings, and perhaps experiencing some new ones. But when P asks, "How can it help me with my problems to talk about myself and my problems?" I will first frame my answer in terms of CUD and say, "By talking about yourself and your problems you can come to understand yourself better, you can become clearer about who you are, and discover things about yourself and about your problems that you didn't know."

U   Suppose he agrees with the efficacy of CUD but questions whether our therapy is the best way to achieve it. "Simply talking about whatever I want to doesn't impress me as the way to gain clarity-understanding and discover."

Me The same claim can be made about free associating, or about analyzing dreams, or reviewing one's childhood— or, indeed, about talking about oneself.

S   They have a certain face validity.

Me   "But I talk to my friends, and it hasn't done much for me, so why should talking during therapy sessions be better? In short, I want you to explain why talking to you for an hour several times a week can lead to any special understanding."

S   "If you think it's just going to be talking, you have another think coming!" I'd say that to myself. My overt response is this: "I can listen to you in a way that others can't; I can listen with only one interest, to understand; I can listen without injecting my opinions and judgments, criticisms, and evaluation, without taking sides and giving advice or guidance." If that explanation doesn't suffice, I have the option of adding that therapy provides a safe place for the airing of any and all issues, that it provides for the free expression of any and all thoughts and fantasies and feelings, every wish, action, memory, and dream is free from external constraint in here, everything can be examined in the same light—to know and understand it. This, after all, isn't usually true for ordinary interpersonal situations.

Us   The point being that if P wants to know what's so special about our therapy, we can tell him. And our answer is framed on the special conditions that it can provide, conditions that boil down to a freedom from constraint. "You can talk freely here because I remain neutral and impersonal, because my sole interest is to understand you and help you understand yourself." At the risk of repeating ourselves too much, we again mention that we have in mind those additional features of our therapy that make it special—transference, resistance, regression, and abreaction—but these cannot so readily be explained to our average P.

And suppose P doesn't agree to the efficacy of CUD. "I know myself already," he says, "and I'm still a mess. I'm clear about my problems, I know what I should be doing and how I should be doing it. There is nothing mysterious about me and my hangups. The only mystery is why I can't profit from the knowledge I have, why it benefits me so little to understand." Or he may claim to know why he has problems, what caused and still causes them, and despite the knowledge the problems remain ("How will it help for me to rehash all that here, to share with you my CUD?").

Let's make it tougher by supposing that P concedes that he has something still to learn and discover; he doesn't know it all, we may be able to show him a thing or two. But he makes this claim: "If CUD could alleviate my problems, then it follows that the amount I've already achieved would have had some commensurate effect on my problems. If anything, however, my problems have gotten worse the more I've thought about them. The more I've tried to figure out, searched, and delved, the more have they grown more painful and unbearable (so I've come to the conclusion that CUD has had no beneficial effects for me)."

Before saying how I'd proceed, I want to point out some pitfalls that lie before us. The most serious is taking the position that P's CUD is faulty ("The trouble is that your CUD hasn't been good enough. I will show you how to do it better, and that will have the beneficial effects you desire"). This is both a big temptation and a big error. We mustn't yield to the impulse to argue with P, and claim he's kidding himself if he thinks he knows himself. Moreover, we shouldn't say it even if we suspect it's true. Whether it's true or not is beside the point. The point is not to challenge—for how can therapy stand a chance when it stands on a difference of opinion? How can we hope to be of therapeutic use to P when there's an underlying challenge (a complicated set of them, in fact) of a show-me type? We want to avoid even giving the appearance of challenging P's claim that he has significant and substantial clarity and understanding.

The first thing I'd ask myself is how come CUD has not worked for him. Now, if therapy was young I would not have an answer, and I'd say as much. I see no reason not to tell him that I don't know why his experience has been that CUD hasn't helped. But notice an interesting thing: this question itself calls for CUD. In fact, "Maybe we can find out why that's been," I could even add. Or does this strike you, and P as well, as a piece of sophistry? "Oh, come off it!" he may exclaim, and then continue to challenge with, "Look, that's just begging the question! If it hasn't helped with my problems, why expect it to help with the question of why it hasn't helped?"

This, of course, is a fair question, but I can answer it in a way that I couldn't answer the other one. The question has now shifted in its focus, and therefore I can now fall back on my earlier answers; I can appeal to the special properties of therapy that make CUD special, and reasonably claim that therapy may have a special efficacy in throwing light on this new question (or this old question in its new focus). After all, P hasn't had a transference neurosis, has he? Has he ever done pitched battle with resistance? How much has he regressed with his friends or in his self-inquiries and deliberations? How much catharsis was possible for him? In this way can I hold out the promise that my form of therapy, with its potentials for such experiences, not to mention my own special ability to clarify, understand, and discover, can help him despite the fact that his experience has been discouraging.

Here's the way I'd respond to his challenge: "I understand your feeling discouraged and pessimistic about the value of gaining clarity and understanding, and of discovering; you've done a lot of it, and it hasn't helped. I don't mean to dispute or minimize it in any way, and neither am I surprised that it happened to you. But I think it's possible for us to understand how come it happened to you. I also believe it doesn't mean that this kind of therapy stands no chance of helping you." This is a useful statement to make, and I would make it first. It will have to be followed up with some equally useful statements, which are specified in the following dialogue.

P Why aren't you surprised it happened?

Me Several reasons. I know how painful and upsetting it can be to dwell on one's problems, examine oneself and one's life. There are unpleasant truths to be faced, bad memories to be remembered, shameful events, guilt provoking acts.

P But I'll be doing the same here, won't I?

Me But you won't be doing it alone, and that could make a
    difference.

Notice that I don't volunteer why, I don't point out that self-inquiry
when conducted by oneself is limited by one's ego, because this
is a complicated issue to get into. If necessary, I can suggest that
there are reasons, like repression and intellectualization.

P   But it hasn't been alone. I've shared them with others.

Me   There's another price you pay then: the other person's
     reactions and feelings.

Here I can tell him about the value of neutrality. It's what I mean
by "price" and another basis for not being surprised it hasn't worked.

P   Okay, now tell me why it doesn't mean that therapy
     stands no chance of helping me.

Me   Because therapy can give you a different perspective on
     your self-inquiry. That your efforts haven't helped
     might be due to the fact that you had only your own
     perspective from which to do it. In therapy that
     perspective can change, because you're not only talking
     to yourself here, you're talking to me, and I can provide
     a new perspective.

"Perspective" is vague. I have in mind "the perspective of psycho-
dynamic theory." Another is less specific: "the perspective of an
observer who is dispassionate, neutral, and impersonal." A third
is quite concrete: "the perspective of someone who can see things
you might not, things like defenses and affects." If P asks for explication, I can give him one or another of these.
    But you're feeling impatient with me; I'm repeating myself and
not getting to the hardest question of all. The challenges I've been
dealing with are likely to occur at the beginning of therapy. When
P expresses skepticism and perplexity then, it's one thing; when
he does it after therapy has had a chance, when it has already run
a substantial course, it's another. Still, everything I've so far written is relevant to what follows.

Here's what provoked this polemic: P has been in therapy for a while, has had a substantial experience of Psychotherapy; he says: *"But this isn't working! How does it work, anyway?"*

I will now make a big assumption: resistance isn't a significant factor here. For our purposes, let's assume that P is experiencing no gains from therapy, and is raising a legitimate issue; he is only asking, "How can that be?"

When P asks how therapy works, and asks it in the context of a complaint that he's getting no better, his question probably means "How come?" "I gather you're asking why this therapy is not working for you," is therefore the first thing to say. He undoubtedly has some answers in mind, as do I. The technical problem is twofold: how to explore his answers and formulate mine.

A good way to proceed is in that order, by beginning with his ideas. The second thing to say is: "I take it you have some ideas about it." If this stands too nakedly as a direct question, I would continue with some speculations as to what his reasons and concerns might be (it's unlikely that I'm completely in the dark as to what they are). My intention is to explore his answers to the question, for it's better to frame my answers in the context of his than impose mine. This doesn't mean I'm not going to give answers, or at least be ready to give them; it means that my answers have to be formulated in the context of his, and I want to be sure I'm answering his actual question (he might be questioning my skill or his own, or the suitability of this therapy or his fitness for it; he might be asking whether his problems are recalcitrant to this or any type of therapy, or whether I'm doing the right thing for him; he might be wanting me to do something more or different; he might be wanting me to give up on him, declare him hopeless; the possibilities are diverse and I have to know them). In short, I want to approach P's question with CUD (and while I am caring and concerned, I'm trying not to be worried and defensive).

Let's assume that this work gets done and my answers get framed in accordance with P's question. What now are my options for answers? How do I steer a course between the Scylla of indifference (disregard for P's well-being and interests) and the Charybdis of nonneutrality (the imposition of my values and judgments)? How do I give answers that are ethical and responsible,

that embody integrity, fit my self-image and definition as a therapist, and don't violate or undercut the spirit and orientation of
the therapy that I've been conducting? Given all of these assumptions, conditions, and caveats, there are three options for an answer. Option 1 is: therapy has insufficiently progressed for its
beneficial effects to take effect. Option 2 is: P's work in therapy
has been insufficient. Option 3 is: my work in therapy has been
insufficient.

Option 1 ("I believe the reason for the lack of good results is
the fact that your therapy is so young") raises the question of
when it will grow up, which often can't be answered by more
than a shrug. It implies the directive, "Wait!" together with a
piece of advice, "Have faith!" There is no way to suggest to P
that he hasn't given therapy enough chance without at the same
time advising him to have patience, and this is true no matter
how "young" the therapy.

I have more to say about option 1 but let's move on to (2). Here
the focus is on insufficient quality of P's work. Insufficient can
mean nonreflective ("You have not been searching enough in your
deliberations"); defensive ("You've been too guarded, apprehensive, circumstantial"); irrelevant ("You've been talking about the
wrong things"). It can be formulated in terms of affect versus cognition ("You've been too intellectual and insufficiently feelingful,"
or, "You've been too preoccupied with feelings and not enough
with understanding"); and it can be formulated broadly in CUD
terms. Whatever the focus, one thing is clear: the onus is on P.
The message is: "Therapy is not at fault, and I am not to blame,
which leaves only the possibility that you are the responsible
party." There's an additional message: it is P's work in therapy that
is being faulted, not his problems or personality; he isn't declared
unsuitable or incapable. But he is being given a directive: "Change
your way of working!"

Thus the first two options imply directives. If P wants results
he must (1) behave differently in therapy, and (2) give it more time.
But so what? Am I not backing us into a corner, and unnecessarily so, with my extreme rhetoric? I am, for I want to make a strong
case in favor of option 3—taking the onus on ourselves.

Before I do that, I need to restore some balance. Options 1 and
2 aren't so bad. They have pitfalls, which are obvious enough, but

also features that are potentially useful and therapeutic. Each can be given in the spirit of information sharing, of notifying P instead of directing or criticizing him—and the mantle of expertise on therapy lies comfortably on our shoulders.

"I'm saying that therapy takes time, but whether you decide to give it more time is entirely up to you," is how option 1 can be put. "I'm telling you that your fear of introspecting is what's responsible for your experience of this not helping you; I'm suggesting that it's the reason, not you should do anything about it, and neither am I criticizing or judging you for it," is how option 2 can be formulated. I can imagine circumstances in which I'd feel comfortable taking such positions, but I can also imagine risking a serious impasse. Therefore, on balance, and for our average P and average course of therapy, I regard these options as measures of the last resort, or at least as having less priority than option 3. This is really the main point I want to make here.

I need to say more about the first two options. If I believed that the therapy was in fact too young, I'd go ahead and say so. True, there is the promise that if P hangs in here he'll see results, but it may be unavoidable. And won't I listen hard to his subsequent material in order to interpret his reactions to those aspects? These interpretations might not suffice, they might prove futile, but what other option was there? (I'm assuming now that the other two options were unavailable for the simple reason that they simply weren't valid, or valid enough.) The same applies to option 2; I may have no other option. If so, I'd make it clear that I was answering the question, nothing more.

Me   Why is therapy not working?—because of the way you're doing it.

P   You mean it's my fault!

Me   I mean only to anwer your question and tell you what I believe. I take it as a reason, not a fault; I know you take it as a criticism and feel that I'm shifting the blame away from me and the therapy and putting it on you. But I see no other way of telling you that, in my

opinion, your way of working in therapy is what's
keeping you from experiencing beneficial effects.

P   Then why haven't you told me? Why do you wait for
me to complain?

Me   I didn't know you were experiencing no beneficial
results. I had no way of being sure the work you're
doing here wasn't going to be effective. This is the first
indication you've given me of it.

P   So you're instructing me to strive for CUD?

Me   It sounds so, but I don't mean to be instructing you.

P   You mean you don't care if I get better or not?

Me   My answer may sound harsh but I'll give it straight. I
care only to understand you; it's the best way to help
you get beneficial results. In that sense I do care. The
best way to do it is to keep from giving you advice or
direction, including telling you how to work in therapy,
which is different from helping you understand and
discover the best way for you to work in therapy.

P   You sound like a fanatic!

But you get the point! So let's turn to option 3, which is the one I
favor. It means saying to myself that my work has been inadequate;
my efforts at CUD haven't been good enough and I haven't pro-
moted the process for P to an optimal degree. Not, mind you, that
it's my fault and I'm to blame; merely that the responsibility lies
with me.

Before getting into the problems of putting this into practice, let me anticipate your reactions. You're thinking that I'm
defending myself against externalizing the blame, so I'm in-
ternalizing it; or I'm retreating to reaction formation in order
to flaunt my virtue; or I'm being teacherly, trying to reassure
you that I, too, have shortcomings, you shouldn't feel so bad
about yours. Well, maybe it's true, to a degree, but I'll remind
you that I'm writing about relative priorities, not about good

and bad ones. To blame P or fault the therapy aren't bad options, they are merely of a lower priority. My preference, or first priority (and from a technical position, at the very least), is to look to myself.

So what does option 3 entail, a confession? Do I say out loud, "The reason this hasn't helped you is because my work has been ineffective"? Do I tell P that my interpretations have been poorly formulated and timed, or that I've mismanaged the transference or inadequately dealt with his resistances? No, I don't want to say any of that. Even if I worded it carefully, I see no useful function, no benefit to P, in my telling him those things; it is quite sufficient to have said them to myself.

What then do I say to him?—nothing special. Yes, nothing special! For the chief function of this option is in what it keeps us from saying—all the things I wrote for the other two. And this, in my strong opinion, is a very useful function.

But you are now feeling exasperated with me. Is my prescription itself "nothing special"? Is business as usual all I'm advocating? Therefore, since it's unlikely that I can effectively say nothing to P, let's consider what I might have to say.

Bear in mind that I have already responded to his complaint by asking for his explanation. That was what I did first. I can therefore assume that he will tell me what he thinks and feels, and since my preferred approach requires of me to say nothing special, I can follow his lead. Moreover, and this is crucial, since I'm assuming that therapy is past its beginning phase, I can expect to have sufficient basis for formulating good interpretations.

Suppose P resorts to option 1 by saying the fault lies with his impatience that therapy has to take time and he doesn't have the time: I would try for an interpretation of why he opts for this explanation. Perhaps he has a history of impatience, perhaps I know something of its dynamics; perhaps he is criticizing therapy for taking so much time; perhaps he's trying to take me off the hook. In short, chances are that I know enough about him to venture a speculation about why he prefers to lay the onus on his own impatience or on therapy's youth.

Suppose he chooses option 2 by blaming himself and his problems. This can raise fresh issues: e.g., either his personality or his symptom is recalcitrant. The former might raise the question,

"Can I alter my biological makeup?" and the latter, "Can I change my past?" The answer to both is no. But the questions can be translated into: "What can one do about the past?" and "What can be done about biology?" And these are answerable. The same answer handles both: "One can bring to bear the powers of CUD."

Here's a way to formulate it: "By understanding the past, by gaining clarity about what happened, and by discovering things about the past one had either forgotten or never knew, one can hope to loosen the grip that the past holds on the present; one can gain in one's control over the present; one can stop being such a slave to one's history." The same can be said about biology: one doesn't seek to change it, only loosen its grip—and what it means "to loosen its grip" can be formulated in a variety of ways. Doing it in terms of freedom (or ego autonomy if you prefer) is my favorite way. I speak of getting free from past events and from biological givens, and I never promise complete freedom—relative freedom is quite sufficient. I make it easy for P to persuade me that his past has played a big role in determining his present problems, that his biological makeup is largely responsible for his personality and symptoms. I am quite prepared to accept that, so I don't feel any need to persuade him otherwise; if that's what he believes, so be it. There's no need for me to impose my theory, my point of view, except when it pertains to the power of therapy itself. Because when he contends that therapy cannot prevail against the past (as distinct from changing it), or against the effects of biology, then my saying I agreed would undercut the basis of the treatment. This, therefore, is a limitation on my unwillingness to impose my theory and point of view: I maintain a firm faith in therapy's power to help against the past and biology—namely to help free P from their grip.

But notice that this conviction requires of me, at most, to continue the therapy. And to paraphrase what I wrote much earlier in this letter, I would not be continuing a treatment that I didn't think was going to be effective. Bear in mind, too, that P probably wouldn't have entered therapy if he believed that it couldn't be effective for him—and he already knew that the past cannot be changed and neither can psychotherapy change one's biology. So what he is now skeptical and perplexed about is this question: "If one cannot change the past and biology, is there anything one can do about them to make life more bearable and productive? I thought therapy was the answer, now I'm doubting it."

My answer, and both to P and to you, is: "I'm not doubting it."

TWENTY-FOUR

THE STAGES OF PSYCHOTHERAPY AND THE BEGINNING STAGE

You've made frequent allusions (in your "it depends" remarks) to the developmental status of therapy, so we already know that our techniques must take it into account. One major way in which Psychotherapy's developmental status can influence our technique is this: once our patient knows how nondirective we are, how nonjudgmental, nonconfronting, and nondiagnosing, we might occasionally relax our posture and loosen our grip on our proscriptions by asking a direct question, probing, and even venturing a confrontational and diagnostic interpretation. For once the task of establishing our neutrality has been completed (although there's a sense in which the therapy would have to be finished before we could make that claim), we are free to behave in ways that might otherwise compromise it. It's not that we abandon our nondirective stance in respect to narrative, but the meanings and ramifications and implications will have changed, and the balance between our countervailing rationales may have shifted.

Chess, too, has stages, a beginning game, a middle, and an endgame; they are analogous in several respects to those of Psychotherapy (certainly, the middle game of chess is no time to abandon technique). Anyway, we're not to presume that our rationales will have changed in any fundamental way; they won't have changed, it's their relevant contexts that will. When we are confident that our patients know that we intend never to give them any advice, we can make remarks that imply it; when we know they know we never pass judgment, we can feel somewhat free to venture diagnostic interpretations, and even confrontations may not crowd them too much. We may now be able to address issues that we weren't able to before, such as defense and resistance to change, for instance, without running the risk of being inconsistent.

All right, Psychotherapy tends to fall naturally, albeit roughly, into three developmental stages. They may be fluid, but these stages are real. More than just a didactic tradition, and far from arbitrary, this subdivision not only helps us formulate matters for ourselves, it can have significant implications for our patients by helping them understand their experience of therapy. We will be giving them interpretations (but often they'll be business remarks) that refer to the stages, and particularly to the transitions from one to the next (e.g., "The impasse you are experiencing reflects the fact that therapy has entered a new stage"). The idea of stages is often meaningful to patients, for the stages have distinctive characteristics and themes (e.g., "Your recent preoccupation with death might be based on the fact that we're now into the final stage of your therapy").

The beginning is when the therapeutic process is set in motion, and also our technical principles. Many of our "rules," in their most stringent forms at least, apply to this stage. It is therefore the most standard of the stages, the easiest to write about, and the easiest to learn. It can also be the most crucial, for it establishes the character of the therapy and foreshadows its course. We introduce and define ourselves to our patients; we show them how our therapy works; they in turn introduce and define themselves to us, and show us how they work.

The middle stage is when we usually encounter the major reorganizations and transformations, the major revelations and discoveries, the major transferences and also the major impasses. By now our patients have had a substantial experience of Psychotherapy, and we have had a substantial experience of them. So our chief work consists in the formulation, elaboration, and also the repetition, of interpretations, and their chief work is working through. This is when the main struggle for and against change takes place.

The beginning is often marked by an undercurrent of optimism and enthusiasm, the middle by an undercurrent of despair and resistance, for the patient's unwillingness to change now becomes manifest, and pits its strength against the healing processes of growth and development. It is now that long-entrenched patterns of behavior are weakened and altered, now that the transference reaches its full intensity and exerts its full force. The middle is therefore the natural habitat of the impasse, and often is inaugurated by a patient's struggles with the question of continuing therapy ("I think that, in part anyway, your misgivings and doubts over whether to continue in therapy have to do with the fact that we've completed the beginning stage of it"). Despite the fact that the shape of the middle varies, and each therapy has a distinctive shape, two of the most common, and also most vital, themes are resistance to change and dependency on therapy.

Finally comes the final stage, the ending, an often difficult and problematic period, fraught with dilemmas and hard questions (such as "What is the nature of the 'cure'?" and "What criteria are available in determining when therapy can be regarded as having fulfilled its purpose?" and "Is a patient ever finished with therapy?"). The characteristic theme of this stage is separation, naturally. It takes a variety of forms, and can be accompanied by regression.

That was your snapshot of three stages, to give us a picture of the issues we'll be studying in our last lessons. The rest of this letter is devoted to the beginning stage.

First off, we should expect that P will expect, at least at the outset, to be interviewed and diagnosed: we are going to examine him and his problems, with questions and probes, to figure them out and treat them. And he may be right in one respect; several diagnostic interviews may in fact be required; it will depend on the nature of the referral and the clinical requirements. If this was the case, we will explicitly distinguish these sessions from the therapy proper, by telling him that we're going to begin with some interviews and afterwards switch over to the therapy proper.

Since our patients will have been interviewed and diagnosed by the clinic, Susan and I will be able to dispense with a clinical interview and launch straight into Psychotherapy. We do have the responsibility for making an independent assessment of P, but we'll be able to do it by observing his behavior during the beginning sessions, for we can hardly help making diagnostic observations even as we're avoiding making diagnostic interpretations.

All right, we now turn our attention to the very first session, and we start at its very beginning. What's our first move? Do we open with the basic instruction? Can we picture ourselves saying, "You can tell me the things you want to," immediately after P has been seated? The natural topic to start with is the reason he's coming for therapy. It isn't, however, the best topic to start with. How much we already know about P and his problems is the best topic to start with, and for several reasons.

One is embedded in our "epistemological cave": everything we know about him is going to be based on what he tells us. So indigenous to psychotherapy is this constraint—and for Psychotherapy it has to be stringently adhered to because the treatment would in fact work best if we knew nothing whatever about P to begin with—that we might want to embody it right away.

Therefore, if P was silent, looking expectantly at us, Susan and I might begin by telling him what we know about him. In your practice, you would tell him what the referrer had told you (deleting remarks of a judgmental and diagnostic nature that were made), and if he was self-referred (your name and number was given to him by a former patient, say), and you knew nothing else about him, you nevertheless would begin by telling him what you know, namely, "I gather so-and-so gave you my name and number." If P simply said yes without elaborating, you would now switch over to, "Please tell me your reasons for seeking therapy."

Since we will know a lot about P, we can say, "I've read the report of the interviews you had; it tells, for instance, of your . . . ," and continue by selecting items from the report. There's no need to give him a comprehensive review of the report, several highlights usually suffice. We're well advised to make our opening statement and say nothing further. There's no need to follow up with any directives for P to say more about the matter (we can ignore the popular advice to say, "But I'd like to hear it in your own words"); if he wants to elaborate on any of the things we've mentioned, fine; if he doesn't, that's fine too. In fact, we have to be prepared for the possibility that he will say nothing after we've made our opening remarks, just receive it in silence and continue to look expectant.

In that event we'll ask him to tell us how he construes therapy ("Tell me your thoughts about the therapy you want and how you expect it to go"); this was going to be our first order of business following P's account of his reasons for seeking therapy. In fact, an argument can be made for the priority of a discussion of P's ideas and expectations about therapy over a discussion of his reasons for wanting it. It may turn out that his conception of therapy was too unrealistic or idiosyncratic, and when he learns what therapy will entail (regular sessions, for instance) he might decide to forego it.

So if P hadn't had a consultation (during which it was discussed and explained), we would begin with a discussion of therapy. Our opening remark would not be in the nature of, "Why are you seeking therapy?" it would be in the nature of, "What kind of therapy are you seeking?" The two questions might be conflated in P's mind, and he might answer them together. But our chief interest—and it will remain our chief interest during the beginning sessions—is to learn what his theory of therapy is. How does he think therapy works? What does he believe it will do for and to him? How does he construe our role? These questions have a certain priority over questions having to do with his reasons for seeking therapy. And the point isn't to educate him, it's to know what his ideas are so that, for one thing, we can correct those of his misconceptions which are business in nature—and if this is what's meant by "educating," fine. All we are doing is making it clear to him what our expectations and requirements are.

For another, we need to know what P's ideas are so that we can take them into account and make sure our interventions are consonant with them. We don't want to work at cross-purposes with him, for which reason it is necessary that we know what his purposes are. (1) He devotes his sessions to complaining about things: he might believe that therapy is a place to get such things off his chest. (2) He talks exclusively about his emotions and feelings and gives full expression to them: he might believe therapy is a place to ventilate. (3) He gives detailed and circumstantial accounts of his daily experiences: he may be doing it because he finds it relieves him. Any interpretation that we offer vis-à-vis (1) particular complaints, (2) particular feelings, (3) daily events, might only serve to bolster his convictions. We might therefore consider it in the best interests of the therapeutic process if we reserved our interpretations for those convictions. Not that we're going to challenge them; we want only to expose and explore them.

Some of them may, after all, be unrealistic, in which case we'd have to deal with them in a businesslike way. Others will be less unrealistic and we may have no other way to deal with them except by affording P an opportunity to experience the therapy as it unfolds. But in either case, in order for us to play a useful role, we need to know what P's ideas are. So here's a little list of average expectable convictions and themes that we are likely to encounter during the beginning stage of therapy.

- Once you have all the facts you will proceed to cure me.

  This is such a widespread misconception that expecting P to have it is prudent. As soon as we hear any hint of this theme, we should not only articulate it clearly but tell him that it isn't how Psychotherapy works.

- I am in for some rude shocks and painful surprises.

  Expecting therapy to be an unremitting ordeal may be based on a felt need for punishment (if not also on a streak of masochism). P might expect us to confirm his most dreaded judgments of himself—that he is cruel, selfish, perverted, and the like. We can disabuse him of these sorts of expectations.

- So it looks like I can't do it myself after all.

  Being in therapy is often taken as an admission of defeat and sometimes it is. Despite viewing therapy as a way of overcoming his problems, P may experience a sense of resignation that is tinged with shame, and the conviction that he was weak and unable to take care of himself.

- Being here means I'm crazy.

  Many of us harbor the fear that we don't think like every-body else does, or that we are quite crazy underneath. This is a fear that's likely to run deep; so even after it was dis-cussed, we should expect it to recur in therapy. P might fear that therapy will not only expose his craziness but will re-sult in his becoming overtly crazy. He might give it expres-sion by asking, directly or indirectly, "How abnormal are my problems?" In our answer to this question we might want to articulate this fear.

- Therapy will make me ordinary, like everybody else.

  Part of a more general theme having to do with unwanted changes that therapy will wring as a side effect. An artist, for instance, may fear the loss of creativity and exhibition-ism, a businessman his loss of ambition. Simply acknowl-edging the fear often has the effect of diminishing it. Whether it is realistic or not cannot be said in advance, but it is safe to say that it's generally exaggerated.

- Can I really trust you and depend on you?

  A question that may reflect a variety of concerns and fan-tasies. What being trustworthy and dependable means should not be taken for granted. Trust in what sense, depend on how? It often means little more than, "Do you know what you're doing?" but sometimes it means more than that, and we can often predict the nature of the coming transference from the form it takes. Sometimes it's synonymous with the larger question, "Do you care?" Here, too, the meanings are vari-ous and run deep. During the beginning stage we can usu-ally do little more than make sure the issue becomes explicit (these questions often come up again during the middle stage, when the major impasses and resistances occur). It's impor-tant for us to know the ways in which P expects us to be trust-worthy and dependable, and essential that we have a clear idea of the ways in which he expects us to care.

- Does therapy really work?

> No matter how well motivated and how urgently felt his prob-
> lems, it's prudent to assume that P will harbor doubts about
> the efficacy of psychotherapy, and it is useful to articulate
> them. It's the rare P who will actually ask us the question.
> After all, the time to have weighed it was before initiating a
> contact with us. So if P becomes preoccupied with the ques-
> tion after therapy has begun, he is probably using it in the
> service of resistance.

When do we give the basic instruction? Often we'll be able to
fit it into a discussion of P's expectations about therapy. Sometimes
it will be appropriate to give only the first part of it—for instance,
if, after telling what he knows about therapy, he says, "What can
you tell me about it?" And if, at any point, he says, "What do you
want me to tell you?" we might say, "It's up to you; you can talk
about whatever you want to talk about." There's no compelling
reason to give the full basic instruction at the outset; there will be
occasion to complete it, if not in this session then in the next. Neither is there any reason not to repeat the instruction; in fact we
should be glad to give it as many times as necessary (it's not uncommon for P to have forgotten everything we said during the first
session).

It may not be necessary to give the basic instruction at all (after
all, inasmuch as it is a directive, we should be glad to dispense
with it). P may not require it (you have conducted full courses of
Psychotherapy without ever having given it once). Nevertheless,
neither should we try to avoid giving it, and chances are that a suitable opportunity will present itself early.

This gives Susan and me an opportunity to raise a question of
ours. What if P asks us to explain the necessity for our nondirective
stance? Such a basic and important an issue as this, it seems to
us that the pragmatic reply is likely to strike him as curt and un-
satisfying. Can we not tell him something of our rationale? We
came up with the following formulation (it could be broken up
into parts):

One of the reasons I prefer to give you no advice, either
in respect to how you behave during the sessions or
outside of them, is because if you followed my advice
then you'd expect me to be pleased, and if you didn't
follow it you'd expect me to be displeased. But my
having those feelings would be of no benefit to you and
could spoil the therapy. I believe, you see, that my
personal feelings and attitudes should play no part in your
therapy, and that's one of the reasons I need to be so
impartial and nonjudgmental. If I were to give you
advice, then I might find it hard to remain indifferent to
whether you followed it or not, and I could hardly expect
you to believe that I really was. In addition, this would
put me in the position of passing judgment on you, and I
think your therapy would go better if I never did that.

It was generous of you to picture for us the most awkward and
difficult of possible openings. We read it with grim amusement.

Us   Please tell me about your interest in therapy.

P   I've decided to try it. [silence]

Us   Please tell me what you have in mind.

P   So-and-so works in my office. He was a patient of yours.
      He gave me your name and number. [silence]

Us   Had you discussed with him your interest in having
      therapy?

P   [nods]

Us   Can you tell me something about it?

P   I don't know what. I can't even tell you what's wrong,
      because everything is. My life is one big mess. [silence!]

Well, a diagnostic interview is already now in order—though if P
was showing little sign of anxiety, we might consider sitting out
the silence and seeing how long he sustained it (Susan could do it,

but I couldn't). And what if we come to the conclusion that P wasn't a good candidate for Psychotherapy? Since we've already examined that question, we use this opportunity to consider the question of how tightly we hold on to P.

When therapy is in its beginning, but also even later than that, we sometimes face the option of referring P to another therapist (or to another form of therapy, or, indeed, of recommending no therapy at all). No matter what considerations form the basis of this option, it's an option we should take seriously and without qualm. If we or P have doubts and misgivings, our attitude should be one of holding him loosely.

Now, lest this be misunderstood, we hasten to add that it isn't quite the same as letting him go easily. There's a fine distinction between holding loosely and letting go easily. The crucial consideration is whose welfare is at stake, and it won't be only P's. "Am I the right therapist for him?" and "Is mine the right therapy for him?" are important questions, but so is, "Is he the right patient for me?" His well-being isn't the only consideration, ours counts too. We might even contend that if ours is compromised, his is bound to be as well.

So *"Hold P Loosely"* is our motto, and it applies especially to the beginning. It isn't an easy guideline, for so many personal and professional issues can be brought to bear on it. For a variety of reasons that are independent of P's well-being, none of us likes to lose a patient. ("Will I be judged for it?" "Will I be able to replace him?") Still, the best time to lose P is at the beginning, before he's developed feelings of dependency and attachment. When therapy is mature, questions of irresponsibility and ethics come into play in a way they don't when it's young.

Which segues nicely to the question of how old should Psychotherapy be, how long will it last, and should we raise this question when P hasn't? We're well advised to find an appropriate moment to ask P what his expectations are concerning the duration of therapy. For one thing, P has a right to know what expectations we have; and for another, we might be surprised to learn what his are (and better we should be surprised early than late).

Our expectations in respect to Psychotherapy's duration are initially rather vague. It certainly isn't possible to say much about it
with much assurance—and that's the first thing to say about it. A
full year at a minimum is a prudent estimation, so we should say
as much ("It's likely to take at least a year or two, and probably
three, but it could last longer"). We make sure to add that it isn't
possible to say in advance with much assurance (if P requires a
rationale, we tell him our experience has shown this to be so).

P might protest that his condition isn't so serious as to merit such
a lengthy course of therapy (the same is true when he learns that
we expect more than one session a week). Isn't there a correlation
between the severity of a medical problem and the duration of its
treatment? "That has little to do with it," we respond, alluding to
P's reference to how bad his problem is. "This form of therapy usually takes some years, and it works best when there are a minimum
of two a week."

But what if he doesn't have the time? What if, for whatever reason, P wants therapy for a circumscribed period—a year, say, or
half a year perhaps? Do we agree to such a contract? It depends.
The therapy won't be complete and P might not derive much benefit from it, but the question is whether he will be at risk and will
the treatment have done him harm if it's curtailed. This depends
on our clinical judgment, and pivots on diagnostic considerations.
We will certainly need time (and supervision) to think about the
matter, so we must tell P this. Rarely would we agree to such terms
without having taken the necessary time to ponder them.

The next matter to ponder is schedule and fee. Here we need
sufficient time—meaning, we have to allow enough time during
the initial session for an interview that might have to be quite extensive. This may require interrupting P in order to do it. So if the
matter hasn't come up and the session has only ten or fifteen minutes left, that's what we'll do.

The main requirement in respect to schedule and fee is that they
should not be too difficult and problematic, either for P or for us.
A schedule that is too onerous and a fee that is too costly are undesirable in themselves, of course, but we have further considerations

having to do with resistance. In brief, we don't want to make it too easy for P to "use" the schedule and the fee for its purposes. He will do it in any case; we merely want to make it more difficult. If the schedule is too disruptive of his life and isn't sufficiently comfortable, then we can expect it to become a focus of resistance, and this resistance will be recalcitrant to analysis insofar as it was based on too much reality (instead of saying, "I wish to cancel the session," or, "I wanted to miss it," P will say he simply had to). The same applies to the fee ("These sessions are too expensive," will not be so readily available, and instead he will only have recourse to, "These sessions are not working," at best).

The same applies also to us, in a way. For one thing, we needn't make it too easy for ourselves to organize countertransference feelings around these reality issues. If it should happen that we look forward to a session with some resentment or dread, it ought to be difficult for us to lay the onus on the schedule's inconvenience. Neither should we want to have good reason to feel put out and irritated when P missed a session (or delays paying his fee). But if it comes down to a choice of relative inconvenience, we should opt for the one that's inconvenient for us; it is more important to keep the schedule and fee from becoming a real source of resistance for P (our own feelings, after all, are our business).

Three times a week is optimal; twice is minimal; once a week is acceptable only in exceptional cases and circumstances. It's quite sufficient to give P our standard reply when he asks why, but our full rationale is that a certain continuity is fostered by more frequent sessions; there is apt to be less focus on current events; the therapy is more likely to become an important part of P's life.

Then there's the matter of paying for missed sessions (the clinic has no policy for it, so it's up to each of us to set one). The regnant consideration is to make sure that our policy protects us from any requirements in passing judgment. We never want to be in the position of judging P's reasons for missing a session; we don't ever want to be distinguishing, or even seem to be distinguishing, between good and bad reasons. Whatever policy we adopt (there are several to choose from), it mustn't be one that hinges on reasons and circumstances; it should be based on criteria that are entirely objective (a day's notice, for instance). Neither should it contain the common clause, "I'll charge you if I am unable to use the time for another patient," or anything of the sort. Not only is this unfair to P but it can call our integrity into question ("How hard did you try to fill the time?" if not even, "How do I know that you're telling me the truth?").

So much for the beginning. Susan and I are left with some questions that many teachers would dismiss as trivial. They are questions like: How do you greet your patients and respond to their "how are you"? How much socially conventional interchange do you engage in (such as comments on the weather and current events)? Do you never say, "I'm sorry," and, "Please excuse me"? What about offering congratulations and best wishes, not to mention condolences? What do you do when P says something humorous and amusing? Do you ever use humor of your own? Finally there's the matter of how you end sessions and do you ever extend them. These issues are bound to be useful for us to think about.

TWENTY-FIVE

VARIOUS AND SUNDRY DETAILS

Us   Yes, the clinic provides a box of tissues in its consulting rooms.

U   My advice: get rid of it!

Us   Your rationale?

U   The clinic also provides a pitcher of water?

Us   Actually, no.

U   No dish of throat lozenges either. So why the tissues? It sends a message, no? And P may weep during sessions, but his throat gets dry from all the speaking, too. Lozenges could come in handy.

Us   He will bring his own.

U   How is it different for tissues?

Us   A box of tissues is standard decor for a therapist's office.

U   Where is it written that it should be?

Us   Isn't this a rather small, if not even trivial, detail?

U   Small, yes, but trivial, not in my opinion. Details count in therapy, they have a way of adding up to something significant. And in Psychotherapy each detail contributes something to its uniqueness, and is therefore valuable on those grounds, too. Besides, I don't regard the tissue box as a trivial detail. I used to provide one—everybody else did and I hadn't given it much thought. It was a patient who alerted me to it, and who taught me that it wasn't so innocent a piece of decor. For her the box of tissues stood in silent rebuke over the fact that she never wept during sessions. "You are expected to make use of me to dry your tears," said the box to her, and, "I wish you'd get rid of it," said she to me. I did.

Me Because it was a distraction for her.

S   You didn't feel it was necessary to take account of the fact that she was thereby manipulating you.

U   As you know, I take a dim view of my colleagues' concerns over being "manipulated" by their patients. At best, such concerns reflect a willingness on our part to teach P a lesson, and I don't think it's a good idea to do that.

S   Weren't your patients distracted by the disappearance of the box?

U   I removed it only for P. Then I phased it out of my practice.

Us Let's discuss verbal gestures that serve a social function. What's your opinion on "hello" and "goodbye"?

U   They simply acknowledge the beginning of an encounter and its ending. Similarly, "please" and "thank you" acknowledge that something was being requested and received. These gestures are therefore no problem for us, in no way can they be taken as a breach of our neutrality.

Us What about "how are you" instead of or in addition to "hello"?

U   It crosses the line. To be sure, it can be synonymous with "hello," and usually elicits a perfunctory response. But in the context of therapy, it can obviously have substantive meaning. When my doctor says, "How are you?" I'm inclined to take it as a question.

Us How about "excuse me" and "I'm sorry"?

U   They may convey more than an acknowledgment that a social transgression was committed, though they may also not. Still, I think we should discipline ourselves to avoid using them, though it can be a difficult habit to break.

Me Difficult is putting it mildly in my case. Are you not willing to make an exception for instances in which we are apologizing for a common social transgression? Say, I accidentally bumped into P when we're crossing paths, can't I say, "Excuse me"?

U   Sure. It's little more than an acknowledgment of what you did. I, however, would probably say, "I didn't mean to bump into you," and skip the excuse me.

Me   What if you belched, or (God forbid) farted, would you not acknowledge that?

U   I see no reason why I should feel I had to. Do you?

Me   P might have found it offensive.

U   He might also find the tie I'm wearing offensive. If so, he is free to tell me. Besides, why should I draw his attention to my having belched, or farted even? He may have been so absorbed in his work that he didn't notice. Just because you were embarrassed by it doesn't mean he has to have reacted to it.

Me   Say I'm late to a session; restricting myself to, "I'm aware that I'm late," is going to be tough, adding "I'm sorry" is so ingrained. If I have to step out of the room for a moment, not adding, "Excuse me," will be impossible. I'm sure Susan could do it.

S   Susan isn't so sure.

Me   I find it hard to take these strictures seriously. I do see how they would make my role definition distinctive, but I'm not convinced it would be worthwhile. I can imagine P reacting with puzzlement, if not amusement, at my idiosyncratic avoidance of common social gestures. He might even regard me as something of an eccentric, if not something worse.

S   I personally think it is worth it. His regarding you as an eccentric is something you and he can work on.

Me   It won't be a business matter, either. You're a big believer in things being grist for the mill. I lean toward the opinion that not everything is good grist, and issues like these might actually interfere with the therapeutic process. Moreover, I think there's a difference between our behaving in distinctive ways and our behaving in ways that are uncivil and may border on the rude.

U   I am not suggesting that you ever do anything that feels uncivil and rude. I'm recommending that you give thought to all of your actions and utterances, weigh their potential significance and implications, and consider whether you might want to try to modify some of them. It can take practice—so many of them are so habitual as to be automatic—but it also takes conviction.

Me   Then to what extent, and how scrupulously, must we avoid conventional gestures that mark an occasion? If the session is on a Friday, say, I won't say, "Have a good weekend," I can picture myself dispensing with it. But if that weekend marks the passing of the year, I mustn't say, "Happy New Year"?

U   As far as I'm concerned, the only thing you mustn't do is say it thoughtlessly. If, after consideration, you decide to, that's fine.

S   I can picture myself not saying it. But if P says, "Have a good weekend," and, "Have a Happy New Year," I do think it would be rude not to acknowledge by reciprocating.

U   I fully agree. Saying, "And you too," usually has no additional meaning than that of acknowledging the gesture. A gesture that is made in reciprocation is significantly different than an initiated one.

Me   So both of you would wait for P to say, "Happy New Year," and simply not say it first. If P doesn't, neither do you; you're going to be as uncivil as P is.

S   You want us to be more civil than he is?

Me   No, but I want you to take account of gestures that can only be initiated by us. One is congratulations when P tells us that he has crossed a milestone, and another is, "Good luck," when he is about to face one. If P tells you that today is his birthday, you aren't going to say, "Happy Birthday"?

S   I don't think so.

U   Then let's discuss these initiated gestures. The critical moment is the first occasion in which they were called for. It's then we must decide whether or not we're going to make these remarks. It would be inconsistent to stop making them later.

S   I see no reason we should make them in the first place. We need only be alert to P's reaction. Even if we have to strain for it, we should look for an opportunity to interpret his reaction to our having failed to make the appropriate gesture.

Me   Why should we want to deal with it interpretively? Isn't this a business matter, inasmuch as it pertains to the way we work? So when P tells me that he passed the exam, or today is his birthday, I would rather not wait for him to become puzzled and irritated (and distracted!) by my lack of civility. I'd rather tell him right away that the remark he expects me to make on such an occasion isn't going to be forthcoming, and explain why.

S   How exactly will you do that?

Me   Not easily. After P told me he passed the big test that he was so worried about, or that he failed it, I find it hard picturing myself saying, "From time to time you will tell me about a milestone you have successfully or unsuccessfully passed. At such times you will expect me to make the socially conventional response like 'congratulations' and 'I'm sorry to hear that.' But I'd prefer to avoid such remarks because I believe they aren't useful." I mean, talk about obsessionality, not to mention uptight!

U   I think you could work out a less stilted, more succinct way of putting it. And why wouldn't you use Susan's technique, make no response and then listen for P's reaction, and then interpret it?

Me   For two reasons: I was responsible for that reaction, and I don't see what P gains from having his response articulated. After all, his response was altogether normal and expectable. Moreover, will my definition of such gestures gibe with his? Say he tells me that his mother is seriously ill, do I define expressions of solicitude as simply conventional gestures? Say she died, isn't it going to be needlessly cold and heartless, if not downright cruel, not to express sympathy and condolence?

U   It would be insensitive and uncaring in the extreme. But I would justify it not in terms of its being the conventional thing to do; I would presume that P's experience has been so devastating as to constitute a crisis for him. Whenever P is in crisis we must not take a business-as-usual approach to him. It would border on the unethical to do so. If his mother had died, the least I could do is express heartfelt condolences, and I would do more than that if it was called for. For instance, if he was so devastated that he needed some advice from me, I would give it unhesitatingly. But whether or not I'd say, "I'm sorry to hear that," when he tells me of her illness, is a matter for my clinical judgment to decide.

Us   If the issue was his having passed the big test, then there's no question of any crisis, and therefore you don't believe that congratulations are called for. And if he had failed it . . . .

U   Then I'd rely on clinical judgment to determine whether it has reached crisis proportions.

Me   My definition of crisis is probably going to be broader than yours, and certainly broader than Susan's.

U   That's unavoidable. Anyway, the question of whether P is in crisis, and also whether therapy is at a point of impasse, is best answered in supervision. But I can say this much in a general way: our failure to follow social convention can certainly be perceived as cold, if not uncivil, though I wouldn't think of it as rude; and sometimes it isn't really useful to avoid the conventional gesture. Still, we will have to draw the line somewhere, and it can get quite arbitrary. The principle, however, remains: all things being equal, and without taking an extreme and dogmatic position, gestures of a socially conventional nature often can, and usually should, be dispensed with. I'd be inclined to agree that P's reaction could be treated as business instead of narrative.

Us   Let's turn now to the way we'll greet him. The arrangement here is that P will wait in the waiting room and we will fetch him; then we'll walk together to the consulting room. What if he chats with us during the trip?

U   If it happened during the prelude to the first session, I would be cordial and engage in the chat; doing otherwise would be taken by him as rudeness on my part. I'd then make sure to raise the issue during the session, as business, of course, and inform him of my preference for no conversation during that period. Whether it's about the weather or about some recent political or social event, or even if it's about something personal to P, I would prefer not to talk about it outside of the consulting room.

Us   And lest you think we've forgotten, the answer to his why not is, "Because this form of therapy works better if we don't engage in conversation like that."

U   P may greet me with a, "How are you?" My correct response is a clarifying question, "It isn't clear to me whether you mean it as a form of hello or whether you expect a personal answer." After all, he may genuinely want to know how I'm feeling. So I can define it as a personal question, and treat it as such—and choose to respond with silence.

Me   Let me play a bit of devil's advocate and protest this level of nit-picking formality. What's the harm, after all, in a bit of social intercourse? Why not simply say, "I'm fine, thank you," and keep things a bit human? Why not share an observation on the weather and current events? Surely, such a rigid formality and stringent aloofness could make things unnecessarily strained and artificial? Can such abstemiousness be all that useful? Is the therapeutic process so fragile that it can't withstand a modicum of civility?

U   All of that is quite true, and if you aren't comfortable with this level of abstemiousness then you should certainly not subscribe to it. Being civil is by no means a serious infringement on our neutrality. So you can go ahead and say, "Thank you," when P has asked God to bless you for having sneezed; you can say, "Fine, thank you, and how are you?" when he has inquired into your well-being. You can give congratulations and good wishes, and the rest. But bear in mind that while there can be no harm in that, there could also be no benefit in it. So you might also venture to abstain; you might give it a try.

Me   Why would I want to do that?

S   In order to experience for yourself the difference it can make; in order to discover for yourself that in a way that is perhaps small but potentially significant, it can contribute to the distinctiveness, if not the uniqueness, of the relationship you have with P.

Us Let's get back to particulars. How will we end sessions? First of all, how will we know the time is up? Glancing at a wristwatch, unless it occurs when the session is really over, is a problem. P is going to spot us doing it, and it will distract him, at the very least.

U   Use a clock and place it where both you and P can see it. Position the clock so that you don't have to avert your gaze much to catch a glimpse of it. That P has to avert his gaze matters less.

Us Don't patients differ widely in the way they end their sessions?

U   They also vary it from session to session. But there's no reason for us to, and we certainly don't want to use the opportunity to pass judgment on the session. If P has had a "difficult" session, or is in the middle of an "important" piece of narrative, your temptation will be to say something like: "I regret that we have to stop now." Even "We have to stop now," can convey a sense of misgiving. Your best choice is simply to say, "The time is up."

We What about when to call time? The clinic has a forty-five-minute policy. Appointments are scheduled on the hour, so we have a fifteen-minute leeway. Should we stick to forty-five minutes?

U   The distinction between being consistent and being rigid isn't easy to draw, and definitions vary. In my view, rigidly adhering to the allotted time serves a number of functions that are irrelevant to Psychotherapy and in no way contribute to its uniqueness. After all, if P tells me he wants to end the session early, I don't want to pass judgment on it and neither do I want to stand in his way. Ordinarily he will say why he wants to end early, but suppose he doesn't. That's fine. In fact, I could infer that he's getting the hang of things; he understands the nature of my neutrality and knows that I require no reason because I'm not going to be "doing anything" with it. He may even ask me to monitor the time and tell him when he needs to stop. That's fine, too, because keeping track of the time is a responsibility that I have assumed.

Us What about extending the session?

U   If it's feasible I see no reason not to. I see no value in rigidly
     adhering to the schedule, both as it pertains to the appointment
     time as well as to the duration of every session. Just as I will
     make changes in the appointment time, so I could, if in fact I
     can, make changes in the length of a session. Of course all of
     these changes will have been made by mutual consent.

S   What if P takes advantage of your flexibility and permissive-
     ness, and he makes frequent changes in schedule—cancels
     sessions, ends them early and extends them late—promiscu-
     ously? Isn't he being manipulative?

Me   Yes, but so what if he is? Isn't this something that can be
     explored and discussed, and stopped if need be, in a business-
     like way?

U   Thank you!

Us   What about interrupting P in midthought, if not in midsentence,
     in order to bring the session to a close?

U   Make sure to do it without apology, that's all: "I do realize that I
     am interrupting, but our time is up."

Us   Some of our teachers would have us suggest to P that he could
     continue with the topic next session.

U   They are obviously not teaching Psychotherapy. Anyway, aren't
     their patients free to do that if they want to?

Us   After "The time is up" comes the goodbye.

U   Use, "See you next time," because this can be pressed into a
     useful service by specifying when next time will be. It changes
     the salutation from a gesture into a useful remark. P, as well as we,
     will sometimes need to be reminded of when the next session is
     going to be taking place. He may have forgotten that we had
     changed the appointment, or we may have forgotten that he did. So
     if we say, "I'll see you next Tuesday at ten," he has an opportunity
     to correct us. Furthermore, he also has the opportunity to say, "Oh,
     I forgot to tell you that I can't make it on Tuesday at ten."

Us   Shouldn't business matters, such as changes in appointment,
     have been discussed at the beginning of the session?

U   I hope it wasn't us who said, "I forgot to tell you. . . ." Yes, business matters that we initiate are best raised early in the session to allow time to discuss them. There's an important corollary: issues that arise early in therapy should be treated as business whenever possible, to allow time to analyze them. This can be quite vital.

Us   Then would you like to give an example?

U   I once had a patient who, during his second session, said, "I wish you wouldn't stare at me." Now, I already knew, from his first session as well as the discussion I'd had with the referrer, that he was paranoid. But I would have responded the same way had I not known it. I treated the matter purely as business, and said, "I will try not to stare," and that was all I said.

S   It wasn't your only option. Your might have inquired into what he meant by "staring." That's businesslike, too.

U   Sure, I might have said, "What do you mean by 'staring'?" But since I knew that P was paranoid, it would not have been businesslike to find out what "staring" meant to him. That would have been taking a "What's your problem?" approach. Instead, I chose to say, in effect, "What's my problem?"

Me   If you hadn't known that he was paranoid, would you have taken that approach anyway?

U   Why not? Instead of staring, say it had been, "I wish you wouldn't keep adjusting your glasses," or, "I wish you didn't pick your nose." I wouldn't think, "What's your problem?" unless, of course, I wasn't in fact adjusting my glasses or picking my nose. But assuming that I was, I wouldn't counter with a question like, "Why do you wish that?"

S   But whether you were "staring" or not is a subjective judgment. So you could have responded with a clarification question framed this way: "I am looking at you, I'm maintaining eye contact, is this what you mean by 'staring'?" Or if you framed it more simply, "What do you mean by 'staring'?" and he said, "What do you mean 'What do you mean?'—isn't it clear?" You might say, "I'm not sure whether you're referring to the fact that I'm looking at you and maintaining eye contact with you, or whether you're referring to the fact that I'm doing it steadily, or whether it's something about the way I'm doing it."

Me   Suppose he now said, "You never avert your gaze, and you hardly ever even blink—and it unnerves me."

S   We have the option of beginning a clinical interview to diagnose the matter.

Me   Precisely how?

S   By asking him whether this was a special problem for him, and amounted to a symptom. "Is this a concern of yours, that people stare at you?"

Me   "Not just at me. People stare at each other in the rudest way. Don't they realize how hostile it is?"

S   "And it 'unnerves' you?"

Me   "Yes."

S   Okay, that went nowhere fast. We certainly don't want to ask him why it unnerves him. "Please tell me more about it," is the best we could say. Anyway, it isn't clear to us why we want the diagnosis in the first place.

U   And the reason for doing the interview and arriving at a diagnostic understanding must be clear. If our reason is to help P understand the issue, and thereby perhaps get some control over it, then it doesn't count as business; it's a therapeutic matter, and interviewing isn't our best way of approaching it. But if our reason is to find out whether, and to what degree, the issue is going to interfere with therapy, and perhaps make it untenable, then interviewing is not only the appropriate way to do it, it's practically the only way.

Me   But the issue can certainly be treated as narrative. After all, P hasn't asked a direct question or made a direct request. It's not as if he'd said, "Please stop staring!" He said "I wish," as he might have said, "I wish you were younger," or, "I wish you didn't speak with an accent."

S   Sure, we can be nit-picking and respond, "It isn't clear to me whether you're asking me to stop staring or whether you're saying that you wish I wouldn't need to stare." But let's assume that it's clear enough that a request is being made, and therefore we aren't dealing with narrative. Incidentally, if that wasn't the case, our only alternative to silence is an interpretation, and we're hardly in a position to proffer one.

Me   But silence is likely to be provocative and tactless, and this gives us another reason to define the matter as business. Let's also assume that we're able to listen well enough without maintaining eye contact or gazing at P—for if that wasn't the case, then the effort would be distracting for us and constitute an incompatibility. In other words, if we had to "stare" the way we do in order to work the way we need to, then P may have to find another therapist, or therapy. So why not simply acquiesce to the request?

U   Some therapists answer this question by raising the issue of "manipulation" and arguing that it's bad for our patients to do it. Others object to bypassing an opportunity to provide some therapeutic benefit from exploring the issue, and this might require not acquiescing to it to begin with. In my opinion, neither of these arguments is convincing enough to override the long-range benefits of treating the matter as business.

Us   What in fact were those benefits for your paranoid P?

U   Well, as it turned out, I was successful enough at not staring during most of the beginning stage of the therapy, and the issue was set aside. It did, however, resurface during the middle stage when, on occasion, P accused me of staring. It was now possible to treat the staring as narrative, and to good therapeutic effect. I was able to tell him that I didn't think I was actually staring, and I was able to suggest that his experience of being stared at was being evoked whenever he was struggling with certain thoughts and feelings. I interpreted it as a defensive projection that was associated with particular memories, and P was able to accept these interpretations and work with them. He came to recognize that his sense of being stared at was a repetition of childhood experiences of being ashamed of his thoughts and actions, in particular those associated with masturbation.

Us   Neat!

U   I am not fishing for compliments. My point is that the achieve-
     ment was substantially facilitated by my having treated it as
     business in the second session. Treating it as narrative would
     have been premature, and promoting it into an impasse, by
     refusing to comply, would have served P badly.

Us   Say P has the habit of being silent at the outset of sessions, and
     say we know that he'll say, "I'm thinking about what to talk
     about," when we ask, "What are you thinking?" Say further, that
     this issue has been discussed, and P has made it clear that the
     opening silence is no problem for him and he preferred that we
     didn't interrupt with our silence-breaking question. What should
     we be doing during the silence?

U   Whatever you want and whatever helps you sustain the hiatus
     with equanimity. This is likely to be a problem between you
     and your superego. During extended silences, whether they
     occur at the beginning of a session or during the course of it,
     you'll face the question of what to be thinking about. I want to
     disabuse you of any sense of should here, aside from recom-
     mending that you should be thinking about whatever you want
     to. What counts is that you remain calm; you have to be
     content to sit in silence; you don't want to be tense, worried,
     impatient or irritated. If thinking about P and progress of the
     therapy doesn't make you any of those things, then go ahead.
     If you want to be thinking about those things, that's good. But
     you needn't feel obligated to do it; there may be no reason for
     you to do it. Accordingly, you should feel free to entertain
     your own thoughts in whatever way you wish. If you want to
     plan your day, fine. If you'd like to have a daydream, fine. So
     long as they sustain your calm waiting there's no reason to
     believe they are the wrong things to be doing. There's no a
     priori reason to believe that the therapy will benefit from your
     being steadily preoccupied with P and his therapy—even
     during the sessions. Our primary task is to listen. Not that
     there isn't often something to hear in P's silence, mind you.
     But just as often we can hear it for a moment, and there's
     nothing more to listen to for the remainder of the hiatus. We

have to sustain the silence with equanimity, and this may actually require us to tune out, so to speak.

Us   How about maintaining our equanimity in the face of humor? What if P tells us a joke or deliberately says something funny?

U   If you can manage it, don't laugh. Don't even smile. After all, you won't weep when he tells you something sad or tragic.

Me   I wouldn't take that for granted.

S   And if we can't manage suppressing a laugh, what then?

U   If it were all right to apologize, that's what I would advise.

Me   You can't be serious! Apologize for laughing at a joke? Even for smiling at it?

U   At the very least, you might feel apologetic because you've responded emotionally to P and it wasn't an empathic response, it was a reactive one. It therefore represents a breach of your neutrality, doesn't it?

Me   That's stretching the concept, isn't it?

S   I really don't think it is. Still, neutrality or no, our faces are bound to register the emotional tone of P's narrative. I can't see how it would be humanly possible for them not to, unless it's going to be a wooden poker-face. I'd think this simply amounts to another limitation on our ability to achieve perfect neutrality.

U   I agree. I would make an effort, though, to acknowledge the humor, especially on the first occasion that occurred, and I'd do the same when P said something that he intended to be taken as sarcastic or ironic. So it isn't that I simply didn't respond to his humor, I didn't laugh, or smile much, that's all.

Me   And it goes without saying, I'm sure, that you never indulge in any humor of your own.

U   It's simply too risky and can too easily backfire. I don't think the gain is worth it, even when the humor was good and it conveyed the point of an interpretation in a economical and pungent way. I have the same attitude toward sarcasm and irony.

Us   Well, we've run out of questions—for the moment, at least. We
     will doubtlessly think of more, and it'll probably be during a
     session with P. If so can we call a timeout and give you a ring?

U   Choose the answer that feels right, observe the effect it has,
     think about it after the session, and—the best of luck!

Us   Thank you!

TWENTY-SIX
RESISTANCE AND TRANSFERENCE

Resistance and transference, whose natural habitat is the middle stage, are psychoanalysts' pet concepts. As such, they are overused, sometimes misused, and to correct for that, ours is a conservative stance toward them. In the interests of doing justice to today's lesson, so dense and difficult is it, Susan and I will settle for a summary, and involve ourselves only in the resistance exercise.

Resistance and transference do play a special role in Psychotherapy. In respect of that role, we must construe them narrowly and treat them conservatively. Resistance should be reserved for impasses, and not denote our patients' unwillingness to change or their "resistance" against the work of therapy; that conflates resistance with defenses. Similarly, transference mustn't be equated with the relationship that patients have with us, and it shouldn't be invoked every time they have a thought, feeling, or fantasy about us. That obscures the fact that transference is a deep distortion of reality.

Resistance, as commonly construed, counts as a disruption of the therapeutic process, and consequently could appropriately be treated with interpretations. Doing so, however, would make it problematic for us, inasmuch as Psychotherapy proscribes the use of diagnostic and confronting interpretations, and those are the only kinds we might apply to resistance—so construed. But if we construe it not as defense but as impasse, then we have a way to treat resistance: in the business mode. This requires us to define resistance in a way that not only limits it to therapy but further limits it to patients' intention to abort it. Viewed as an impasse of this magnitude, resistance becomes a business matter, for the interpretive mode must never be used for the purpose of influencing their actions, and quitting therapy clearly counts as an action.

275

Transference, on the other hand, counts as narrative. But to treat it and still satisfy our criteria for using good interpretations, we must distinguish between "the relationship" and "the transference." The latter has to be restricted to patients' ideas, wishes, fantasies, and feelings about us (while countertransference refers to those we may have about them), and will have nothing to do with the former.

Resistance is a notorious concept, in that it gets used to fend off challenges to our theory, and it should never be used for that purpose. It can be subtly and egregiously self-serving in our clinical work, too. Patients want to quit therapy for many reasons, and only one of them has to do with resistance. Moreover, there are many reasons we might not want them to quit, and only one of them is because they are in a state of resistance. It goes without saying that we may have a stake in holding patients, as, indeed, we might have a stake in letting them go. Perhaps more than any other feature of our work, resistance calls into play not only our clinical judgment but our professional and personal integrity.

A useful first step, in studying the subject, is to speak crassly of patients' "bad behavior," in order to draw a distinction between two categories: behaviors that are bad "only" for them, and behaviors that are bad "only" for their therapy. When it comes to the former, we can distinguish between those that are bad in the short run and those that are bad in the long run. Psychotherapy can be relied on to prevail against the latter, but not against the former, and if these behaviors can't be changed by our approaching them as business, then another form of therapy has to be considered.

So let's imagine P reporting an action that we deemed bad for him in the short run. It involves, say, walking in New York's Central Park when it's dark. So we shift into the business mode, and say, "I want to interrupt and ask you whether you are aware of the dangers of that." If P were to respond, "What dangers? I don't understand," we would say, "Well, it seems to me that you might be running the risk of being mugged." If this came as news to P, then things could proceed normally. (And if he said, "I know it, so why would you want to point it out to me?" we'd reply, "You made no mention of the danger, so I didn't know whether you were aware of it.")

But suppose he responds, "I didn't think that I had to mention the danger because it seemed so obvious," and then says, "Now I'm wondering why you mentioned it." We are obliged to tell him (we did, after all, impose the topic), and we might use an interpretation for the purpose ("I wondered if you were intending to invite a mugging," for example). But we could also remain in the business mode by appealing to the issue of caring ("If I think that you're acting in a way that's dangerous to you, why shouldn't I mention it—do you suppose that I simply don't care?"), or the issue of distraction ("I felt worried for your well-being, and, among other things, this worried feeling distracted me")—and this has to be our choice. It stands the best chance of influencing P's habit.

Moreover, it is what we would do when P's behavior pertained directly (even indirectly) to therapy. Say his walk in Central Park took place at dawn, and only when he was on his way to a session; we'd have reason to label it acting out, and this might require the business treatment: "I mentioned it because it has to do with your coming to therapy, and the reason you'd be inviting a mugging has to do with your wishes, fears, and conflicts about being in therapy." In other words, the issue is now also a matter of resistance, and therefore we regard it as having the status of an impasse.

We could, of course, venture an interpretation, but it's too easy to imagine it being fruitless, in that P refuses to acknowledge a connection between his habit and his therapy—and then we'd have no choice but to broach a connection. Besides, the straightforward response to his question, "Why did you mention it?" is the one we gave, and it is never good technique to offer an interpretation when the patient doesn't want or welcome one—and whenever acting out is the topic, that is likely to be the case. Acting out, provided we want it to stop, is best treated with proscriptions. Not all behaviors that might be considered acting out (like discussing sessions with friends, or reading up on therapy, or getting married) merit being proscribed, only those that pose a serious threat to the integrity of the therapy.

One of our timing criteria is that the interpretive mode should be avoided when we are feeling emotionally aroused—when we

feel taken aback (as distinct from surprised) by something patients
have said, when we feel excited (as distinct from moved) by their
narrative, and when we feel anxious (as in concerned about their
well-being). When we feel worried about a patient, it isn't always
a countertransference problem, it can be based on real dangers that
we perceive. This worry counts as a major distraction and merits
being treated in a businesslike way.

All right, now we turn to "bad behavior" that threatens the therapy:
resistance proper. Here, too, we draw an important distinction:
patients might be aware of their wish to abort therapy and of their
intention to actually quit, and they might not be. If they are aware,
then our approach must clearly be the businesslike one. But if they
have no inkling that they want to quit, the approach we might best
take is not so obvious, though according to the foregoing argument,
it might be the business mode nonetheless. This doesn't mean we
won't face serious problems dealing with the matter regardless of
which approach we take. To help with these problems, we study,
by way of exercise, a form of resistance commonly called a flight
into health.

A Flight into Health

Therapy is in the middle stage. P is exultant, but his affect seems
strained and his speech is somewhat driven.

> Boy, am I feeling great these days! I don't know what
> I'm doing here any more, everything is going so well.
> I've been getting to my classes, even the morning ones.
> I finished the history paper and handed it in on time,
> and I'm working on my English paper. For the first time
> in a long time I can sit down and work without getting
> restless and jittery. Is that ever a great feeling! [pause] I
> spoke to my father last night, and for the first time in
> years he didn't get to me. It was almost a human
> conversation! I didn't get my usual feeling that he was
> bugging me about everything. He made only one remark

that got to me; when I told him how well I was working,
he said, "You're a macher, eh?" [pause] But I brushed it
off, didn't let it upset me at all. I felt like yelling, "And
you're a shlemiehl, eh!" and hanging up. But I bit my
tongue and shut up. [pause] I was talking to Joey
yesterday, and he said he never saw me in such good
shape. You know what he said? Therapy has done me a
lot of good; that's what he said. I'm a new man. I'm not
so tense and uptight any more; I can laugh and fool
around and let myself go. [pause] And it's really true.
It's really great!

"So it's time to quit, eh?" (a variation on this succinct interpretation is "Then what are you still doing here?") immediately leaps
to the tongue. We'll bite it back, of course. It's curt, and would certainly be taken as sarcastic, at the least. Besides, we're dealing with
resistance (it's the assumption we're making here), and resistance
is too serious a matter to be treated either succinctly or lightly.

We're working with a resistance that P is not acknowledging.
Still, the logic of his narrative is this: "Because I am doing so well,
because I have improved so much, it is pointless to continue with
therapy." (It could be transposed into its mirror image, "Because I
am doing so badly, because I haven't improved at all and in fact
have gotten worse, it is pointless to continue with therapy," and
we'd face the same problems.) We could articulate this message—
and we probably should, as a first step toward exploring the resistance—but it can be regarded as only a preliminary step. For when
P concurs with our interpretation, we will have to take further steps
toward the resistance, whose logic is different. Instead of, "I am
better, therefore I want to quit," the logic of the resistance is, "I
want to quit, therefore I am better."

How do we take those further steps? Do we move straight into
the business mode and provide P with an explanation of resistance
and its multifarious ways? That would be my inclination. It seems
to me he's in no condition to hear an interpretation, and any interpretation I'd give would meet with mystification if not outrage. I
certainly don't want to throw cold water on his improvement and

say anything that would seem to cast doubt on his rosy appraisal of his mental health; I'm sure it would only make matters worse, not only for P but for the therapy. Neither do I want to shift into a diagnostic gear and say anything about his feelings (they are strained, for instance, and his excitement is forced and has a driven quality to it). So the best option, in my opinion, is to switch over to the interviewing mode.

Susan prefers to stay with the interpretive mode, to help P recognize that his condition was serving a resistive function. She would rather he discovered the phenomenon than learned about it. And she's willing to speculate, even resort to confrontation. She would proceed under the conviction that, in the long run, the interpretive approach will be more advantageous than the didactic one, provided, of course, it was also effective in ensuring that there was a long run. So she suggested that we look for the best line of interpretation, and we experimented with several. None of them seemed to work well, until Susan hit on a promising idea.

The idea sprang from your parenthetical remark, that every form of resistance, be it a flight into health, a flight into misery, a flight into distrust, or that remarkable one called resistance in the form of free association, is likely to strain our neutrality (if not also our credulity) and invite interpretations that are diagnostic and confrontational. Not only are we apt to experience some skepticism at the rosy picture P painted for us, we may also sense that the resistance will be recalcitrant to good interpretations.

For one thing, the narrative contains no hint of any doubt on P's part that his improvement is anything but genuine, and there is no reason to believe that he would accept any intimation on our part that things weren't as rosy as he thinks they are (so this rules out interpretations such as, "I have a hunch you're trying to convince yourself and me that you no longer need therapy, everything is rosy"). We have to accept his claims and not challenge the validity of his documentation, not excluding the conversation with his father, his description of which is of a somewhat different order than his description of his other gains, and his conclusion that it reflected an improvement is open to question in a way that they aren't. His father disparaged him, as he apparently always has, and P had the impulse to respond in a familiar way, but instead he did something new, he brushed him off and simply shut up. This new behavior was apparently a success, yet we might sense that it was forced. So we might be tempted to exploit the interchange and press it into the service of articulating the resistance and defending an inference that all was not so well. Moreover, it has dynamic content, along with intriguing intimations of transference, which offers us something concrete to work with. It's a tempting target.

Nevertheless, we regard it as a risky choice, if not a potentially serious error. P regards the interchange with his father as another example of his improvement. That's why he described it to us, and we don't want to make him regret having done it. If we use this material at all, it will have to be with special circumspection—and especially so since it touches on transference. Regardless of whether P's response to his father was an improvement or not, his father's attitude toward P's successes may have a bearing on what P might feel ours is. We might draw the inference that he intended to provoke us to challenge him the same way his father did. In fact, we might speculate that he included a description of his father's sarcastic mocking in order to evoke in us a similar reaction, or perhaps even a dissimilar one.

The fact remains that no matter how clearly and accurately we articulated this transferential theme, it can be regarded as only a preliminary step toward formulating the resistance. Since the hallmark of resistance is the impulse to flight, and flight is commonly motivated by fear, all it might take to transform the transference interpretation into a resistance interpretation is to add, "Perhaps a part of you is afraid to continue therapy and wants to quit now." That, alas, is pure speculation. There is no hint of any fear in the narrative, and neither is there a clue as to what P might be afraid of.

Our key problem, then, is finding an approach to the resistance that is sufficiently direct and still protects the integrity of the therapeutic process. The approach will have to be confrontational (P has no idea that resistance is afoot, so the idea will have to be imposed), and the process will be compromised to that extent. But here's what

Susan suggested for a solution: our confrontation needn't be directed at P's claims and documentation, instead it can address his overriding feeling, which is optimism. That, in her opinion, is likely to have the fewest disadvantages, and if done gradually and in stepwise fashion, the greatest chance of success.

Susan suggests that we approach the resistance from an empathic understanding of what P is feeling: optimistic. The feeling reflects not only his good condition but also the assumption that the condition is stable (the underlying logic is that of the optimist). So the question we'd raise is, "Things are going well, yes, but what makes you feel so sure they will continue that way?" We would not put this question to P, of course; it's too flagrantly a challenge. But we have an even better reason for not asking the question: we already have the answer! He feels so sure things will continue to go very well *because* that feeling subserves his wish to be finished with therapy. The nice wrinkle is that we don't have to justify the answer by casting doubt on his improvements; the basis of his optimism is valid enough, only its logic is "vulnerable," and it could provide the leverage that we need to articulate the resistance.

Susan's approach (which you will like inasmuch as it's quite close to yours—and we've taken the liberty of appropriating several of your recommendations here) can be schematized as follows: P is feeling optimistic and therefore is questioning the point of continuing the work of therapy; his optimism is also subserving a prior wish to be finished with therapy, or an impulse to flee from it (or from us). To put this schema into practice, we could begin with a remark that focused on the optimism: "You are feeling well, doing well, and it is making you optimistic. I gather you are feeling so optimistic that you are thinking that you do not need to work any more in therapy."

After P had responded, presumably in the affirmative, we would venture a doubt-casting remark directed not at the improvements or at the interchange with the father but at the optimism. It will have to be a confrontational interpretation, but it can be formulated in a way that minimizes the side effects. "I want to raise a question about the way you're feeling optimistic," we might begin. "You have made big improvements, and that makes you feel great. I do appreciate that. And I know that it may seem strange to question your optimism. But what do you think of the possibility that one of the reasons your optimism is so high is that you no longer wish to work in therapy but want to be finished with it?"

It would come as no surprise if P heard us challenging the improvements; if so, we'd make it clear that we weren't. Neither would we be surprised if he misunderstood the resistance formulation and we had to explain that we were suggesting that it was his wish to be finished that was "causing" his optimism, at least in significant part. In our view, the interpretation was not so confrontational as to leave him no easy way out. He could agree that it is strange, if not also foolish, to question his optimism. Say he put it this way: "Yes, I do think it's strange; but since you don't, please explain." Or say he reacted with a baffled, "You are asking me to consider the possibility that I have gotten better in order to be finished with therapy, and I find that a very strange idea. As if there were something wrong with that! Did I not come to therapy to get better? Frankly, it seems paradoxical, if not crazy, to me. So I wish you'd tell me how it could be."

We would now have two options. One is to emphasize that we weren't speaking about his having gotten better, we were referring to his optimism. The second is to follow the didactic route by notifying him about the flight into health phenomenon. The nice wrinkle here is that the didactic explanation, since he had literally asked for it, won't be taken as a gratuitous act of supportiveness. It will, however, cast us into a teacherly role. So if we had so far avoided didactic explanations in the therapy, Susan would prefer that we took the first option. To be sure, our interpretation transmuted the resistance from being a flight into health into a flight into optimism but this might only be a temporary expediency.

If P were to react to this with resentment, feeling that we had thrown cold water on his improvements, we could point out that he himself probably had some doubts about them (why else would he accuse us of something we didn't do?). If, on the other hand, his reaction was little more than obstinacy (he had no sense that his optimism was suspect, and refused to entertain the possibility that his wish to withdraw from therapy came first), we might be able to prevail on him to suspect the intensity of his obstinacy. Then again, of course, we might not. But if our efforts failed, the outcome would be no different than if we had said nothing to begin with—he'll quit therapy. Within the limits of tact, judiciousness, and professional responsibility, we did all we could.

All right, we have probably done all we could with the topic of resistance, so let's turn our attention to transference—and here is where the lesson turns polemical. "Transference is a phenomenon of *potentially* great therapeutic impact," you write. "But in order to realize its potential, we must treat transference with the utmost respect." This means we have to protect and husband it, as we do the interpretive mode, and not squander or corrupt it. Neither should we magnify it, blow it out of proportion, and thereby attenuate it. In your view, we have good reason to be especially conservative, if not extremely cautious, in approaching it.

Many therapists lean on it too heavily; many teachers insist that it play a central role in each and every therapy, and that none can be considered psychoanalytic if it hasn't trafficked, and heavily, in transference. Yet, not only is it a sometime event, it isn't encountered in every Psychotherapy—not in a clinically significant way, at least. There is no reason to believe that a course of Psychotherapy, in order to be effective, has to have any transference involved. Some patients form intense and persistent transferences, others form weak and transient ones, and there are those who form none that are significant enough to merit being called transference.

When patients say, "I love you," and say it to their lover, it isn't transference, but it is (according to a widely held view) when they say it to us. Not only does this imply a definition that pivots on an arbitrary distinction but it vitiates the distinctiveness of transference. For suppose P loves every person who plays an important role in his life, is his love for us so special that it merits a special concept? Moreover, when he says, "I believe you are in love with me," and says it to his lover, P may have grounds for the belief, but when he says it to us, the basis of his belief is significantly different. Not only haven't we expressed a love for him but we haven't behaved in ways that meet the criteria of being in love (although, of course, according to some criteria they might). Furthermore, we're in a good position to say, "But it isn't true that I'm in love with you, therefore your conviction is based not on truth but on transference." Likewise, a distrustful P might distrust us as he distrusts everyone, and there'd be nothing special in his saying, "I distrust you"; he says the same to everyone who matters to him. If he says, "You distrust me," that may be what he tells everybody, except here we are well positioned to say, "But in fact I don't distrust you, so you are engaged in a deep distortion," and this might merit a special concept like transference.

Transferences may be episodic or chronic. The former (sometimes called "transference reactions") are discrete experiences that may take on the character and proportions of an "analytic experience." As such, they often occur in regressed and altered states of consciousness. (Here are three examples: (1) "I'm having a vivid image of you sitting behind me masturbating. It's ridiculous and spooky, but it feels as if you're actually masturbating!" (2) "You are feeling contemptuous of me; you find me disgusting, and it's making me feel nauseated. This is crazy but I'm really nauseous!" (3) "I was daydreaming before you opened the door, and when I saw you, I had the impression that you were in a bad mood. Maybe it was the expression on your face, but my impression was very intense and I felt frightened." In each instance, P's experience was based not on reality, and therefore could only have been based on transference.) These experiences take a variety of forms and can be articulated as: "It feels as if I'm cuddling you, threatening you, abandoning you, smothering you, biting you, swallowing you; it feels as if you're my breast, my penis, my feces." These can be powerful regressive, or near psychotic, experiences. They implicate primitive defenses of the introjective and projective varieties.

The chronic transference (provided P isn't severely disturbed) is likely to take forms that are more benign, and only deserves to be called a "neurosis" when it is pervasive and debilitating. Often it is reflected in overweening dependency feelings, usually accompanied by idealization; sometimes it takes a paranoid form and implicates feelings of fear and dread; sometimes it is narcissistic in nature and involves fantasies of merging. But whether it calls for special measures on our part or whether we treat the transference neurosis no differently from P's regular neurosis, is the question.

Do our timing criteria need to take account of transference? Is transference, in either its episodic or chronic form, so special that we must compromise our basic technical principles in respect to it? (Or, put another way, is "compromise" an ill-chosen word here?) To be sure, when the transference episode has the proportions of an "analytic experience," we do treat it specially. But when P says he distrusts his father, we don't rise to the occasion with an interpretation, we treat it as narrative and as we treat all narrative, according to our criteria of good timing. Similarly, if he says he distrusts us, we might treat it no differently; just because it might be a piece of transference doesn't mean we have to jettison our timing criteria. Moreover, if P says, "I distrust my father," we may well think, "You distrust me," but we'd say it aloud only if saying it aloud satisfied our timing criteria; it has no special status in respect to timing.

Compare "My father distrusts me" and "You distrust me." We might be tempted to say, "You believe your father distrusts you," when P says the latter, and, "You believe I distrust you," when he says the former. But there is this crucial consideration: we can invalidate the latter in a way that we cannot the former. Whether P's father distrusts him is something we can only speculate about (and of course we never should), and the same is true for P (only his father can say for sure whether he distrusts him). But when it comes to whether we distrust P, we are in a privileged position to know and speak the truth. In this respect, then, transference has a special status; it gives us a way out of our epistemological cave.

The key question is whether we want to escape it. Our answer is the familiar "it depends." No blanket yes will satisfy us, in part because it won't satisfy the requirements of neutrality, and so we'll reserve our clinical judgment and apply it case by case and instance to instance. Moreover, we will also accept as our guideline the dictum, *"Keep the Transference in the Background!"*—when it *is* there, of course. For just as we husband the interpretive mode, making sure never to corrupt and squander it, so we vouchsafe the transference; and just as we give priority to well-timed interpretations, and would rather miss an opportunity to interpret than to interpret prematurely, we prefer to pass up an opportunity to define our patients' experience as constituting a transference rather than misidentify it. The hazards of misusing it, and thereby diluting its *potential*, are greater than the risks of overlooking it.

This is the main reason we keep the transference in the background—and trust that we won't fail to discern it when it's in the foreground. Chances are better that we will "see" it, and so will our patients, when it counts than that we'll be blind and deaf to it. It isn't all that subtle a phenomenon and really isn't very difficult to discern. For one thing, transference episodes may constitute "analytic experiences," which are readily discernable. And we will then treat it specially, yes, but no differently from any "analytic experience," which not all patients have, and those that do don't have one often. The same can be said for transference episodes.

Patients may not experience a transference neurosis, either, in the sense of a chronic transference that has the proportions of a neurosis. Instead, they have a relationship with us that isn't distorted in a way that their other relationships are. Their everyday relations with people who matter to them are bound to be shaped by early experiences with significant caretakers, and this might be taken to mean that all of them are "transferential." It follows that their relationship with us is necessarily "transferential," and therefore nothing special.

And there is, of course, a relationship between us and our patients (how could there not be?), and it's a "real" one (of course!). Our thesis is merely that it needn't and shouldn't play a role in the vital work of therapy. Instead, it may play a vital role in business—which is also vital to Psychotherapy. So if they adopt a passive-submissive posture vis-à-vis us, or a hostile or seductive one, these are characteristics of their relationship with us that are properly regarded as business issues rather than narrative ones, falling thereby in the same category of actions—insofar as they are actions, that is. Insofar as they are ideas, wishes, attitudes, and feelings, they count, of course, as narrative. But those aren't, strictly speaking, "the relationship"; they are what they are, our patients' thoughts, wishes, fantasies, impulses, and feelings vis-à-vis us. A relationship, after all, is a two-way affair, a transference is not. Not only is it conceptually better to maintain a clear distinction between them but it also makes a substantial and significant difference in respect to our making good therapeutic use of patients' transference experiences.

This is not to say that their relationship with us cannot become transferential in the strong sense of the term. But then it merits being called a neurosis and therefore a transference neurosis. Whatever the reasons may be, and they are probably based on an interaction between the patients (their problems and their personality) and the structure and dynamics of therapy (its potential for fostering regression and our neutrality), the fact remains that a course of Psychotherapy can be complete and effective without a patient having had a transference neurosis. In that event we must be content to work with the neurosis that he or she had to begin with.

Imagine P speaking about a pending vacation from therapy and dreading it because his wife doesn't understand his need for independence. In fact, she doesn't understand him at all, in sharp contrast to guess who. "I have you pegged as someone who knows who he is, so you don't step on people and smother them," says P. Were we to now say, "Perhaps if I were as understanding as you suggest, I wouldn't be so inconsiderate as to take a vacation," it would be a sharp and incisive intervention, but a curt and sarcastic remark like that is likely to throw him on the defensive.

Then what about, "I wonder if in ascribing special powers of understanding to me, you aren't viewing me as someone special on whom it's all right to let yourself become dependent"? Inasmuch as it speaks of "special powers of understanding," it may be ambiguous. Psychotherapy does entail a unique relationship with patients and a unique role definition for us; we are in fact "special," we do show "special understanding." P's regarding us as the one who understands him in a special way and who doesn't step on him, is based on an important piece of reality. Such facts should not be overlooked. They pose technical problems in any attempt to interpret a transference, and not only an idealized one.

We could approach this one by distinguishing our being an ideal therapist from our being an ideal person. P provided for this distinction by picturing us as perfect in our personal relationships. So we might say, "I gather you picture me not only as a special therapist but also a special person, someone who treats his friends and family well," and soon we could offer an interpretation that began, "I have an idea about your wish (or need) to see me that way." We might mention that he had, of course, no way of knowing what our outside behavior was like, and therefore the generalization he drew wasn't unreasonable, but we could point out that he might have inferred that only our behavior toward him was special.

Transference interpretations should be formulated around patients' wishes and needs; articulating the distortion will often be insufficient. But it needn't be done all at once. Usually the articulation can be offered and the rest deferred because their reaction to it may be strong, or they may want to complete it themselves and perhaps explore its basis. (They may, of course, reject it altogether.) Transference episodes, because they evoke strong feelings, have to treated with special tact. If the therapy is young, we might preface our interpretation by saying that we appreciate what P is experiencing and how frightening it is. A transference reaction is a deep distortion of reality, and he might sense it.

Moreover, when we, too, sense it, we won't be prone to take it personally. We are liable to have reactions of our own when we become the object of a transference. If it's an idealized one, for instance, we might have the wish to shake it off, inasmuch as it makes us guilty or embarrassed, perhaps evoking narcissistic fantasies and conflicts of our own; and when the idealization is accompanied by feelings of dependency on the therapy, which is often the case, we are prone to additional misgivings and guilt. Not only must we keep such feelings under control but we have to keep from conveying a sense of defensiveness, a wish to push the patient away and disclaim responsibility for his or her dependency.

Imagine P, who isn't a latecomer, being late and saying he could have made it on time today but didn't try ("It didn't seem worth the effort"). After a pause and "I bet you're angry," he says he would ask whether it was true but feels sure that we wouldn't tell him, adding, "You probably wouldn't even give me an interpretation like, 'So you want me to be angry at you, eh!'" We now offer this interpretation: "I gather you believe that that interpretation is correct." "Maybe—I don't know," he responds. Then he speaks of how badly things are going, "I just seem to be getting worse, so what's the use!" He tells of having had another fight with his father, this time not about his doing badly in school but about his sleeping late. "It really bugs him when I sleep till noon, he gets all excited. I'm getting fed up with it. I wish he'd resign himself to the fact that I'm an adolescent and adolescents sleep late. He blew up when I said that, flew into a royal rage. I got scared at how furious he got when I said, 'Tough shit!' I thought he was going to hit me." Now P's voice rises to a whine and he's virtually crying as he speaks of how his father has always treated him off-handedly, as if he didn't matter to him, always making promises that he never kept—"So naturally I wasn't going to be his good little boy. I mean, what the hell does the man expect!" P gasps for breath and takes a minute to regain his composure. With a look of anguish, he mutters, "Boy, I'm such a mess!" and looks imploringly into our eyes. What can we say to him?

We could draw a parallel to his father in the motif of indifference, and say something to the effect of: "I, too, treat you in an offhand way, and so you aren't going to be my 'good little boy' and come on time or get better," or, "You wish I would pay attention to you, just as you tried to get your father to stop treating you in an offhand way." We could speculate that a reaction of anger is better than nothing: "You expect I'll be like your father, that you'll have to be a good boy here, too, and it still won't matter, I still won't care about you; provoking my anger by coming late would at least show that I cared about you—just as your father notices you only when you can provoke his anger." We could infer a mo-tive: "You want me to comfort you just like you would want your father to do." We could infer an affect: "You are feeling angry at me because I'm becoming important to you, and you're afraid I'll let you down as your father does." All of them would be good in-terpretations, but none of them is the best interpretation. They sim-ply draw a superficial parallel between P's father and us.

P apparently has a need to cast us in the same image as his fa-ther, as the one who disapproves in anger, disappoints, and breaks promises. But the fact is: we do *not* disapprove and disappoint, we *don't* break our promises, we *never* react in anger, and P already knows it! This raises the possibility that he is experiencing us not as being like his father but as being *unlike* his father, and this might be what is actually driving the resistance; it might answer the ques-tion, What is he so afraid of that he wants to flee the therapy? That we aren't going to fulfill his transference needs, is the answer: he fears that we are never going to be like his beloved (and be-hated) father. This formulation of the transference isn't any more com-plex than the direct parallel, and neither is it as superficial, but it serves two useful functions at once.

For resistance sometimes takes the form of transference, and the transference often serves as a defense (it's one of the tricks played by the ego). And while transference can become a resistance, more often than not it serves the function of exactly keeping patients tied to us—it keeps them in therapy instead of motivating them out of it. This is true not only when it's "positive" (they regard us as a nurturing, loving, and perhaps all-powerful figure), but also when it's "negative" (viewing us as a demanding, even critical, figure, for instance, could spur them on in the work of therapy). Still, there is no a priori way of saying what function a particular transference is serving, though it often appears to be serving the interests of remembering and reminiscing in disguised and transformed ways. This is the earliest formulation of transference in psychoanalysis, and it's still the most powerful one.

Moreover, P's resistance cannot be explained by distrust alone, it has to be formulated with respect to the therapy as a whole and especially to the therapeutic process. The process contains the seeds of resistance; it has an inherent inertia; there is a resistance against Disclosure and self-inquiry, a resistance that is indigenous to making significant changes and therefore enlists a patient's defenses. As a working hypothesis, this formulation has important ramifications.

So, to return to the transference, we keep it in the background. We don't fish for it or ferret it out, we wait for it to surface and to matter, and only then do we deal with it—no differently than the ways in which we deal with all of our patients' mental content, and according to the timing criteria we apply to it: when it impedes and impairs the therapeutic process, then we address it as we do all impediments and impairments of the therapeutic process, and when it assumes the proportions of an impasse and threatens the therapy, then we address it as we do all impasses that threaten the therapy.

Finally, what about countertransference? It's also an overused and misused concept. We do have to deal with it, but in a way that needn't implicate our patients at all, for they may not be implicated. Moreover, though we can have both "countertransference episodes" as well as "countertransference neuroses," we need not have either, and we certainly should never have the latter. Why, after all, should we? The reasons our patients have transference experiences are in no way applicable to us—we have no reason to distort and defend.

But the fact is, we do distort and defend. We should not, however, impose it on our patients. It must remain our problem and our business. This doesn't mean that we cannot use it to good therapeutic effect, for it can be a useful signal. But it can't always be relied on, doing so is apt to be highhanded, and usually we don't really need it. In any event, countertransference episodes should be used carefully and cautiously, if not also warily. For example:

> I am feeling, say, distrustful of P, and I suspect it may be
> my distortion. All right, but isn't there something P is
> doing to provoke the feeling in me? Well, maybe there isn't,
> and it's nothing more than my personal problem vis-à-vis
> him. The possibility remains, however, that it's a response

to something that he is doing. Still, I must carefully steer a course between the Scylla of distorting what he's doing and misreading his mind, and the Charybdis of overlooking what he's doing and blinding myself to some important mental content of his. After all, I, too, am capable of disavowing defensively and projecting—I'm not perfect.

Whether our experiencing a countertransference doesn't always reflect a flaw or defect in our work is a debatable question. In your opinion, generally it probably does. Therefore this is something that properly belongs in our supervision (and/or our therapy) and not in our patient's therapy. ("That, in any event, is my basic position, and I regard it as a prudent one.")

TWENTY-SEVEN
THE ENDING STAGE

Dear Uncle,

Our final lesson. Fittingly, it's on the ending. This stage, not only is it not a brief one but it raises some of Psychotherapy's most basic issues and difficult problems. In order to do them justice, Susan and I will resort to each of the literary techniques and devices that we've used in our letters. All that's missing is an exercise, but we made one for ourselves, as you will see.

The Perils and Problems of the Ending

Introduction

The ending has the most problems and is the most ambiguous of the stages. Not only does it evoke some of our most basic human problems but it raises some of Psychotherapy's. Separation is the most basic of the human problems, and Psychotherapy's are: (1) Does our treatment have a natural conclusion, and if so, what are its characteristics? (2) What marks the cure?

My colleagues generally agree that psychotherapy has a natural conclusion and that separation is likely to be its main theme; they disagree on how best to approach the ending and on the nature of the cure. Indeed, the concept of cure is widely rejected as inappropriate for our service. Moreover, not only is the ending stage marked by disputes among us but also between us and our patients. It's not uncommon for patients to believe that their treatment is in its final stage at a time when we've judged that it was still in the middle, and for them to resist acknowledging the ending when we've judged that they were there.

294

Because it evokes profound feelings, patients may be motivated to avoid the experience of the ending. They might arrange for circumstance to conspire against it (by taking a job in another city, for instance); they will decide to terminate precipitously (for such excellent reasons as that they feel all better, for instance). And we, too, will find ways of avoiding the ending, for it evokes feelings in us as well.

A common way of short-circuiting the ending is to set an arbitrary date for termination, or one that is based on extrinsic circumstances. I'm referring to the practice of having termination coincide with the onset of a vacation (typically, the summer). That seems sensible: take advantage of an already scheduled termination, and simply transform it from temporary to permanent. This isn't always an evasion of the ending but it often is—and when our professional-economic needs play a part, it always is. Optimally, extrinsic considerations (like our need to replace the patient—and in your case it might be your going on internship) should play no part in the matter. It's always unfortunate when they do, for it prevents the ending from running its natural course; a valuable opportunity for promoting our patient's well-being will have been lost.

**Criteria for Termination When Extraneous Factors
Play No Part**

From P's perspective, they are usually related to his reasons for having entered therapy and what he expected to achieve. The question I will now raise is: Must we share this perspective?

Us By "share" you mean articulate P's reasons and expectations, or do you mean tell him what ours are?

U   Both. P will rarely feel that all of his expectations were fulfilled. What complicates the matter is, they often change during the course of the treatment. Therapy will have uncovered problems that weren't salient at first, or else altered the hierarchy of his problems, making certain of them less pressing and raising the urgency of others. It also happens that the symptom that motivated him into therapy persists, but its role in his life changes in a way that allows him to live with it. What also happens is that as the ending approaches, new problems arise. Sometimes this happens out of a need to forestall termination.

Us   In any case, the critical question is likely to be, "When have I been cured, or more accurately, cured enough?"

U   When has P gained the strength to live well enough without therapy? When has he gained, or regained, sufficient involvement with, and control over, his inner and outer realities? When is he autonomous enough? These questions are always hard to answer, and a degree of uncertainty is bound to remain.

Us   But we're sure that there's a radically different way to formulate the matter, and that you will now argue its merits to us.

U   It does not involve judgments about cure, achievements, or expectations; instead it revolves around our conception that psychotherapy in general, and Psychotherapy in particular, has a natural developmental course.

Us   You've told us that therapy has naturally occurring stages of maturation. Just as there's a beginning and a middle with distinct defining characteristics, so there's an ending.

U   But I never mentioned that the development of Psychotherapy can be substantially unrelated to—can stand substantially independent from—P's condition.

Us   And what do you mean by "P's condition"?

U   Nothing less than this: Psychotherapy can run its full course without there being substantial alteration in his behavior and experience outside of it. And that, you may well believe, is outrageous.

Us   We know better than that by now. You're proposing that Psychotherapy can be divorced from reality. You're claiming that P can enjoy a full and meaningful therapeutic experience without at the same time changing his "real" behavior. You are braving the challenge, "What then was the point of the enterprise?"

U I'll brave it, for though it doesn't happen that often, when it does happen, it needn't follow that therapy was without efficacy; the effects may reveal themselves only after it was completed. The majority of our patients do change during therapy, and some very dramatically. There are some, however, who do it afterward.

Us You're aware, we gather, how question begging, if not self-serving, this point may seem, insofar as you seem to be defending the efficacy of Psychotherapy in all cases.

U It may seem glib to contend that if the benefits of the therapy weren't apparent by the time it's finished, it wasn't conclusive evidence that the therapy was without efficacy.

Us It brings to mind the cognitive dissonance phenomenon, exemplified in the greater faith that members of a millenial movement show after the predicted event fails to occur—they too move the date ahead!

U But we have clinical evidence for our prediction, so it's more of a postdiction.

Us Do we have any clinical theory for it?

U Naturally. One explanation centers on the transference neurosis and its resolution. P might have had an intense transference, and couldn't resolve it sufficiently during the analysis. If that's the case, there may have been little change in his condition while treatment was in progress. When it's over, however, the transference may "loosen its grip," and changes can then occur.

Us Your having started with this explanation would suggest that it's your favorite one. What's another?

U The onus is put on P's use of the therapy as a large-scale defense against change. Instead of having put his energies into making changes, he has put them into doing therapy. Only when therapy is no longer available does he face the necessity of change; up until that point, being in therapy exhausted his motivation for it.

Us The trouble with that explanation is that it seems to minimize our responsibility for having "dealt with" the issue during the course of therapy. After all, whenever we do discern it, we must take steps to dissipate it.

U Yes, and it's far from uncommon. Therefore, unlike the resolution of the transference, if therapy continued to be used as a defense against change, and against living too, it was flawed. Still, therapies are flawed, some more seriously than others, so there's the possibility that this one could have persisted despite our concerted efforts.

Whatever the reason, changes in our patients' psychological condition might occur only after therapy is concluded, and it is useful to discuss this with them. The alternative, after all, is to forestall termination and continue therapy (referring them to another therapist is tantamount to continuing therapy), which can be a mistake. Patients may remain in treatment for too long when the criterion of change is the ruling one. When psychotherapy continues for too many years, it can change its chief function; it can become a way of living for the patient, if not a crutch. I don't mean to take a sanctimonious attitude toward protracted therapy. There are patients who continue to need it, for whom being in treatment serves a vital function. We have to be prepared to make the appropriate clinical judgment for such cases. But we also have to be prepared to make the judgment that a patient has had sufficient therapy, and continuing may not only be without benefit but even detrimental. This isn't an easy judgment.

There's an alternative that amounts to regarding termination as a kind of trial. Just as the beginning can be viewed as a trial period, so the ending can be viewed as revocable. There remains, after all, the possibility that our patient could return at a later date. (We'll soon consider whether it's prudent to proceed on the assumption that a patient is going to be finished with Psychotherapy. Since my answer is no, it has direct bearing on this issue.)

The Earmarks of the Ending

The earmarks of the ending are often as distinctive as those of the beginning. This is particularly true when it is substantially taken up with the issue of termination. But the ending can be distinctive in other ways as well; as, for example, when P turns his efforts to consolidating his gains and his attention to the future. I'll take up the distinctive features of the ending in the context of examining the transition from the middle.

That transition may be marked by a major impasse based on P's sense of an impending change of direction ("I've come this far, so far so good, but where do I go from here?"). The therapeutic process may seem to have come to a grinding halt, and P experiences a sense of perplexity that can be understood as an unwillingness to face termination. For the ending can provoke a major struggle—both within him and between him and us—that is based on the question, "Where do we go from here?" When we answer the question with a reference to termination, we should therefore do it judiciously and tactfully—and then steel ourselves for a struggle.

Sometimes the transition is marked by a burst of intense therapeutic work, the very opposite of an impasse. That makes it difficult to discern. We can be guided here by a sense of something paradoxical happening: the middle has apparently run its course, and just when it's time for the beginning of ending, P renews the work of the middle with surprising intensity. Sometimes the intensity will have a strain to it that will be the clue, but sometimes it won't; all we can go on is our sense of surprise and paradox.

The ending may be heralded by a topic that's new, or one P had mentioned at the outset but not again. It may have a clear reference to termination (as, for an easy example, an obsession with thoughts of death), but the reference may be obscure, if not absent, and the only distinctive feature may be its novelty.

It's not uncommon for the transition to be marked by a regression of some sort. Typically, it takes the form of the return of an old symptom, even the one that originally brought P into therapy, which had subsided after treatment began. When this happens after the middle has apparently run its course, we can take it as a likely sign that the ending is at hand, for its function is typically to prevent that stage from occurring—and it is vital that P be made to recognize that fact (for example, "Just as it was this phobia that led you to start therapy, so it is now this phobia that keeps you in it"). It sometimes happens that the symptom never subsided but was kept out of therapy, then it is invited in, so to speak, to serve its big function. We might experience a sense of "Why now? Why did it wait so long?"

Occasionally, it will be a mental experience—a dream, a fantasy, the recovery of a memory—that ushers in the ending. The content of that experience often bears a direct relationship to the new stage of the treatment. This can be unmistakable when it revolves around the theme of separation, or of mortality, or of everlasting union. If the theme is more obscure than that, we may have to listen hard for it. If we are alert to the function of such an experience, we will more likely hear it. Here are a handful that are rather obscure (they give an idea of what "clear" ones are likely to be):

- I've been obsessed with the memory of my first day at school. I have no idea how come, because there was nothing traumatic about it. I looked forward to going to school. I was excited when the time came.
- I had a fantasy that you needed a heart transplant and mine was the only heart that would be suitable for you.
- I had this weird fantasy. I was an astronaut, in training, practicing moving around in the weightless condition.
- My dream was strange. I was riding an escalator, going down, and when it came to an end, I kept on going down.

The Problems of the Ending

Not only P but we, too, will have feelings and conflicts about the ending. Some will amount to opposition to it, others the opposite; some will be based on countertransference issues, others on issues surrounding our professional work. Instead of spelling them out, I'll merely point out that we can expect to have problems of our own, and therefore we prepare ourselves for the ending by examining our mind and heart, for there are bound to be feelings and conflicts that could influence and shape the ending that P experiences.

Having resolved our conflicts, we turn our full attention to P and his feelings about terminating, which can also go both ways.

Whatever they may be, it is vital that he acknowledge his part in the advent of the ending, that he see it as the product of his own activity, in significant part at least. Ideally, just as he played an active part in starting therapy, so should he play an active part in ending it. But it's quite typical of him to experience it as our decision. "You want to be rid of me," and, "You are giving up on me," are complaints we can expect to hear, and they are likely to be made because he refuses to acknowledge that it was his experience that led us to judge that the ending stage had been reached. We should therefore be in a position to say, in good conscience, "It was my idea, yes, but it was based on your experience of the therapy."

P might reject that claim ("I see what you based it on, but I disagree that it means what you've said"), and contend that he can't be in the ending because he doesn't feel prepared to terminate. The basis of this feeling, the meaning of his "I'm not ready," will then become the topic, and the question may be raised, "Not ready for what?"

Before addressing the topic, we might take the precaution of determining how P construes the ending. Does he believe it's a brief period, little more than an extended goodbye? If so, his feeling unprepared for it can be based on that simple misconception— after all, one doesn't begin saying goodbye until one is ready to depart. When we tell him that the ending isn't a brief farewell, it's a full stage of therapy that can take months, if not a year, our aim isn't to reassure him but to lend weight to the issues of termination ("The issues that are going to be brought to the surface by the pending termination are of utmost relevance to your psychological well being; they merit a thorough working through").

But P will have already worked on these issues; there've been temporary terminations during the course of therapy. The summer vacation typically provides an opportunity to deal with separation, and can be regarded as a trial termination. The value of so regarding it is twofold: separation issues will not be novel during the ending; the ending will not be entirely taken up with termination—for when it is, we are open to the criticism that we weren't active enough in listening for termination themes during the therapy.

In the majority of cases, such themes will have been uncovered and analyzed before the ending was reached, and this means that we will be offering no new interpretations about separation and separation anxiety. We'll be repeating, amplifying, and articulating interpretations that we'd had occasion to make before and after summer vacations or interruptions due to illness, and the like. Still, when therapy terminates for good, there can be no easy recourse to the expectation that it will resume. The rhythm of the weekly schedule, of the holiday and summer vacation schedule, quickly establish themselves for patients, and that rhythm often serves to structure the separations, and organizes defenses against separation anxiety. Termination proper, however, can take on the properties of irrevocability and finality.

Even when its ingredients are familiar, the ending can provide patients with a profound experience of separation. Paradoxically, it's this profundity that can limit its analysis and resolution. What I mean is this: only death is irrevocable, psychotherapy can resume (if not with us then with another therapist)—and just as the transference might not be fully resolved, so separation is ever relative.

On Modifying Our Technique

A member of the class was presenting a case that had reached the termination stage. Our teacher, the wise and experienced analyst, was sucking his lemon and looking sourer than usual, for the presenter was describing how she'd been modifying her analytic stance in deference to the final stage. "One of the modifications I have decided on," she said, "is to be less silent and speak more."

"What will you be speaking about?" inquired our teacher.

"Well, for instance, P described his plans for the summer. So I told him I was planning to spend the summer in Europe," said our presenter, and there was an note of pride in her saying it.

"You told him maybe where exactly in Europe?"

"No. He didn't ask."

"I'm not surprised. He also didn't ask, in the first place, what your summer plans were, no?"

"Yes. I decided to tell him, anyway."

Unable to contain his exasperation, the analyst said, "What is it between you and P, a friendship suddenly? Not only do you decide to be less silent, you decide also to be less impersonal."

"I will show him a more human face."

Our teacher winced at this, but let it go. He scanned the table. "Would anyone like to give a rationale for such measures?"

"To help P resolve his transference," one of us offered. "Another rationale could be to actualize his problems over separation," another offered. "P learns to separate from a real relationship instead of an artificial one." "And a third reason is that he's already had enough experience of the analytic mode, and maybe now he could use something a bit different." This was contributed by the class wit, wearing a wicked grin.

Our teacher, with a rare smile, said, "Fine! Two rationales is plenty. Let's begin with the first one. The transference is still in full bloom; P needs our help in resolving it; so instead of giving him good and useful interpretations, we stop being such a blank screen and we start filling in some of the empty blanks. That's an improvement?"

No one dared respond to this rhetorical question. Instead, we all settled back to listen to a lecture on transference. His point was that if interpretation and working through were the ways to resolve the transference during the middle stage of analysis, they remained the ways to do during the ending. Any changes in our "real" behavior could only impair and impede the resolution. "And tell me, by the way," I remember him saying, "are you maybe prepared to act nasty if P, it happens, has an idealized good-mother transference? And since when do we playact, we are students of drama?"

I also remember this: "It happens often during the ending, P sees changes in us; we seem more friendly and relaxed, less inhibited and removed. The interpretation we could now offer him will draw attention to the fact this perception is based on changes in him and not in us. If we have maintained our regular position, it is he who is the more friendly and relaxed, less inhibited and removed. If, however, we have not maintained our regular position, we have lost the chance to help him see a piece of his intrapsychic reality."

On the subject of separation, our teacher had a jaundiced view. Too much was made of separation anxiety, and, as far as he was concerned, it was little more than a manifest form of castration anxiety. In fact, too much was made of separation anxiety because it was a handy way to mask the underlying castration anxiety. You see, the wise and experienced analyst saw no connection between separation and death, so he refused to give separation a special status.

After this discussion, during which the presenter was conspicuously silent, he turned to her and said, "Have we covered all the bases? Is there not something else you did or plan to do?"

Our hapless colleague was in pain—and loath to say anything other than "No, that's enough, please leave me alone!" Except there was one more thing, and she chose an unfortunate way of speaking of it—by breaking our teacher's cardinal rule which was never to make mention of supervision and lay any responsibility on the supervisor. She said this: "My supervisor suggested that I might consider a reduction in frequency of sessions, to reduce the intensity of P's dependency on the analysis and maybe gradually shift the balance from therapy to living."

"You blame her because you take it for granted I will disapprove of the measure. She advised you to raise this possibility with P?"

"No, she just advised me to support it if P raised it."

"Then I'm sorry to tell you that I don't disapprove. To introduce such a measure, is one thing, to agree to it is another. I do not disapprove, for not only is it no modification of any analytic technique but it's a business matter and would in no way spoil P for further psychoanalysis. So if it came up as his idea, and if you judged it could serve a useful practical purpose without diluting the vital work of the ending—and that is the critical consideration—you could agree to it. Otherwise, I recommend you stick with a business-as-usual approach throughout the entire course of the ending. Not only won't it hurt P in the short run but it will be much better for him in the long run."

Well, Uncle, this covers today's lesson—and all of our lessons, as a matter of fact. There are lots of loose ends, of course, but practicing and listening will teach us how to tie them together. Besides, will we not be engaged in studying psychotherapy until we retire from the field? So we'll end with an overdetermined question and a closing exercise.

Does the Last Session End the Therapeutic Process?

S   In my opinion, no.

Me   Let's make it unanimous. But what accommodations are we prepared to make in respect to it being P's last session?

S   None at all, I would think. I see no reason for any. I can even picture us making a strong interpretation during the session.

Me   Even though there are going to be no more sessions afterwards?

S   It's because so many sessions have gone before. Moreover, Psychotherapy may be coming to a close, but the therapeutic process extends beyond it. P has learned a way to experience himself and examine his mind and his actions.

Me   So, whether it is prudent to proceed on the assumption that P is going to be finished with psychotherapy can be construed in two ways. One has to do with the continuation of the therapeutic mode in the absence of formal therapy sessions. The second has to do with the possibility of his resuming at a later date, either with us or with another therapist.

S   And both of them must be taken seriously, for every therapy is flawed, some more than others, and every therapy, and every P, will arrive at a position that is short of the ideal in one way or another. Further attempts are therefore always possible.

Me   Advisable?

S   It depends. The shortcomings will not always merit the cost of further therapy. In some cases the disadvantages of prolonging therapy will outweigh the advantages, in others they won't. Still, the fact that P might potentially benefit from a further course of therapy has to remain as a real consideration. If it does, then two consequences follow: the termination of Psychotherapy needn't wait until perfection has been achieved, and the ending should not be conducted in such a way as to "spoil" P for further therapy.

Me   I think we may be losing sight of the fact that the experience of separation actually takes place after termination, not before. In a vital sense, then, P must confront the experience, must learn to deal

I. H. Paul

with it, after the final session is over. Separation is something each of us must achieve alone.

S   That's a good point. If we bear in mind that separation proper is what P faces on his own, we will vouchsafe the therapeutic process so that he has it available for such important purposes.

Me   We mustn't overlook the fact that P had all along been using the therapeutic process between sessions. We hope he has.

S   The final session, then, can be expected to be no different from the preceding ones, with the possible exception of the parting exchange, the goodbye and farewell.

Me   "Our time is up" won't suffice for the occasion. I suspect there will have to be some sort of ceremony.

S   I doubt there will have to be anything called a "ceremony."

Me   No grand summing up, no resume of the therapy, eh?

S   We would think not.

Me   No parting words of advice?

S   Little more than a wish for good fortune is called for.

Me   All right, then let's try our hand at constructing a closing scenario.

S   Let's do two of them, one with errors and one without any.

Me   Counterpoint it is!

Mistake

P   Well, I guess this is it, really it. [pause] I'm feeling some different feelings.

T   What are you feeling?

P   A melange of mixed and messy feelings. One part sadness, one part gladness, a bit of anguish, and a bit of relief: stir them up and simmer, and voila!—mixed feelings. But you know what, this session wasn't as bad as I imagined it would be. I was dreading it, expecting to feel nervous, at least. And embarrassed. But that hasn't happened. Not until this minute, anyway. And even this minute it isn't that bad. Strange to say, but I'm feeling good.

T   So you're not feeling any of the anger with me that you've been feeling over the past few weeks?

P   Maybe I am. But most of it is gone. Now I'm just scared.

T   Scared of being alone, without me and without therapy, eh?

P   Hey, I just remembered a dream I had last night! I'd completely forgotten it till now, and suddenly it comes back to me. Oh, that's great! So let's see now, how much time do we have left? [glances at clock] Ten minutes. Oh well, then I guess we're going to have to have another session next week to work on it. [smile]

T   I don't think that's advisable.

P   To tell the dream or not to tell the dream, that's the question.

T   Might it not be a going-away present for me?

P   You're marvelous! Because I was at a party of some sort, and maybe it was a birthday party—and you were there, so maybe it was yours. Anyway, the fragment I recall was my unwrapping a big box, and it might have been a present. It was one of those Chinese boxes-within-boxes. All eyes were on me as I opened each box only to find another, slightly smaller one, inside; and each unwrapping revealed another box. But I never got to see inside the final box because I awoke too soon.

T   It was empty, I'm sure.

P   Perhaps. Nothing left—nothing left to give you.

T   So the idea of a birthday might just reflect how you feel about this final session.

P   This is my day of birth, eh?

T   Don't you want me to wish you a happy birthday?

P   Yes, but no many happy returns, please. [pause]

T   Look here, you're wondering whether this is really going to be your final session with me, or whether you will come back to me at some future date.

P   That's true. I was thinking yesterday about what you said awhile ago: there was always the possibility that I could come back for more therapy if I felt I needed to. I guess that made it easier for me to accept termination. But I feel a bit guilty about it too.

T   It sounds like it lends a false note to our ending. Maybe the empty box in the dream means I've been tricking you.

P   [big sigh] I do hope I'm really finished with therapy, but I guess I'm still conflicted about it. [silence]

T   Then why don't you keep in touch in with me, give me a call in a couple weeks, say.

P   Yes, I'd like to keep in touch with you. That's all right, is it?

T   Oh, sure! I'll be happy to hear from you.

P   I guess you think I'm going to need it.

T   But I'm afraid our time is up, we'll have to stop now.

P   Thanks for everything. It's been a rough ride but—a good one. I really appreciate everything you've done for me.

T   I know. Anyway, take care of yourself and be well, and good luck!

Correct

P   Well, I guess this is it, really it. [pause] I'm feeling some different feelings.

Us   Mixed feelings, I take it.

P   A melange of messy feelings. One part sadness, one part gladness, a bit of anguish and a bit of relief: stir them up and simmer, and voila!—mixed feelings. But you know what, this session wasn't as bad as I imagined it would be. I was dreading it, expecting to feel nervous, at least. And embarrassed. But that hasn't happened. Not until this minute, anyway. And even this minute it isn't that bad. Strange to say, but I'm feeling good.

Us   Strange because you know that the prospect of being alone—without me and without therapy—frightens you.

P   Hey, I just remembered a dream I had last night! I'd completely forgotten it till now, and suddenly it comes back to me. Oh, that's great! So let's see now, how much time do we have left? [glances at clock] Ten minutes. Oh well, I guess we're going to have to have another session next week to work on it. [smile]

Us   [warm smile]

P   To tell the dream or not to tell the dream, that's the question.

Us   I have a hunch that the dream might represent a sort of going-away present—for both of us.

P   I think you're right, because I was at a party of some sort, and maybe it was a birthday party—and you were there, so maybe it was yours. Anyway, the fragment I recall was my unwrapping a big box, and it might have been a present. It was one of those Chinese boxes-within-boxes. All eyes were on me as I opened each box only to find another, slightly smaller one, inside; and each unwrapping revealed another box. But I never got to see inside the final box because I awoke too soon.

Us   I think you realize that it might have been empty.

P   Perhaps. Nothing left—nothing left to give.

Us   I wonder, then, whether the idea of a birthday reflects how you feel about this final session.

P   This is my day of birth, eh?

Us   I suppose, then, I should wish you a happy birthday. [smile]

P   [laughing] Thank you, doctor. But not, if you please, many happy returns. [silence]

Us   Are you wondering, perhaps, whether this is going to be your final session with me, or whether you might want to return in the future?

P   Yes. I was thinking yesterday about what you said awhile ago: there was always the possibility that I could come back for more therapy later on, if I felt I needed to. I guess that makes it easier for me to accept this termination. But I feel a bit guilty about it too.

Us   As if it lends a false note to this ending, perhaps. Maybe the trick boxes in the dream also have that meaning.

P   [big sigh] I do hope I'm really finished with therapy, but I guess I'm still conflicted about it. [silence]

Us   Our time is up now.

P   Thanks for everything! It's been a rough ride but—a good one. I deeply appreciate what you've done for me.

Us   Thank you. And the best of luck to you.

> Thank you—and best of luck to Us!
> Simon and Susan

INDEX

311

Letters to Simon (Paul) vii, vii*n*
Life and Work of Sigmund Freud (Jones), 137*n*
Listening (by the therapist)
  activity-passivity of, 211–12
  and distraction, 19, 81, 94, 114, 201
  impassively, 213–14
  with an interpretation in mind, 220–21
  and remembering, 212–13
  and therapists' orientation to session, 210–11
  to vs. *for*, 83, 97, 212
  and understanding, 211, 236. *See also* Patient, listening by
Love, 284–85

"Mai komashmalon?" 210–11
Manipulation, 113, 261, 268, 271
Memory, 135, 145, 159, 212–13
Meno, 129, 132–34, 145
Mental content, 133, 159–62, 180–83. *See also* Mind
Metapsychology, 23, 135, 150–51, 184
Middle stage of Psychotherapy, 248–49, 299–300
Mind, 29, 42, 131, 133, 140, 161, 182–83, 186. *See also* Mental content
Mood, 165
Motives, drives, and wishes, 159, 182–83. *See also* Volition

Narrative, 43–46
  and business, 43–46, 53, 79
  and Disclosure, 139, 144
  as fiction and story-telling, 142
  and interpretation, 45
  theory as, 142–43
  transference as, 276, 286

Neutrality, 10, 29, 37, 40
  as being nonselectively responsive, 121–22, 273
  blank screen theory of, 37, 121, 303
  and business, 13, 46–47
  and caring, 56, 110–11, 240–241, 243
  as desireless, 10, 210
  as ideal and relative, 10, 102, 121
  as limited to narrative, 46, 53
  limits of, 13–14, 37, 100–01, 110–11, 273
  and normative formulations, 109
  and patients' credulity, 46, 112, 122
  and patients' expectations, 39, 47, 58, 105–06
  with respect to action, 73–74
  "with respect to content," 10, 100–05, 153, 206–07
  in respect to interpreting, 454, 110–11
  in respect to resistance, 103
  and social amenities and civility, 261–66
  and therapists' expectations, 10, 105–06, 198
  and therapists' integrity, 72, 240–41
  and therapists' personality and impersonality, 109–15, 121–22
New York Times, the, 118
Nondirective therapy, 28
Nondirectiveness (of Psychotherapy), 27–29, 43–45, 101–02, 108
  limits and temporary suspension of, 37, 57, 89
  with respect to action, 28–29, 73–74

technique for explaining, 48, 254.
See also Directives and directiveness
Normality and normative formulations, 109, 181, 199, 253

Pappenheim, Bertha. *See* Anna O.
Patient, the
activity-passivity of, 28, 38, 301
compatibility and qualifications
of, 11–12, 61, 231–32, 256
expectations by, 47, 164, 203,
210, 249–53
freedom and autonomy of, 10–12,
28–29, 40–41, 99, 123, 219
identity as "the patient" of, 149
listening by, 87, 207, 214
questioning by, 2, 5–9, 56, 237
repetitiousness of, 191
theory of, 78, 142–43, 150
vulnerability of, 146, 148, 157.
See also Silence, of patients
Paul, I. H., viin
Paying for missed sessions, 258–59
Penis envy, 185–86
Perception, 83, 141–42, 151–52
Portnoy's Complaint (Roth), 168,
168n
Practice, 15–17, 22–26, 34, 215
Pragmatic rationale
In my experience, 13, 53, 104
It's a fact, 24–26, 181
This form of therapy works better
if . . . , 13, 266
Principles of Psychoanalysis
(Fenichel), 137, 138n
Projection, 188–90
Psychoanalysis
clinical theory of, 151, 184–86,
247
didactic mode in, 135–38
directiveness in, 10, 37

efficacy of, 139
the "fundamental rule" of, 10, 27,
37–38
genetic theory of, 186
history and evolution of, 134–36
as idealistic, 151
metapsychology of, 23, 135,
184–85
modifications of technique in,
36–38, 233
neutrality in and nondirectiveness
of, 37
resistance in, 36, 137–38, 275
structural theory of, 33
timing in, 217–18
topographic theory of, 186–87,
189
transference in, 36–37, 135, 284,
291
Psychopathology, 16, 22–23, 130,
231–32
Psychotherapist, the. *See* Therapist,
the
Psychotherapy
"core event" in, 32, 130–32,
136–40, 145–46, 149, 184
definition and goals of, 16, 25,
28–31
duration of, 256–57
efficacy of, 296–97
as a form of psychoanalysis, 27–
30, 36–38
length of session in, 267–68
modifications in, 57, 233, 302–04
nondirectiveness of, 4, 27–30,
37–38, 43–47, 101, 208,
213–14, 254–55
and patients' activity-passivity,
171–72, 207
patients' freedom and autonomy
in, 236
problems of ending of, 294–95